THEATER
IN THE
AMERICAS

A Series from
Southern
Illinois
University
Press
ROBERT A.
SCHANKE
Series Editor

THE THEATRE OF SABINA BERMAN

THE THEATRE OF
SABINA BERMAN

The Agony of Ecstasy and Other Plays

Translated by
Adam Versényi

With an Essay by
Jacqueline E. Bixler

SOUTHERN ILLINOIS UNIVERSITY PRESS
Carbondale and Edwardsville

Library of Congress Cataloging-in-Publication Data
Berman, Sabina.
    [Plays. English Selections]
    The theatre of Sabina Berman : The agony of ecstasy and other plays /
Sabina Berman ; translated by Adam Versényi ; with an essay by Jacqueline
E. Bixler.
       p. cm. — (Theater in the Americas)
    Includes bibliographical references.
    Contents: Yankee — Puzzle — Heresy — The agony of ecstasy.
    1. Berman, Sabina—Translations into English. I. Versényi, Adam.
  II. Title. III. Theater in the Americas.

    PQ7298.12.E68 A618 2002
    862'.64—dc21

                                      2002018759
    ISBN 0-8093-2457-1 (cloth : alk. paper)
    ISBN 0-8093-2458-X (pbk. : alk. paper)

Printed on recycled paper ♻

For
ELENA and NINA

CONTENTS

◆

TRANSLATOR'S ACKNOWLEDGMENTS

The best work in the theatre is always a curious mixture of hard-won creativity and serendipity. My thanks go first and foremost to Sabina Berman for creating these works whose worlds it has been my pleasure to enter and to translate. My thanks go to Diana Taylor, who first introduced me to Sabina Berman's work when she asked me to translate *The Agony of Ecstasy* for a collection of plays in translation by Latin American women playwrights that never came to fruition. I am extremely pleased that these plays are finally being published and made accessible to an English-speaking audience. As any translator for the theatre knows, one's task is not only to translate the words themselves but to create speakable, theatrically vibrant language for the stage. That task cannot be done alone, and I am grateful to the members of the Duke–University of North Carolina Working Group on Latin American Theatre and Film who helped me hear these plays; Sharon Mújica, who provided invaluable help with certain colloquial expressions; and the members of my Latin American Theatre class at the University of North Carolina–Chapel Hill over the years, whose responses to these plays have reconfirmed for me time and again that Sabina Berman's work deserves to be known and produced not only in the Spanish-speaking world. This volume is one step in that direction. Its faults are my own. Finally, thanks to Sue, as always, my first reader and proofreader extraordinaire.

TRANSLATOR'S INTRODUCTION

●◆

Objects: a moustache, a Cartier watch, a pistol. Poetic images: hair like a black silk lightning bolt, a wounded nightingale. Snatches of song, lyrical dialogue, raucous humor, suggestions of mystery and menace, forceful characterizations, theatrically rich situations. These were some of my initial impressions when I read *The Agony of Ecstasy,* Mexican playwright Sabina Berman's collection of three short playlets, for the first time. Each of these short pieces, small jewels in their own right, demonstrated the hand of a mature playwright at work and left me yearning for more. Having been asked to translate *The Agony of Ecstasy* for an anthology of plays in translation that never came to be, I searched for and found Berman's other plays, becoming familiar with a distinct theatrical voice and a diverse corpus of work.

The four plays in this collection—*The Agony of Ecstasy, Yankee, Puzzle,* and *Heresy*—are the works that established Berman's reputation in her native Mexico and demonstrate the capabilities of her nation's most prominent female playwright at an early point in her career. *Yankee, Puzzle,* and *Heresy* all won the coveted Mexican National Theatre Prize, while *The Agony of Ecstasy* has generated the most critical commentary in academic circles, with portions of it published and performed abroad. Each play explores a different facet of Berman's dramaturgy, with *The Agony of Ecstasy* focusing on sexuality and gender, *Yankee* providing a kind of psychological realism, *Puzzle* probing Mexican political and social conditions since the Revolution, and *Heresy* rediscovering the historical presence of Jews in Mexico since the sixteenth century. The range of subject matter and theatrical approaches present in these four plays reflects the complexity of Mexico itself, where hovels stand side by side with luxury high-rise hotels in Acapulco, the megalopolis of Mexico City exists a world apart from the sparsely populated countryside, a technologically sophisticated Subcomandante Marcos becomes the media voice of an indigenous peasant Zapatista rebellion outflanking the seasoned politicians of Mexico's long-ruling Partido Revolucionario Institucional (PRI) government, and the PRI—in power since 1928—finds itself ousted by a coalition composed of the probusiness, socially conservative PAN party (Partido Acción Nacional) and a variety of forces on the Mexican left who together elect Vicente Fox to the presidency.

Sabina Berman herself is fully representative of her country's complexity. The daughter of immigrant Polish Jews in a predominantly Catholic country, she is both native and recent arrival, both Mexican citizen and social anomaly. She is the commercially successful, critically acclaimed playwright who was seriously considered by President-elect Fox for the post of minister of culture in his new administration until she made clear her proabortion, feminist beliefs and enraged Fox's conservative backers. Not only a playwright but also a novelist, poet, journalist, director, and actor, she shifts professional shape like the mythic *nahual*—a creature from Aztec mythology able to change form at will. This chameleon-like ability to alter form is what makes her dramaturgy so vibrant, as well. It never remains static, enclosed, or incarcerated in a particular dramatic, cultural, or linguistic form.

Perhaps the first question any translator must ask is who is the "target" audience and how does it differ from the "source" audience? What makes theatre effective for one versus the other? When does translation shift into adaptation? How does the process of negotiating cultural boundaries reposition the work? Walter Benjamin has written that each text contains a limited degree of "translatability"—the essence of the work retained in translation. He speaks of "translation as a mode" by which the translator looks for linguistic "kinships," trying to create an "echo of the original" rather than impose "the royal robes" of translation in which translation overwhelms the original intent.[1] In approaching Berman's work I have alternately assumed and discarded a variety of roles: translator as dramaturg, translator as adapter, translator as playwright-director. In all of these guises I have also tried to avoid the all too common tendency in translation to "explicate" the text, smooth out its original inherent roughness, and eliminate its ambiguity.

The process of translating these plays has been one of constant negotiation carried out in conjunction with Berman and with her full consent. My substitution of "Come on baby, light my fire" for snatches of a Mexican popular song in *The Agony of Ecstasy* results in a cultural reference for an English-speaking audience that carries the same weight as the original for the Mexican audience. More radical choices, however, have been avoided. During a symposium and festival celebrating Iberoamerican women playwrights in Cincinnati, Berman attended a staged reading of *The Agony of Ecstasy* that I directed at a theatre across the river in Covington, Kentucky. Afterward, she wondered whether the Catholicism underlying the second playlet, "The Love Nest," would carry the same resonance for North American audiences unfamiliar with the kind of Catholic society Mexicans take for granted. Berman suggested that I make the man in "The Love Nest" into a Rev. Jerry Falwell—type figure, thereby creating a conceptual frame for the piece closer to the sensibilities of a largely Protestant society. Such a change felt to me to cross the boundary from translation to adaptation, particularly for the first time the play was appearing in English translation. Such a context makes it incumbent upon the translator to present the play in question as close to the playwright's original intent as possible. Berman's suggestion, however, is one that future directors might want to explore, particularly if they have steeped themselves in the nature of the play as presented here.

Other aspects of translation were also thoroughly discussed: What is the cultural ambience of a place like Puerto Vallarta in *Yankee*? What is the effect of locating the play's action there? What are the shape and size of the unfamiliar *piolet* (a mountaineer's ice pick) with which Mornard stabs Trotsky in *Puzzle*? How were the scenes with Mornard in prison that call for characters to speak Russian or Persian performed: one language spoken with foreign accents or multiple idioms used in a single scene? What do the *cante hondo* and *palmadas* in *Heresy* sound like? Do they have cultural equivalents elsewhere? The translations presented here contain my answers to these questions and my solutions to these problems. The intention has always been to provide performable translations that capture Berman's own voice and particular theatrical approach.

Berman's corpus of work is, in many ways, concerned with the corporeality of her characters. What constitutes who they are, how is their consciousness created? In a Berman play, character is never fixed; it is always fluid. We are shown just how fragile identity can be, how provisional one's sense of self can become. In *The Agony of Ecstasy* Berman's focus is upon the meaning of gender itself and, by extension, sexual politics. In "The Mustache" a couple who seem to have exchanged their gender-based characteristics—He is described as an "effeminate man," She as a "masculine woman"—also share a false mustache. The mustache, an article of disguise that belongs to her, is used by both of them as a means of providing certain attributes that their own undisguised personalities lack. When he wears the mustache he is converted into a suave, debonair Don Juan who leaves behind his apologetic and pusillanimous personality to carry out a series of sexual conquests. She uses the mustache when her confidence and strength leave her and she needs to ward off unwanted suitors.

Throughout this first playlet, identity is presented as provisional in a variety of ways. As they discuss his latest conquest, it is plain that She, who insists upon her utter self-sufficiency, lives vicariously through his adventures. Each of them repeatedly suggests that it is not the opposite but the same sex that the other is attracted to, and the action moves effortlessly from description to reenactment, to dreamed-for fulfillment, ending with a formal technique—an indiscriminate alternating of lines of verse—that dramaturgically demonstrates how fully merged the two have become. By the end of the one-act it is clear that this relationship is one of absolute symbiosis. No separate personas exist, and the lines of gender are indistinguishable. He and She have become one.

The second and briefest of the three vignettes, entitled "The Love Nest," investigates similar themes in a very different way. The entire vignette consists of a wealthy businessman's harangue of his kept whore as she dresses for an evening out. This man of wealth and power who prides himself on controlling all those around him is driven to distraction by this woman who blithely prepares, seemingly unconcerned with the abuse he continually spews at her. The businessman's impatience is further increased by a telephone call to his wife to tell her he will be late. When his wife puts his teenage daughter on the phone it is clear that his two worlds have merged, the one tainting the other. His illicit lovemaking is momentarily checked by the appearance of his idealized daughter, his conception of her virginal purity momentarily stained by the presence of his whore. The more he insists on organizing and commanding the women around him, the less effect he has on them.

As the playlet continues it becomes progressively apparent that the prostitute is consciously irritating him. Her drawn-out dressing ritual is, in essence, an extended form of foreplay leading to the climax in which he rips off the clothes she has arranged with such care. Berman's writing here carries within it the strong suggestion that both the businessman and the prostitute are playing roles, that this is a ritual in which they engage on a frequent basis, and that for him she is simply another facet of womanhood along with his wife and daughter. Whether idealized or vilified, none of the women is allowed her own identity, yet the man who believes himself to possess the ability to control their identities is revealed to be without control over his own. Crossing himself and calling out praises to his wife, he plunges into the prostitute's arms, completely losing himself in the sexual activity she has brought to a fever pitch.

The final short playlet of this trilogy, "The Pistol," investigates the same themes from another angle. In it another married couple confront the emptiness of their relationship and the way in which they have remained together largely out of cowardice. Their unfulfilled dreams have become submerged into the daily routine, their initial love for one another is now a leaden weight. The catalyst for these discoveries is a pistol the husband brings home with the explanation that a friend's house has recently been burglarized. The pistol creates consternation in the wife, so much so that the couple carry out a series of farcical attempts to conceal the pistol from each other, leading to the climactic moment when she fires it at an intruder who turns out to be her husband, disguised. When he staggers off the stage, wounded and bleeding, only to return a few minutes later completely unharmed, she no longer knows who she is or what is reality. During the play's final moments, when he removes the pistol from his robe and hides it in a manner reminiscent of a Hitchcock film, it becomes apparent that he has been playing a series of roles, establishing a cycle that will soon repeat itself. The purpose of all of this activity, however, is obscure. The husband's motivation is open to a variety of interpretations. Is the pistol, as he suggests, an instrument of deliverance for both of them in that it provides the possibility of salvation from their painful existence by merely pulling the trigger? Or is it, as the wife fears and the slightly sinister quality of some of the husband's lines and activity suggests, the tool by which he will divest himself of her suffocating presence, killing her and blaming her death on an intruder? The opening moments of "The Pistol," in which husband and wife stand back to back and pace off in classic dueling posture, provide a potent visual image for what we subsequently discover to be the nature of their marriage.

Where gender and sexuality are the focus of *The Agony of Ecstasy,* the body itself becomes the focus of *Yankee.* The dirty diapers and constant bodily needs of a newborn infant are juxtaposed against the adult character Bill's inability to control his own bodily functions or to clearly express to the couple Alberto and Rosa who he is or what he is doing in Puerto Vallarta. The setting of Puerto Vallarta—a location built almost exclusively on tourism—is no accident on Berman's part, for the larger "body" of Mexico itself is also under investigation here. In a country where reruns of U.S. television series pervade the airwaves, Hollywood films dominate the movie theatres, and blond, blue-eyed models hawk products to a largely mestizo and indigenous population in commercials, the presence of the Yankee Bill represents more than his intrusion into Alberto and Rosa's relationship. Bill embodies the North American invasion of Mexican culture in all its complexity and confusion.

Bill is a U.S. citizen who suddenly appears to offer his services as a handyman to a young couple living on the outskirts of Puerto Vallarta. Obviously undergoing some ill-defined inner turmoil, Bill provides us with a series of contradictory explanations as to who he is and what he is doing in Mexico. He is variously a U.S. Marines deserter, an English teacher, a disillusioned Vietnam vet, a tourist, an employee of the U.S. Embassy, a CIA agent. Each successive scene cancels out the identity established in the preceding scene until we are left with a man who has so many identities that he has no identity. The only constant, and the reason that he has turned to Alberto and Rosa, is his desire to establish a sense of self, to quiet the confusion raging within him.

Bill's presence creates the crucible out of which new facets of the Indian Alberto and the mestiza Rosa appear as well. Their relationship, Alberto's commitment to his writing, and mutual responsibility for their child are all put into question by Bill's arrival. Rosa, the descendant of a combination of foreign and indigenous ancestors, both employs and comforts Bill, seeing in him a need similar to that of her own newborn child. Her actions anger Alberto, her indigenous husband, who cannot accept the foreigner's presence in either his home or his nation at the same time that he (as Bill points out) writes novels thoroughly imbued with Western European existentialism. The play builds to its final climax in which Alberto, the disengaged novelist who writes for writing's sake, becomes the voice of an indigenous communal demand that Bill tell the truth. When Alberto, now converted into a guerrilla-like figure, interrogates Bill, demanding to know his true identity, Bill explodes and in a single violent motion that appears to be a product of trained precision, attacks Alberto. As Rosa happily climbs the stairs toward them the play's final ambiguous image is that of Bill cradling Alberto's inert body in his arms. Is Alberto dead? Has the yawning maw of need that has been Bill finally learned how to nurture others? The only clear thing is that the presence of the Yankee has brought destruction.

In *The Labyrinth of Solitude* the Mexican poet, essayist, and cultural critic Octavio Paz famously put forth the notion of the Mexican populace as a people who have adopted a series of masks in the course of which they have lost sight of who they are. Berman has remarked that she considers herself a "Pazian," but in *Puzzle* and *Heresy* she seems more interested in demonstrating the nature of masks themselves and their effects on society than in Paz' focus on what society loses when people put on masks.[2] *Puzzle* and *Heresy* both deal with historical events but not in a documentary fashion. As Freddie Rokem has written in *Performing History,* his study of plays about the Holocaust and the French Revolution, "performances about history frequently also draw attention to different metatheatrical dimensions of the performance, frequently showing directly on stage how they are constructed."[3] Both of Berman's plays lay bare for us how history, as well as the play's own performance, is constructed.

In *Puzzle* Berman explores the conundrum behind Leon Trotsky's death by assassination in Mexico in 1940. Trotsky's dead body appears in the play, but it is the mercurial body of the assassin, Jacques Mornard, who performs a seemingly endless series of personas, a parade of masks, that dominates the play's action. In the course of the play the actual assassination is reenacted twice, each time with different emphases and explanations for the acts that take place. That the assassination is reenacted for us, first in the version given by Trotsky's lover Natalie, second as reconstructed by a committed Mexican Stalinist whose high position in the penal system gives her the power to protect and clear the suspected murderer, is important because these reenactments are themselves performances within the larger performance of *Puzzle*. It is this insistence on performing, on acting, on assuming different roles that emerges most strongly from *Puzzle*. As the reenactments are plays within a play, thereby blurring the line between illusion and reality (who is performing for whom?), so too does the majority of the play involve Colonel Salazar's attempts to solve the puzzle of the true identity of Jacques Mornard, the confessed assassin. In a much more profound fashion than Bill in *Yankee,* Jacques Mornard is a man with so many identities that he lacks any true identity. Where Bill's internal angst establishes him as an individual, albeit an ill-defined one, Mornard's endless series of identities, of roles that he adopts, cancel one another out until he becomes a kind of corporeal tabula rasa.

The true battle being waged in *Puzzle* is over who will control Jacques Mornard's identity, who will possess the power to define him. The Colonel dubs him Mr. X, refusing to accept any of the contradictory explanations offered and carrying out a campaign of psychic and physical torment designed to break his resolve. Just as firmly, the prisoner holds to his persona of Jacques Mornard, a kind of Ur-identity that encompasses within itself all explanations as to who he is and what his motives were for killing Trotsky. Juxtaposed against the Colonel's insistence on lack of identity and Mornard's insistence on an identity that is all-inclusive are the various characters who establish a single, fixed identity for Mornard in relation to themselves. The prisoner fiercely adheres to his chameleon-like ability to assume an identity that fits the context, rejecting both those who would dam his fluid sense of self and the Colonel, who would remove the flowing river of persona entirely. In essence Berman constructs Mornard as a character with the same proclivity for masks indicated by Paz, yet Mornard's masks lack any kind of cultural connection.

The play's last moments suggest that the Colonel, at the ebb of his power, does in fact win control. Told by his superiors that Mornard is to be removed from his custody before he has been able to complete his investigations, the Colonel resigns his command and then, with a hand-picked escort, accompanies Mornard to the prison yard. Mornard is informed that they are about to stage his attempted escape, the result of which will be the prisoner's death. The Colonel permits Mornard one last cigarette and lights it for him. The cigarette, however, is one that we have seen the Colonel roll himself in a previous scene. It contains a plug of gunpowder that, as Mornard draws on the cigarette, explodes in his face. To the background of the Colonel's laughter we see our last image of the prisoner, his face burnt by the gunpowder, blackened beyond recognition, an X, unidentifiable as he is led away. Mornard's final mask is a void, his faceless body an image akin to the emptiness that Jacqueline Bixler suggests lies at the heart of the construction of history present in the "official story" of Mexican education and political discourse for the greater part of the twentieth century. That discourse is also one that has excised the presence of Jews from the history of the Mexican body politic. The "official story" depicts Mexicans as the descendants of European Catholics, indigenous converts to Catholicism, or a mixture of the two. In the last play of this collection, *Heresy,* Berman explores the history of Mexican Judaism masked by the official discourse.

Heresy depicts a family of *conversos* (Jewish converts to Catholicism) who secretly continue to practice Judaism. Journeying to New Spain, they establish a new life in Mexico only to be denounced to the Holy Inquisition by the spurned suitor of one of the female members of the family. The play's focus is the interplay between the family's exterior mask of Christian respectability and its interior commitment to Judaism. This split sense of self is most forcefully presented in a series of encounters between the two brothers, one of whom has become a Dominican monk. After their father's death the lay brother demands that the Dominican hear his confession. The monk refuses, knowing the danger that such a confession could pose for him both legally and spiritually. The two brothers then come to blows in the middle of the monastery, physicalizing for us the internal turmoil that each of their family members experiences.

The brothers' physical violence toward one another is an aspect of the strong emphasis on the human body that pervades *Heresy* and the other plays in this collection. In *Heresy* the official hostility toward heretical faith is shown by a series of scenes in which the Inquisition interrogates people by means of physical torture. At the same time that the adult son Luis attempts to circumcise himself as a demonstration of his faith, the family's overseer whips a Chichimeca Indian laborer for attempted escape and corpses are prepared for burial according to Orthodox Jewish ritual. Each of these actions leaves its mark on the body, physicalizing for us how a society that demands adherence to a single creed or code deforms its own inhabitants. The culmination of this progression comes toward the end of the play when the Inquisitors parade the naked body of Luis' mother in front of him and all the other prisoners before she is put to the rack. With this theatrical image the masks are all stripped away as she desperately attempts to maintain her faith and the cynical Inquisitors' single-minded attempts to assert their dominance are laid bare. The play's final image is an auto-da-fé, a conflagration in which the heretics' bodies are literally turned to ash and dust becomes dust. Berman's theatrical reconstruction of their history resuscitates their memory and exposes the lacunae in the official discourse of the nation.

The theatre distinguishes itself by its use of the presence of the live human form. Visually arresting, dramatically compelling, Berman's plays are always theatrically present as they embody her shifting perspective on the labyrinthine twists and turns of Mexican society and plumb the depths of our deceptive souls. Whether it is the physicalization of what it means to be interrogated and to interrogate in *Yankee;* the final enigmatic image of a soldier alone on stage, silently aiming his firearm at an undefined threat that potentially emanates from the audience in *Puzzle;* the manner in which the family narrates its own "heretical" actions in *Heresy;* or the sheer variety of techniques, from song to staged tableaux, that appear in *The Agony of Ecstasy,* it is evident that Sabina Berman's theatrical acumen matches the depth of her dramatic design. It is this combination of theatrical technique with a kind of subject matter, that of self-definition, which cuts across cultures that ultimately makes these plays translatable. These are not plays simply to be read but to be performed. Consequently, they do not depend exclusively on language for their effect but incorporate an entire realm of theatrical discourse within their staging. Pleasingly written, they are playful and pleasurable in performance.

These four plays that established Berman as a significant voice in Mexican theatre are also the foundation on which all of her subsequent work for the stage has been built. A feminist perspective on sexuality and gender, a constant questioning of the meaning of identity, a frequently searing and satirical treatment of official discourse, and a resuscitation of historical presences willfully ignored are all characteristics of Berman's dramaturgy found in both these early plays and her later works. This collection provides English-speaking audiences with an introduction to Berman's plays. It is hoped it will spur other translations of her works. This collection also challenges readers to approach Berman's Mexican theatre on its own terms rather than expect immediate accessibility or complete familiarity. Translation is always a two-way street.

NOTES

1. Walter Benjamin, "The Task of the Translator," *Illuminations* (New York: Schocken Books, 1969).

2. Octavio Paz, *El laberinto de la soledad* (Mexico City: Fondo de Cultura Económico, 1973).

3. Freddie Rokem, *Performing History: Theatrical Representations of the Past in Contemporary Theatre* (Iowa City: U of Iowa P, 2000: 7).

FROM ECSTASY TO HERESY
The Theatre of Sabina Berman
Jacqueline E. Bixler

Of European Jewish descent, Sabina Berman was born on 21 August 1955, in Mexico City, where she continues to reside today.[1] Following the footsteps of several family members, she entered the university as a psychology major but was soon drawn to the theatre, where she started taking classes in scenography, acting, and playwriting. As the final project in one of these classes, she wrote her first dramatic work, a monologue titled *Esta no es una obra de teatro* (*This Is Not a Play*, 1975). After several years of working with director Abraham Oceransky and studying acting and dramatic composition with dramatists Héctor Azar and Hugo Argüelles, Berman wrote the plays that constitute the present collection of translations: *Suplicio del placer* (*The Agony of Ecstasy*, 1978), *Yankee* (1979), *Rompecabezas* (*Puzzle*, 1981), and *Herejía* (*Heresy*, 1983). While the first piece, with its playful treatment of gender stereotypes, has received more critical attention from U.S. scholars, *Yankee, Puzzle,* and *Heresy* all won the coveted National Theatre Award and granted Berman a place in the group that Ronald Burgess later labeled the "New Dramatists of Mexico," which includes Oscar Villegas, Víctor Hugo Rascón Banda, Jesús González Dávila, Miguel Angel Tenorio, and Oscar Liera. These young dramatists, all born between 1954 and 1973, share not only an affinity for one-act plays, sociopolitical criticism, and the humorous use of colloquial language but also the influence of older dramatists such as Rodolfo Usigli, Emilio Carballido, Luisa Josefina Hernández, Hugo Argüelles, and Vicente Leñero.

During the past twenty years, Berman has become the most prolific, original, and daring of her theatrical generation. Although she is not the only woman writing theatre in Mexico, Berman has had unprecedented success in staging and publishing her works and in gaining international recognition. She has consistently defied and challenged the patri-archal order of things with penetrating and humorous studies of the battle for sexual or political power and with commercial successes like the blatantly anti-*machista Entre Villa y una mujer desnuda (Between Villa and a Naked Woman)*. In addition to nearly twenty dramatic texts, Berman has written poetry, narrative, chronicles, and movie and televi-sion scripts.[2] One of her latest endeavors involved interviews with several Mexican women who had against all odds reached positions of considerable power. These interviews, which received the 2000 National Journalism Award, were televised and then published in a book titled *Mujeres y poder* (*[Women and Power]* Mexico City: Hoja Casa Editorial, 2000). One of Mexico's most politically involved writers, Berman is presently creating a series of television programs that discuss the 11 September 2001 terrorist attacks and Mexico's role vis-à-vis its powerful Northern neighbor.

Sabina Berman is Mexico's foremost female dramatist and, gender aside, sits among Emilio Carballido, Vicente Leñero, and Hugo Argüelles as one of Mexico's most prolific and commercially successful playwrights. It is rare not to find at least one of her plays listed among Mexico City's theatrical offerings. Berman's fame has spread to Europe and the United States, where in addition to stagings, both in Spanish and in translation, her theatre has received considerable critical attention from scholars of Latin American the-atre. In a country in which cultural functions are usually controlled in some fashion by the government and where it is difficult to stage theatre, either due to lack of political sup-port or lack of funds, Berman has had remarkable success not only in seeing her works reach the stage in the hands of talented directors such as Sandra Félix, Antonio Serrano, Héctor Mendoza, and Abraham Oceransky but also in seeing them published. Her plays are, however, highly theatrical and clearly designed with the stage in mind. Consequently, texts like *Krísis* or *Aguila o sol (Heads or Tails)* call for a competent reader who can "trans-late" the language of the text into a virtual stage production.

Summary of Berman's ever-growing corpus of dramatic works is difficult owing to a stylistic and thematic variety that ranges from the psychological realism of *Yankee* to the antirealistic street theatre of *Heads or Tails,* and from the playful study of sexual roles in *The Agony of Ecstasy* to the tragic triangle of *Muerte súbita (Sudden Death)*. There are, nonetheless, several features that repeat themselves throughout her production: a fine flair for dialogue, a predilection for black humor and irony, a distrust of all official dis-course, an interest in personal and national identity, a need to transgress sexual and the-atrical boundaries, and a profound awareness of the inherently theatrical nature of Mexican history and politics.

Despite a noticeable overlap among some works and a tendency to repeat certain dra-matic forms and thematic preoccupations, other factors make it difficult to describe the trajectory of Berman's theatre. The main obstacle is the author's bewildering habit of reworking earlier texts, extending them, and often even changing the title. This tendency applies in particular to her early works, such as *Un actor se repara* and *Esta no es una obra de teatro (An Actor Takes Note* and *This Is Not a Play)*, *Bill* and *Yankee*, *Suplicio del placer* and *El jardín de las delicias (The Agony of Ecstasy* and *The Garden of Delight)*, *Rompecabezas* and *Un buen trabajador de piolet (Puzzle* and *A Good Hand with an Ice Pick)*, and *Herejía* and *En el nombre de Dios (Heresy* and *In the Name of God)*. In addition to plays that have undergone several changes in title, other works later became the basis for longer plays, such as *El gordo, la pájara y el narco* and *Krísis (The Fat Man, the Chick and the Drug Dealer* and *Crisis)* and *El polvo del tiempo* and *La grieta (The Dust of Time* and *The Crack)*. While this propensity for endless revision is maddening to her critics, it ultimately needs to be recognized as the mark of a perfectionist. This very same professional work ethic is no doubt the reason for Berman's repeated success in obtaining the coveted Premio Nacional de Teatro.[3]

Although her name is always included among the New Dramatists of Mexico and her first works were published along with theirs in various collections of *Teatro joven de México (Young Theatre of Mexico)* edited by Emilio Carballido (Mexico City: Editores Mexicanos Unidos), Berman has always followed her own artistic and professional path. While she recognizes a broad influence of certain American and European playwrights (Shakespeare, Molière, Tennessee Williams, Beckett, Stoppard, Ayckbourn, and Neil Simon), she belongs to no particular dramatic school or group and owes no favors to anyone. To the contrary, she has repeatedly run the risk of offending the same cultural organizations and institutions that could offer patronage. *Heads or Tails*, for example, was commissioned by the Mexican government as part of a plan to "educate" the rural population with respect to national history, in this particular case the history of the Spanish conquest of the Aztec empire. The final product, which makes a mockery of the Spanish conquerors, was, however, not at all what the officials had in mind, with the result that they refused to fund the stage production. A later play, *Krísis (Crisis)*, suffered months of delay when Berman was unable to find anyone willing to provide a theatre space for her scathing attack on contemporary Mexican politics.

During the 1980s, in particular, Berman wrote several plays that scrutinize, criticize, and subvert what has come to be known as Mexico's "official history," that is, the history espoused by textbooks and the PRI (Partido Revolucionario Institucional), the party that uninterruptedly dominated Mexican politics from 1928 to 2000. In *Puzzle* (1981), *Heresy* (1983), and *Heads or Tails* (1985), Berman exposes histories that have sat dust-covered and repressed for centuries while attacking others that have been told only from the viewpoint of the victors. Foregrounding the re-presentation of history and its ideological implications, Berman often employs a complex mixture of historical facts, narration, music, parody, and the popular street theatre known in Mexico as *teatro de carpa*. In each instance, she stylizes history to foreground its representation and to remind her audience that events from the past acquire their meaning through their representation, whether it be on the page or on the stage. *Heads or Tails,* for example, is a postmodern revision and parody of the Conquest of Mexico in which Berman borrows heavily from Miguel León-Portilla's book, *La visión de los vencidos ([The Broken Spears]* Mexico City: Universidad Nacional Autónoma de México, 1992), to flip the coin and give the Aztecs the main role and the dominant voice. In these "historical" pieces, Berman pokes fun at the dominant historical narratives by presenting history as a play of perspectives, a malleable substance that takes form according to the intentions and ideology of whoever writes it. In the end, what interests the author is not history itself but rather the process of its own making.

In several plays of the 1990s, such as *The Crack* (1990), *Between Villa and a Naked Woman* (1993), and *Crisis* (1996), Berman successfully integrates her two main preoccupations: the eternal battle for power and sexual relations between the genders. *The Crack* is a farce with distinct absurdist echoes in which Berman attacks Mexico's political system, in particular its crumbling bureaucratic structure and the endless rhetorical blah, blah, blah of those who inhabit that structure. The metaphorical "crack" of the title is the enormous rift that appeared in the bureaucratic temple of the PRI in 1968 and continued widening until the building fell to the ground in the elections of 2000. In what is without a doubt her most commercially successful play, *Between Villa and a Naked Woman,* Berman uses the figure of Pancho Villa to attack not only one of Mexico's most sacred nationalistic myths but also the traditional control that the *macho* has enjoyed in the relationship between genders. *Crisis* offers a political parody of the famous "Crisis," a term that Mexicans have used for years to describe, summarize, and justify all of their current economic and political woes. With obvious references to the presidency of Carlos Salinas de Gortari (1988–1994), Berman opens the sewer to the personal story of the Salinas brothers and to that of the generalized corruption that has permeated Mexico's political system. She relies on irony, black humor, and the inherent theatricality of the Mexican political system in this merciless parody of Mexico's most sacred institutions.

In three recent plays—*Molière* (1998), *¡Feliz nuevo siglo, doktor Freud!* (*Happy New Century, Doctor Freud!,* 2000), and *65 contratos para hacer el amor* (*65 Contracts for Lovemaking,* 2000)—Berman takes advantage of European literary and scientific history in her continuing inquiry into the themes of power and sexuality. In the highly metaliterary *Molière,* she brings back to life Racine and Molière and their long-standing literary and theatrical rivalry in order to juxtapose comedy and tragedy, two opposite (or maybe not so opposite) ways of seeing reality. Ultimately, the play transcends its own metatheatricality in conveying the seductive nature of power both within the world of theatre and in the world beyond. Like Molière and Racine, contemporary Mexican dramatists, Berman among them, vie for audiences, theatre spaces, and subsidies. In *Happy New*

Century, Berman utilizes the figure of Freud, the famous case of Dora, and the transition to the twentieth century to suggest with a large dose of irony that the situation of women has changed very little in the last one hundred years. Berman's most recent piece, *65 Contracts,* is a logical extension of *Happy New Century,* as she continues to explore sexual relationships. In this play, she adapts Arthur Schnitzler's *La Ronde (Der Reigen,* 1900; translated to English by Eric Bentley, *La Ronde: Ten Dialogues.* New York: S. French, 1954) and the circular and ritual structure of la ronda ("the round") to present a chain of couples, all of whom end up copulating after an intense dialogue of negotiation. Through these tragicomic dialogues, the author underscores the blurred borders between love and passion, fidelity and infidelity, legal contracts and contracts of passion, heterosexuality and homosexuality.

Although the present collection of translations is limited to Berman's earlier theatre, the selection exemplifies the stylistic and thematic range of her dramaturgy, from the relative realism of *Yankee* to the sketchy absurdism of the trio of playlets contained in *The Agony of Ecstasy.* The latter conveys her interest in issues of gender, identity, and sexuality, treating them with humor, playfulness, and absurdist overtones.[4] The three one-acts share a number of features: a focus on the couple, always named simply *El* and *Ella;* a third, invisible character, whose threat or outside influence is made present through continuous reference; the foregrounding of the object on which the title is derived (moustache, Cartier watch, and pistol); and a combination of gender-related topics and gender-based role-playing. As the title seems to suggest, the characters illustrate that there can be no pleasure without a certain amount of torture, a dichotomy that forms an integral part of the warlike game between the sexes that continues to play out in subsequent works.

Yankee, Berman's first full-length play, displays a fine early talent for dialogue and character development. The building suspense, the final ambiguity, and the complex triangle of emotional relationships point the way to the later play *Sudden Death,* which likewise involves the intrusion of an unexpected and enigmatic male guest on a writer and his heterosexual partner. The complicated and shifting relationship between the writer and his (this would-be writer is always masculine) reality is one of Berman's most consistent concerns. Most notably in *Yankee, Sudden Death, Between Villa and a Naked Woman, Molière, Crisis,* and *65 Contracts,* she presents a frustrated writer who nonetheless tries to use his intellect and language as weapons in the eternal battle for sexual or political control, or both. Wielding his overblown intellect, the writer of *65 Contracts* states that his main objective is "ajustar el lenguaje a los hechos. Fundir pensamiento y carne" ("adjust language to facts. Fuse thought and flesh"; *65 contratos para hacer el amor,* unpublished, 7; sc. 1). Yet in each play it is precisely this need to talk, this eternal blah, blah, blah, that complicates matters, whether they be sexual or political.

Puzzle and *Heresy* are two of several plays of the 1980s and 1990s in which Berman takes up the cause of the defeated victims of little-known histories. In the first piece, she builds a complex puzzle around the assassination of Leon Trotsky, who found asylum in Mexico in 1937 after being expelled by Stalin from the Soviet Union. Despite his pledge not to meddle in politics, Trotsky continued to enjoy the political limelight in the revolutionary aura of the Lázaro Cárdenas presidency and had a close, albeit troubled friendship with muralist Diego Rivera. Just three months after an assassination attempt led by painter David Alfaro Siqueiros, in August 1940 Trotsky was fatally stabbed with an ice pick by one Ramón Mercader, a Spanish Stalinist posing as a Belgian Trotskyite named Jacques Mornard. Rather than try to piece together the puzzle or to propose a "true" history, Berman presents multiple recreations of Trotsky's assassination, which suggest that history itself, much like theatrical performances, changes according to the desires and the ideology of the historian or director. By the end of the play, we know even less than before about the identity and motives of Trotsky's assassin. Our only certainty is that history is a malleable substance that changes over time and according to the whims and political motives of its writers. Although the figure of Trotsky may initially strike the audience or reader as being somewhat removed from contemporary Mexican reality, *Puzzle* seems almost prophetic when one considers the similarly incomplete and manipulated investigation that took place after the 1994 assassination of presidential candidate Luis Donaldo Colosio.

In *Heresy,* Berman exposes yet another distorted and repressed history, the little-known story of the inquisitorial persecution of Mexico's colonial Jews. Through fragmentation and an unrealistic style, the author not only underscores the duplicity and contradictions of the Spanish Inquisition but also attempts to "heterogenize" the history of these events by granting a voice to those who have been silenced for the past four hundred years. Berman relies on dusty volumes of New World history to relay the fact that there *was* a Jewish presence in Mexico long before World War II and that the Inquisition was not limited to European soil.[5] Although the Inquisition was not nearly as active in the New World as it was in Spain, it did reach the Americas, starting in Mexico as early as 1571. Most of the persecuted were Portuguese colonists who had publicly embraced the Christian faith while secretly practicing Judaism. When Portugal rose up against Spain in 1640, many of Portuguese descent were tried by the Inquisition as traitors and heretics. In 1649 alone, thirteen Jews were burned at the stake in Mexico City. The most sensational case was that of Don Luis de Carbajal, the head of a wealthy, aristocratic family of false converts. Through the fragmented presentation of various relationships among family members, church officials, and political figures, Berman makes it clear that the Inquisition was not entirely a religious matter and that it was in fact often used as a pretext by church and government officials to appropriate power and property. *Heresy* represents a complete departure from *Yankee* in its fragmentation, stylized presentation, and use of narrators. Particularly effective is the "vista desquiciada" (upside-down view) of act 3, scene 12, which conveys the historical distortion that Berman treats in this play, as well as others, such as *Between Villa and a Naked Woman, Crisis,* and *Heads or Tails.* Instead of attempting to present a new "truth," Berman theatricalizes the dusty facts to emphasize the purposeful distortion of a history that historians had already twisted to homogenize and unify Mexico's society, as well as its history.

Through *Puzzle, Heresy,* and other "historical" plays, Berman suggests that during its run of seven decades, the dominant political party, the PRI, created an "official history" that upheld the myths of nationalism and satisfied its own political agenda. As the author herself said in an interview with Lydia M. Gil, "Right now we are in a period of transition [. . .] and we have to revise all those things they taught us in elementary school" (p. 35, translation mine; "Entre fronteras: Entrevista con Sabina Berman," *Dactylus* 13 [1994]: 29–36). It is indeed interesting how many times Berman resorts to historical figures, both well known (the Salinas brothers, Pancho Villa, Freud, Moctezuma, and Molière) and obscure (the Carbajal family, Trotsky's purported assassin), to contextualize her historical, literary, ontological, and sexual concerns. The early plays contained in the present volume not only established Berman's place among Mexico's leading playwrights but also set the stage for her continuing exploration of issues related to personal and national identity, sexual relationships, the writing and rewriting of history, and the eternal struggle for power, whether it be for sexual dominance, textual authority, or political control.

NOTES

1. Berman's nationality owes to the twists and turns of history. In her semiautobiographical novel, *La bobe* (Mexico City: Editorial Planeta, 1991), she narrates the fascinating story of her Jewish ancestors' escape from religious persecution. En route to San Francisco when the Japanese bombed Pearl Harbor, their Japanese ship was forced to dock in Mazatlán. Had their ship set sail any earlier, Berman would most likely be a U.S. citizen.

2. She has also directed a number of plays, including a few of her own *(Between Villa and a Naked Woman, Crisis,* and currently *65 Contracts for Lovemaking).*

3. Berman has won this prestigious national award no less than three times: *Yankee* (1979), *Puzzle* (1981), and *Heresy* (1983). She won the counterpart for children's theatre in 1982 with *La maravillosa historia del chiquito Pingüica (The Wonderful Story of Little Pingüica).* Other prestigious awards include the Premio Juan Ruiz de Alarcón (1999, *Molière*), the Premio Rodolfo Usigli (1998, *The Crack*), and the Premio de la Asociación de Críticos (1994, *Between Villa and a Naked Woman*).

4. Although the original version of *The Agony of Ecstasy* (1985) contains three plays ("El bigote" ["The Moustache"], "La casa chica" ["The Love Nest"], and "La pistola" ["The Pistol"]) linked under the subtitle *Tres obras de un acto sobre un tema (Three One-Act Plays on a Single Theme),* a later edition (1994) adds a fourth play titled "Los dientes" ("Teeth"). To add to the confusion, yet another

edition from the same year likewise includes "Teeth" but for some reason excludes "The Moustache." In terms of historical accuracy and thematic unity, I believe that the current collection contains the most judicious choice of texts.

5. In 1991, Berman extended *Heresy* and retitled it *In the Name of God (En el nombre de Dios)*. The most notable differences involve length, structure, and technical elements. The later play also includes flamenco dancing and singing, both of which complement and help convey the characters' inner torment.

THE THEATRE OF SABINA BERMAN

THE AGONY OF ECSTASY
Three One-Act Plays on a Single Theme

●◆

Each play deals with a couple and an absent third person. A minimum of two and a maximum of six actors are required for performance.

ONE. THE MUSTACHE

HE: Effeminate man.
SHE: Masculine woman.

HE and SHE both wear their hair cut short and dyed a red mahogany color. They are svelte, beautiful, and elegant—and they know it. They speak and move with leisurely assurance. They look astonishingly alike.

The action takes place in the main room of a hotel suite. A little table on which can be found a tea service and two cups. Two chairs. A door that leads to the bedroom from the main room. It is morning.

When the lights come up SHE reads the newspaper, seated at the table. From time to time she takes a sip of tea. She wears white silk pants and shirt. After a while HE appears, dressed exactly the same as SHE. HE enters through the door to the bedroom. HE is still drowsy. HE approaches her and kisses her on the cheek.

HE: Good morning, dear.

SHE nods. Continues reading. HE sits down.

HE: Excuse me. I mean for getting up so late. I think I had one too many last night.

I

SHE turns the page. HE watches her every movement.
>HE: In a bad mood?

SHE shakes her head no. Continues reading. HE keeps watching her.
>HE: There's something different about you today. As if something was missing or . . . Is your shirt new?
>SHE: Drink your tea. There it is.
>HE: It's cold.

HE gets up with the cup. Goes to a flower pot and pours out the tea. Sits down again. Tilts the teapot. There isn't any tea left. HE looks at her for a long time with rancor. HE observes the still steaming tea in her teacup. SHE takes a sip. HE looks at her with controlled anger.
>HE: I know what it is. You're not wearing your mustache.

SHE lowers the newspaper.
>SHE: My mustache? Of course I'm not wearing my mustache. You have my mustache.
>HE: Me?
>SHE: You've got my mustache on your face.

HE touches his lips.
>HE: Ah, yes. Excuse me, I'm sorry.

SHE continues reading. HE is deep in thought.
>HE: Could you tell me why I'm wearing your mustache?

SHE suddenly lowers the newspaper. Folds it energetically. Looks at him firmly.
>SHE: You've forgotten about last night?

HE refuses to look at her.
>HE: Do you want it?
>SHE: No. What for?
>HE: I thought you liked wearing it.
>SHE: Liar. You know perfectly well that I use it only so that I won't be propositioned. Only for that. So men don't try to pick me up when I don't feel like it.
>HE: I forgot. I'm sorry.
>SHE: You didn't forget. You wanted to annoy me.

2

HE: That's not true. I swear. You know I forget things.

SHE unfolds the newspaper.
SHE: Wretch.

Pause
SHE: I lent it to you last night, remember?
HE: The mustache?
SHE: You wanted to impress that brunette at the next table and asked me to lend it to you. You saw her while we were eating dinner, and since the brunette was alone, you decided to approach her and pick her up.
HE: I did this? I approached her and picked her up? I don't even remember seeing a brunette.
SHE: Incredible. *(Pause)* . . . She was wearing a white chiffon, neckline, sleeveless. Her eyes were green, her lips full . . . almond-colored skin. . . . And her hair, long, jet, fell over her shoulders like . . . like a black silk lightning bolt.
HE: *(Maliciously)* And I was the one attracted to her?
SHE: You're insinuating again . . .
HE: No. Nothing. Really. I'm sorry. Are there any cookies?
SHE: You are so infantile. Just because I'm a woman that doesn't mean that I can't enjoy another woman's beauty. I admire good things when I see them. A beautifully set jewel; a purebred colt; a sky splashed with white stars . . . And I don't have to take them home to enjoy them. I contemplate beauty from afar. . . . I let it be. . . . You, on the other hand, who, due to your preconceptions, can only appreciate certain kinds of beauty, see something admirable and want to possess it, consume it, use it up.

HE laughs joyfully.
HE: I'm sorry I've made you jealous.
SHE: Jealous? Me? *(SHE laughs.)* Me, jealous? Jealousy and I are like oil and water: we don't mix. I was the one who lent you the mustache.
HE: That's true. You're right. It's just that sometimes I can't believe that you're so liberal. Sometimes I irritate you only to prove it, you know what I mean?
SHE: We're two independent people. Our agreement . . .
HE: Yes, but you never take advantage of our agreement. I do it all the time, all the time, and you never, neve . . . *(Moans.)*

3

SHE: *(Vehemently)* Can't you behave like an adult? Why do I have to do the same things you do? We are two people, each of has his or her own tastes and desires. Each of us is free to do as we please.

HE: You're right, you're right. I didn't mean to offend you.

SHE: I didn't mean to offend you. You never want to offend me and you're always doing so.

HE: Excuse me.

SHE: And then you feel guilty.

HE: I'm sorry.

SHE: What good is it if you're sorry?

HE: Pardon me.

SHE: An independent person never asks to be pardoned for what he does.

HE: Excuse me.

SHE: An independent person does what he wants and doesn't ask to be excused because he has no regrets.

HE: I'm sorry.

SHE: What do I care if you're sorry?

HE: You're right. Excuse me.

SHE: Don't ask me to excuse you!

HE: All right, I won't! Pardon me.

SHE: You're driving me crazy!

HE: I'm sorry!

SHE: I'm going to explode!

HE: It's my neurosis!

SHE: So I have to suffer?

HE: I'll throw myself off the balcony! I'll never bother you again!

SHE: Coward!

HE gets down on his knees and implores her.

HE: Excuse me already! Please . . . I can't stand it when you're irritated with me. . . . What would I do without you? I'm so weak. . . . I'll never become an independent person without your help.

SHE strokes his hair.

SHE: *(Sweetly)* Well, dear, you managed to be independent yesterday.

HE: The only thing I managed to do yesterday was to get so drunk that I can't remember a thing.

SHE: You don't remember, but I saw it and I'm telling you. You approached her table and seduced her. You were so sure of yourself that you didn't even wait for her to ask you to sit down.

HE: She must have thought I was rude.

SHE: No way. She was enchanted by your confidence. It was a pleasure to watch you. Such elegance in every gesture. What "charm, mon cherie." With delicious arrogance you called the maître d' and ordered: "Champagne, Brut '52. And have the musicians play Strauss."

HE: Strauss! *(HE hides his face in his hands.)* Good god, how tacky!

SHE: How right. All you had to see was the enthralled look she gave you to know that Strauss was exactly the tone for her. Sweet little girl. She looked at you as if in a dream.

HE: At me?

SHE: Of course at you, who else? With the mustache on, you were irresistible. That's why you asked me to lend it to you.

HE: Yes, the mustache does look good on me. I'm more sure of myself with the mustache. I know that when I'm wearing our mustache I'm irresistible. And then, what did I do next?

SHE acts out what she has to say as if she were him and HE were the brunette.

SHE: You served the champagne. You toasted. You stroked her hands. You smiled at her. You leaned against her naked shoulder and began to whisper in her ear . . .

HE: *(Whispering)* What?

SHE: *(Whispering)* What do you mean "what"?

HE: *(Whispering)* What did I whisper to her?

SHE: *(Whispering)* What?

HE: *(Whispering)* Yes, what? What? What?

SHE: How am I supposed to know what you whispered to her! I couldn't hear what you were whispering from across the room.

HE: No, of course not, excuse me. But you watched.

Playing his part once more, SHE stands.

SHE: Shall we dance?

HE accepts the invitation.

SHE: *(Taking him in her arms)* The Blue Danube.

HE: *(With nervous laughter)* Oh my god, how tacky! *(They dance.)*

SHE: Sweet little girl. She stared at you as if she were in a dream. When had she ever been approached by such a handsome man? She was like a feather in your hands. Your fine hands, your expert hands . . . *(SHE caresses his back, his shoulders, his waist, his buttocks, and, finally, between his legs.)* . . .

HE: You saw it all . . . *(SHE breaks the embrace. Sits down. Lights a cigarette.)*

SHE: Well, almost. The rest took place behind closed doors.

HE: You mean . . . ? But . . . we'd barely met.

SHE: Well . . . what do you want me to say?

HE: But so easily?

SHE: A naive little girl. Don't judge her too harshly.

HE: I can imagine what she must have thought when she entered our suite. She must have been amazed.

SHE: *(Irritated)* You were polite enough not to bring her to our suite. You took another room for the two of you.

HE: Yes, of course, excuse me. . . . And of course I didn't tell her that I was staying in the hotel but took another room to let my wife sleep.

SHE: Your memory's coming back?

HE: Simple logic. She would have found it monstrous. There aren't many people as liberated as you and me. Everyone else demands an absolute, crippling fidelity. They are so insecure about their own worth that they think that if their partner meets someone else that they will be abandoned. That's why they get jealous. Appreciating someone else is taken as treason. They say: it's either you and me, bound together by a thousand vows, or you by yourself and me with someone else. Ah, how beautiful it is to be us. *(They both sigh.)* Liberated, refined, beautiful, and with everyone else within arm's reach. Although sometimes . . . I don't know . . . sometimes.

SHE: *(Irritated)* Sometimes what?

HE: Sometimes I feel guilty for being so beautiful and so refined and so socialist. . . . But even deeper down I'm convinced that we shouldn't fight poverty; that poverty is sublime and ugly people are tender. I believe that the smell of rancid urine and rotten apples in decaying cities is the odor of the soul . . . a soul that I can't find inside myself . . .

SHE: Shall I get you an aspirin for your hangover?

HE: *(Pointing to the newspaper)* I'd rather have the cultural section.

SHE: Society or Sights. This paper doesn't have a cultural section.

HE: An aspirin then.

SHE: Go get it.

HE: Where are they? The bathroom or the kitchenette?
SHE: The pharmacy.
HE: I could call room service. *(But HE doesn't do anything. Pause.)*
SHE: Do you know why you don't remember things, dear? It's because you feel so guilty about your absurd little adventures that you prefer to forget them.
HE: My adventures don't give me a bad conscience. It's yours . . .
SHE: But I don't have any.
HE: That's precisely what bothers me: you don't have any. You preach to me about free love, even about its social value: that it's a way to free the masses . . . a way to distribute a bit of beauty, but you never . . . I hope it doesn't bother you if I remind you, you never share yourself with anyone. I beg you, for me, for my mental health, share yourself soon.
SHE: Not for you nor for anyone else will I ever do anything that isn't my own personal desire.
HE: If I saw you act like a liberated woman I wouldn't feel bad in the mornings.
SHE: How dare you? You want to limit my freedom by asking me to act like a free woman when I'm so free that I don't need to act free!
HE: You've never felt the urge? Really?
SHE: Not yet.
HE: Not even once? Not for a single minute?
SHE: No.
HE: Do you promise me that the next time you see a good-looking man, a very good-looking one, that you'll take off the mustache and let him seduce you?
SHE: I forbid you . . . that is, I suggest . . . moreover: I assure you that when the day comes that I want a man to approach me and seduce me, that I will approach him and seduce him first and that I will do it so quickly he won't even realize that I've had him and thrown him away.
HE: You promise?

Pause

SHE: Besides, it's your fault I use the mustache. If you introduced me as your wife . . . if you didn't leave me alone to go to other tables . . . I don't want anybody else, I'm liberated enough not to want anyone else, and you leave me alone and they proposition me. . . . I put the mustache on because I don't have a husband to scare off unwanted suitors.

HE: But you're contradicting yourself. You push me into these adventures and suddenly now . . .

SHE: So I'm contradicting myself. What do you want me to do? I'm a complex person.

HE: *(Maliciously)* Have you seen how women look at you when you're wearing the mustache? How they smile? . . . You're irresistible with the mustache on, and you know it. You enjoy it.

SHE: And just what are you insinuating, my dear?

HE: Well, sometimes it makes me think. You notice only beautiful women. You point them out to me, you advise me to approach them. . . . *(SHE stares at him firmly. HE takes it back.)* It's not true. I was joking. Don't look at me like that. I can't stand it when you look at me like that. It's obvious that you don't like women. If you didn't like men you wouldn't like me, right? And it's plain that you like me because I'm a man. Answer me. Tell me that you like me because I'm a man.

SHE: I like you.

HE: Say the whole thing. Say: I like you because you're a man.

SHE: I already said I like you.

HE: Say it word for word. Say it: I like you because you're a man.

SHE: I think that's obvious as well.

HE: Obvious. Only to you. I can't see myself. I can't see myself through my eyes. I can see myself only through your eyes, and when you look at me like that, from head to toe . . . *(SHE looks away.)*

HE: No. Look at me. Tell me what you see.

SHE: You can't make me . . . *(HE makes her look at him.)*

HE: Tell me, what do you see?

SHE: I see that you're weak. Insecure. That you can't behave like a person independent from me. And even so, I love you.

HE: Because I'm a man.

SHE: Because you can't behave like an independent person. Because you're weak. Insecure. Because you need me to know whether or not you're a man. *(Pause)*

HE: You made me like that. I wasn't like that before. You've changed me day by day. Next to you I'm nobody. But as soon as I move away from you . . . *(HE moves away.)* . . . I'm someone else. Yesterday, for example. You were sleepy, you didn't want to have anything to do with me that night, so I went and got another woman. Another woman more woman than you, gentler, fresher, younger. Her lingering nudity, you should have seen that

8

little girl naked in front of me, looking at me as if in a dream. Mmn. My hands over her smooth skin. What wonderful skin, so soft. Her breasts. Her belly. Her pubis. Her thighs. Her long, long back. Her quivering, open mouth waiting for me. Sweet little girl . . .

SHE: Sweet little girl.

HE: You can't imagine the pleasure it was to linger in caresses. How wonderful it was to feel her in the net and to be able to take her or leave her. Her hair falling between my fingers, falling like . . .

SHE: Like a black silk lightning bolt.

HE: What freedom: to be able to take her or leave her. What freedom . . . I felt her unbutton my shirt . . . I let her kiss my chest . . . I lowered my face to hers . . . I said, "Open my pants with your teeth." "With your teeth," I said! "My cock. Take it. Grab my cock, little girl! No, no whimpering, for pity's sake, no. Go away, but no tears!" I felt her wet cheek against my abdomen, her trembling hand, warm, entering my clothes, searching . . . searching . . . finding . . . kissing it. She kissed it! She kissed it, she kissed it, she kissed it . . . Prince Charming awoke! *(Pause)* The shame . . .

Lighting shifts to something that suggests the dream. SHE kneels down. SHE crawls around on her knees with her hands before her in the air as if she were blind.

SHE: *(Like a little girl)* Where's my nightingale? I'm tired of looking for it in the dark.

HE: The shame . . . *(SHE approaches him.)*

SHE: Oh, do you have it? Do you have my nightingale, weeping willow? Ay, it's dead. *(Lighting changes to something else that suggests the dream.)*

HE: *(Very gently)* I hate you like I've never hated anyone, like only I can hate you. The way that I hate you when I know that you've pushed me into confronting another person's disgust, with all its infinite pain.

The following lines are spoken indiscriminately by HE or SHE. Each verse is a complete whole.

HE or SHE: *(Alternating, without emotion)*

It's an ugly world. Other people are ugly.
They demand that you be someone else. They don't want you as you
    are.
No one accepts you like I do.
I love you.
You love me.

I alone understand how painful it is to be you.

I am you.

I love you in me.

I know your shame.

You are my shame.

Hide me.

Don't go with the others. Go prove to yourself that they don't love
you.

Only I love you. Understand: only I, only I, only I love you . . .

They both get up, fix their clothes and hair. Lighting changes back to normal.

HE: You cried in your sleep last night. I came into the room and I heard
you crying in darkness. Were you crying for me?

SHE: I dreamed I was a little girl again. I was blind and I was searching,
feeling my way, for a nightingale in the forest. I don't remember if I found
it. I don't remember. *(They caress each other.)*

HE: You're beautiful. Like a marble goddess, cold and beautiful. When you
wear the mustache you're made of flesh but still dangerous: do you want it?

SHE: No. What for? There's no other woman tonight to tempt me. But if
you want to take it off . . . There might be a man who appeals to you, and
if you want him to approach you, you have to take off the mustache.

HE: No. I like you more than any other man today. You're irresistible with the
mustache on. Put it on. *(HE puts it on her himself. HE caresses the mustache.)*

HE: Like a black silk lightning bolt . . . *(They kiss each other on the lips.)*

Blackout

TWO. THE LOVE NEST

HE: A mature man, ostentatiously dressed, obsessed with his
own importance.

SHE: Her measurements are 5-90-60-90—respectively of the
head, chest, waist, and hips.

*A tiny apartment. HE waits while SHE gets ready in front of the mirror. SHE wears a
bathrobe.*

HE: Aren't you ready yet?

SHE: *(In a spent voice)* Almost ready.

HE: What do you mean by almost? Five minutes? Two hours? A week? A century? A millennium?

SHE: Almost ready.

HE: How many hours a day do you spend in front of that mirror, huh? Don't you know? Of course you don't. You've got a Cartier watch on your wrist, but you never look at it. Fifteen rubies, white gold works, ticking uselessly. Do you know how much it cost me? No, you don't know. Did you ask me how much I paid for it? No, it's rude. It's bad manners to measure. Numbers are vulgar. Let the poor measure, not you. Do you know how much you've cost me each year? What do you care. You're just like my wife. She's known for years that I cheat on her, but as long as she doesn't have to worry about money she doesn't care if I'm unfaithful. All women are alike. Billfolds for hearts. But what each of you don't know is that you're not rich. You don't own a thing. You only receive. I'm the rich one. You are my luxuries: my Cartier watches. I'm the only one who pays here, are you listening to me? Ah, when I die. I'm sure you've already calculated what will happen when I die. My wife thinks that she'll get everything. What do you think? Am I going to leave you anything? Shouldn't I compensate you for those best years of your life that you've given to a guy, who, even in your wildest dreams, would never have asked you to marry him? Well, what do you think? My wife thinks that she's going to get everything. Fool. Well, she's right she's going to get everything. Everything. Nothing for you, what do you think about that? Everything for her. Including you, of course. I wonder what she'll do with you. Well, I can imagine, slut! Do you hear me? Damn it, I want you to listen when I'm talking, I'm paying you for that as well. I'm not your Cartier watch going tick tock tick tock for nothing. Do you hear me?

SHE: Yes, my love.

HE: *(Imitating her)* Yes, my love. Love? Who do you think you're fooling? Love has nothing to with what goes on in this house. You're mine not because you love but because I bought you. Understand?

SHE: Yes, dear.

HE: Cynic. How much longer? Don't you know? No, you don't. You couldn't even hazard a guess. Try. Make the effort. You're not going to faint trying to think. Well?

SHE: Almost ready.

HE: Do you know how much time I spend in front of the mirror each day? Exactly five minutes. One to wash my face and brush my teeth. One to comb my hair. One to shave. And two more to get nostalgic looking at my double chin. Har, har, har. Laugh at my joke. I'm not your Cartier watch going tick tock tick tock in vain.

SHE: Ha, ha, ha.

HE: I don't have time to contemplate myself in the mirror. I work, did you know that? Like the hands on your Cartier, I turn and turn without stopping the whole blessed day. And for what? To keep useless women. Women whose only job is to be women, shit. Yes, you're my luxury, my white gold Cartier, but I can throw you away whenever I want to. Did you hear me?

SHE: Ha, ha, ha.

HE: What are you laughing about? That wasn't a joke, it was an insult. At least your Cartier doesn't go tock when it should be going tick. When I insult you I want to hear you suffer. Is that clear?

SHE: Yes, doll.

HE: Doll! So you think I'm your puppet? Stupid.

SHE: Ay.

HE: Imbecile, is that what you call suffering!

SHE: Ay!

HE: Cretin.

SHE: Ay!!

HE: Moron.

SHE: Ay!!!

HE: That's it. Very good.

SHE: Thanks, angel.

HE: Go to hell.

SHE: Ay!!!!

HE: I'm really going to send you to hell one of these days.

SHE: Ha, ha, ha.

HE: That wasn't a joke, you . . .

SHE: Ay!!!!

HE: Let me finish, damn it. You . . . Besides, telling you I'd send you to hell wasn't an insult either. It was a warning.

SHE: So what should I do? Laugh or cry?

HE: You're warned by a warning, nothing more.

SHE: How do you do warned?

HE: You open your eyes very wide and feel your heart beating very rapidly and . . . Do I have to explain everything to you? *(Going to the telephone and dialing)* Christ. I don't know how you survive from day to day when I'm not here. You're nothing more than a cow lying in a pasture watching life go by as if it were a train. *(Into the phone)* Hi. It's me. Yes, me. Listen dear, I'm in a business meeting that looks like it's going . . . That wasn't a joke, what are you laughing about? As I was saying, I'm in a meeting with the president and several businessmen and bankers, and it's going to be a while longer. . . . I don't know, maybe half a year. The president has proposed to make us work now, all of us, for the common good of the nation without paying any attention to the time and effort that this patriotic enterprise involves. Yes, now you can laugh. . . . No, don't put her on. Please don't put her. No, no! *(Transition)* Hi, daddy's little itsy-bitsy extra precious chestnut. . . . No, daddy's going to get there very late so give yourself a kissy-wissy on your little hand and then put the hand with the kissy-wissy on your forehead from me. Then get into your pj's, get into beddy-weddy and dream about the sweet little virgin and the . . . What do you mean there aren't any virgins?! Listen, you little punk, you may be eighteen years old, but you're still innocent and pure, is that clear? *(Hangs up.)* There aren't any virgins anymore. Son of a bitch! How much longer??! You still don't have any fucking idea?! See if you can't hurry it up. I'm not your Cartier watch going tick tock tick . . . *(SHE comes out of the dressing room, dressed, made up, and dazzling.)*

HE: *(Speechless before her beauty)* Tick tock, tuck . . . *(Singing)* "Come on, baby, light my fire . . . "

SHE: Well, how do I look, kitten?

HE: *(In a beautiful tone)* Horrible.

SHE: Horrible, my Arabian sultan?

HE: Horrible. It took so many hours in front of the mirror to look like that? Like a pornographic Christmas tree?

SHE: You don't like me anymore?

HE: No. But if I return you to where I bought you they're not even going to give me back the cost of the wrapping. My god, how frustrating you are. You go out of your way to provoke me! I'm only glad that when I die, my wife will get you. Maybe she'll be able to make something out of you. She's really a good woman. A wise woman. What difference does it make to her if I'm unfaithful as long as I give her what she needs to keep our house up in a dignified fashion. She's resigned herself to everything so that I look good before the world, so that my children don't have to hide their faces because of me. My wife *(Crosses himself.)* is a wonderful woman. You, on

13

the other hand . . . Look at you. Filth. Get rid of these showgirl's feathers. Do you want my children to have to hide their faces? How can you dare to go out with me with your hair looking like that? Look, I'm going to show you a picture. . . . Yes, here it is, look at it, it's a picture of my wife. Learn it by heart. Look how she puts herself together to go out with me. See? Each detail arranged so that they'll say, "What a couple, so reserved, so stable, so respectable," . . . shit. Have you seen your neckline, slut?

He grabs hold of her neckline, and the dress rips, revealing her rotund nudity, barely covered by skimpy underwear.
> HE: But what a whore, my god, what a whore!
> SHE: You don't like me anymore, dear?

HE pulls her to an armchair and lays her down. HE arranges her roughly, as he pleases, while threatening:
> HE: Women like you should be locked up. Destroyers of happy homes. High-priced call girls. Parasites feeding off the national economy. Corrupters of morals. Harlots. (If my wife ever gave me permission to do what I'm doing, I'd kill her!) Venomous snakes. Emissaries from Satan. (When you come, be careful not to bang your Cartier, understand? Fifteen rubies are worth more than all of your abject, filthy, evil-minded, paranoid, sexual treachery, is that clear?) *(Just before falling between her legs, crossing himself:)* My wife's a wonderful woman!

Blackout

THREE. THE PISTOL

> HE and SHE: A young married couple who consider themselves to be old.

The action takes place in the living room. A table. A bookcase. A sofa. A door to the kitchen. A door to the bedroom. A door to the street. Windows. Nighttime.
They stand back to back, taking a step with each sentence, as if in the preliminary moments of a duel.
> SHE: I don't understand.
> HE: I don't understand.
> SHE: I don't understand.

14

HE: I don't understand.

SHE: I don't understand.

HE: *(Turning around)* What don't you understand?

SHE: *(Turning around)* I don't know. I simply don't understand. What about you, what is it that you don't understand?

HE: The same as you.

SHE: That's not possible. How can you not understand what I don't understand when I don't understand what I don't understand?

HE: Wait. I think I remember something. I came home one night. I had a package under my arm. Do you remember?

SHE: A little . . . I asked you, "What's that?" *(Here the memory becomes present action.)*

HE: Are you talking about this package? It's nothing.

SHE: What do you mean, nothing?

HE: It's a package.

SHE: What's in it?

HE: Nothing. Nothing important.

SHE: What is it? Tell me. Why don't you tell me?

HE: It's a pistol.

SHE: A pistol?! Why have you brought a weapon home?

HE: It's a low-caliber revolver. This city gets more dangerous every day. Last night a friend of mine was mugged. In his own home, two guys with stockings over their heads . . . *(SHE gets even more upset.)* What's the matter?

SHE: Nothing.

HE: Tell me.

SHE: I'm going to get dinner. *(Goes into the kitchen.)*

HE: You're the one who's always complaining about secrets . . .

SHE: *(Coming out)* Let's eat out.

HE: At this hour? Didn't you make dinner?

SHE: Serve yourself. I have a headache. I'm going to sleep.

HE: What's going on?

SHE: Nothing. *(SHE goes into the bedroom.)*

HE: Nothing? María. María! *(To himself, alone)* I'm sick of this. I can't put up with it any longer! . . . Calm . . . *(SHE enters, very agitated.)*

SHE: I'm scared. They mugged your friend in his own house last night.

HE: Come here. *(HE embraces her.)* Let's go to bed.

SHE: Don't you want me to get you some dinner?

HE: You've got a headache.

SHE: It's okay.

HE: I don't want to bother you.

SHE: We could go out.

HE: I'm not hungry anymore.

SHE: Really, I don't feel that bad. I can make you something quick. An omelet?

HE: No, I'm not hungry anymore, really.

SHE: A steak?

HE: No.

SHE: Some fruit?

HE: What is there?

SHE: I'll look. *(SHE goes into the kitchen.)*

HE: Any apples?

SHE: No.

HE: Melon?

SHE: No.

HE: Bananas?

SHE: There isn't any fruit.

HE: All right, an omelet, then. *(Pause. SHE returns from the kitchen. Wrings her hands nervously.)*

SHE: We're out of eggs. Do you want a steak?

HE: I'm not hungry.

SHE: Why are you lying? You just asked me for an omelet.

HE: I'm not hungry anymore.

SHE: You asked me what kind of fruit we had.

HE: I'm not hungry anymore.

SHE: You wanted an omelet.

HE: All right. Make me an omelet.

SHE: I just told you there weren't any eggs.

HE: I'm not hungry.

SHE: Why are you lying?

HE: I don't want steak.

SHE: Let's go to bed.

They continue speaking monotonously, without listening to each other.

HE: Not just yet.

SHE: I'm sick of being so bored. This monotony. When did it begin? . . .

HE: Know what, María?

16

SHE: What?

HE: I don't know. I mean . . .

SHE: What?

HE: It doesn't matter. Let's go to bed.

SHE: You really don't want . . . ?

HE: No.

SHE: Nothing?

HE: Nothing.

SHE: Turn off the light.

HE: Let's go . . . *(HE turns off the light. They go into the bedroom. HE comes back out, walking about in the dark. SHE sticks her head out.)*

SHE: Who's there? *(Pause)* Humberto? Where are you? *(Pause)* Humberto!

HE: Here, here. I'm here.

SHE: Why did you take so long to answer? What are you doing?

HE: I was looking for some fruit.

SHE: There isn't any fruit. I told you that before when you asked me.

HE: I forgot. *(HE heads back into the bedroom. SHE scrutinizes him from head to foot from the doorway.)*

HE: What are you staring at?

SHE: Nothing. *(They go in. They close the door. A few minutes later SHE comes out. SHE moves about in the dark trying not to make any noise. HE sticks his head out.)*

HE: María! *(SHE stops, petrified, looking at him.)*

HE: What are doing out here, María?

SHE: I was . . . I was making sure the windows were locked.

HE: And?

SHE: I haven't looked yet. *(SHE checks them.)*

HE: Why don't you turn on the light? Should I turn on the one in the bed-room? *(HE turns it on.)*

SHE: They're locked.

HE: And the door?

SHE: It's locked, too.

HE: Oh, the pistol. *(HE picks up the package that he left on the table.)*

SHE: What are you going to do with that?

HE: Unwrap it.

SHE: Where are you taking it?

HE: To the bedroom.

SHE: What for?

HE: I bought it in case a thief breaks in. I'm not going to leave it here at the entrance. . . . *(SHE shivers.)* What's wrong, María? You're very nervous.

SHE: That story about your friend upset me. The mugging.

HE: Me, too. That's why I bought the pistol.

SHE: It's idiotic. Some guy breaks into your house, and without even knowing why you wake up dead.

HE: Yes, it's idiotic.

SHE: *(Looking around)* How fragile it all is.

HE: Let's go to sleep.

SHE: Leave the pistol here. Weapons scare me.

HE: Don't be a child. It's a beautiful pistol. Look. Compact, light.

SHE: Don't play with it; it could go off.

HE: I'm glad you reminded me. *(HE aims at her. SHE backs up, terrified. HE fires. It isn't loaded. HE laughs.)* It isn't loaded. Oh, for Christ's sake. You used to have a sense of humor. *(HE smiles sadly. Goes back to the table. Takes out a box of bullets and begins to load the pistol.)*

SHE: Don't load it.

HE: What's the use of having a pistol if it isn't loaded? Have you seen these little bullets? They're wonderful, aren't they?

SHE: What do you mean, "wonderful"? It's terrible that something that small could end all this.

HE: I shouldn't have told you about the mugging.

SHE: You shouldn't have brought that pistol into this house.

HE: *(With the pistol in his hand)* Let's go to sleep.

SHE: *(In the doorway to the bedroom, crying)* Please . . . *(SHE covers her face with her hands.)*

HE: *(Irritated)* All right. All right. I'll leave it in the living room. *HE puts the pistol behind some books. Goes into the bedroom. SHE takes her hands away from her face, goes into the living room. Looks around.*

SHE: I knew it. You were lying. It isn't here.

HE: I put it away.

SHE: You hid it? Where?

HE: What do you want to know for? It's better if you don't know where it is. That way you won't get upset each time you go near it.

SHE: Tell me where it is.

HE: I don't want to.

SHE: Tell me.

HE: That's enough, now. I've got things to do tomorrow. I want to sleep.

(If the light is on, HE turns it off. SHE begins to look for the pistol in the dark. HE sticks his head out.)

HE: María? *(SHE hides behind the sofa. HE walks through the room.)* María? *(SHE runs into the bedroom and locks the door behind her. HE raps on the door with his knuckles. No answer.)* Don't be a child, María. Open the door. Did you think that . . . María, please, why would I want to . . . to you? . . . To my wife?

SHE: You hate me.

HE: *(Softly, in an understanding tone)* María.

SHE: It's true, isn't it? I understand. I'm sick . . . my fears . . . my anxieties . . . You wish you hadn't married me.

HE: María.

SHE: I didn't deceive you, Humberto. I wasn't like this when we met. But if you wanted to get rid of me . . . you didn't need to . . .

HE: María.

SHE: All you had to do was tell me, I swear. Divorce . . . I wouldn't have asked you for anything in return.

HE: All right.

SHE: All right, what? A divorce, that's what you want?

HE: That's enough now.

SHE: We made a mistake, that's all. Mistakes are human.

HE: Do you want a divorce?

SHE: Yes.

HE: Very well. We'll see my lawyer tomorrow. You want to divorce me?! But, why?

SHE: You don't love me, that's why.

HE: Me?

SHE: You.

HE: I love you, I still love you.

SHE: I weigh you down, I'm bad . . .

HE: You're not bad, you don't weigh me down.

SHE: I'm very difficult to live with, more difficult each day . . .

HE: Living together is difficult, María. I never expected it to be easy.

SHE: I feel guilty for being who I am with you. I don't want to feel guilty about being who I am. *(Pause)* Humberto?

HE: I forgave you for everything in advance when I married you. *(Pause. SHE opens the door. Gives him the pistol.)*

SHE: I'm sorry. I'm very sorry. It was sort of . . . an attack . . .

HE: Forget it. Let's go to sleep.

SHE: That story about the mugging frightened me.

HE: Yes . . .

SHE: I was uneasy.

HE: Let's go . . .

SHE: *(Begging)* The pistol . . .

HE nods, gritting his teeth. HE leaves the pistol on the table. They go into the bedroom. SHE comes out. Checks the windows. Goes to the pistol and picks it up. SHE's about to put it behind the books when a noise at the front door causes her to jump. Suddenly, a face appears at one of the windows. SHE screams. Fires several times at the intruder. The intruder shouts and disappears. We hear stumbling steps hurrying toward the front door.

SHE: Humberto! Humberto! *(The stranger enters; his bleeding face is covered by a stocking. SHE recognizes him.)* Humberto! *(HE stumbles into the room as he talks, pausing because of his wound.)*

HE: I went out . . . through the bedroom window. I was coming for the . . pistol. *(HE stretches out his hand, asking for the pistol, but SHE backs up a step. Explaining:)* It's just that . . . María, understand. It wasn't enough for us to separate. How? After so much . . . unhappiness . . . just say good-bye?

SHE: I . . . It's not my fault that . . .

HE: Fault! Don't be so superficial, for Christ's sake. . . . Who wants justice? . . . *(Docilely, SHE lets him take the pistol. HE aims.)*

HE: Make cold the face that . . . has seen me since I was . . . until I'm now no longer . . . young. Since I no longer have . . . hope. Since I no longer . . . no, not anymore . . . I am able to . . . For so many days. All those behind me. All the ones I have left. There are too many . . . Mondays. Do you understand, María? Too many . . . too many friends that no longer . . . didn't make it. And those few who did are . . . too many. You understand me, don't you, María? *(SHE nods.)* Yes . . . you understand me. I . . . I promised you too much. You can't even imagine. I told you half, the other half . . . I kept it, enjoyed it alone . . . everything that I was going to give you . . . because you must know that I was going to give you everything, I was going to . . . and after every failure there you were, there you are, a mirror . . . cracked. . . . Let's see if I can change the face . . . *(HE fires. But the pistol's empty. HE breaks out in laughter.)* I can't do it, I tell you. Don't move!

SHE: I'm going to get something from the medicine cabinet.

20

HE: No! It's not like I thought, but at last we will be . . . in two separate worlds. Don't move, I said!

SHE: I'm going to the medicine cabinet.

HE: Don't move or I'll . . . *(HE laughs, firing the empty pistol.)* Click! No, really . . . nobody's going to . . . . save me from this. I can see my . . . heart . . . in little pieces . . . The bed . . . I'm going to die like those . . . diverted in . . . bed . . .

SHE: Lean on me.

HE pushes her away, staggers toward the bedroom. HE turns out the light. For a moment SHE doesn't know what to do in the darkness. Then SHE turns on a small lamp. SHE sees a bloodstain on the rug and tries to clean it off with her saliva and hands. After that, SHE painstakingly wipes hands on the wall. Says: "How stupid." SHE takes off her bathrobe, goes into the kitchen, wets it, and scrubs the wall with it. Says: "Now the robe's stained. . . ." SHE picks up a lighter and sets the robe on fire, throwing it out the window. SHE watches it burn. HE comes out of the bedroom and turns on the living room light. HE seems to be fine, no trace of damage. SHE is so scared that she can't even scream.

HE: My god, what are you doing?!

SHE: Humberto!

HE: What's burning?!

SHE: My robe.

HE: Why are you burning your robe, María? *(SHE just trembles, terrified.)* Good god, don't get scared.

SHE: *(Embracing him)* Humberto! *(SHE starts to laugh nervously. Tries to get him to laugh. Tickles him, to no avail.)* Laugh!

HE: *(With a touch of repugnance)* But, what's with you?

SHE: Laugh.

HE: I can't. *(SHE is suddenly terrified again.)*

SHE: Then . . . you're wounded?

HE: *(Smiling)* Me?

SHE: I must have dreamed it all.

HE: What?

SHE: I took you for a thief and you . . .

HE: I what?

SHE: Nothing.

HE: You wounded me?

SHE: Nothing! *(Pause)* I shot you with the pistol you brought home.

HE: I brought a pistol home? What a dream.

21

SHE: You didn't bring a pistol home? *(Pause)* A low-caliber pistol wrapped in . . . what do they call it?

HE: *(Sarcastic)* Black butterflies.

SHE: Wrapping paper.

HE: What color was it? What color was this wrapping paper?

SHE: Uhh . . . Gray. Yes, gray.

HE: Rose.

SHE: Rose? No. Yes? Of course. A pale rose. A very pale rose. A very pale rose? Very pale, dear? A very pale rose?! *(HE stares at her firmly.)*

HE: I don't know. We're talking about your dream. And that's why you burnt up your robe?

SHE: . . .

HE: María, tell me, I'm not going to scold you, I promise. That's why you burned your robe?

SHE: It was stained with your blood . . .

HE: But now it's ashes. . . . Ay, María. You didn't like it anymore or what?

SHE: I told you, it was stained with . . . *(HE sighs.)* It's just that . . . I . . . Before, I . . . It used to be that when I woke up from a dream it was so easy. I was in one place and with a little movement, as small as lifting my eyelids, there I was in another place, completely different, serene, as if it weren't . . . strange . . . Now I open my eyes and I can't tell if I'm closing them. . . . I need help.

HE: You need to rest. Come on, let's go.

SHE: Anything would be better than going crazy. I'd rather die.

HE: I know.

SHE: *(Scared)* You know?

HE: What's the matter? *(SHE trembles uncontrollably.)* María, María, please.

SHE: You want to make me crazy.

HE: Me? But you're not going crazy. You have anxiety attacks; that can be fixed. There are pills for that. Where are you going? *(SHE searches behind the books but doesn't find the pistol.)*

SHE: It was hidden here . . .

HE: *(Amused)* The pistol? Is that where you hid it in your dream?

SHE: That's where you hid it.

HE: In your dream.

SHE: No, before. In what I thought wasn't a dream . . . in what I was sure wasn't a dream . . .

HE: Come on. Let's go to bed. *(Embracing her)* My little girl. You'll see,

22

tomorrow will be another day. *(HE takes her by the hand and leads her toward the bedroom. They enter the bedroom; HE lays her down on the bed.)* I'll cover you up. There, there, rest. *(HE can be heard humming the rest of the lullaby . . .)*

> "Señora Santana;
> why does your boy cry?
> For an apple . . .
> . . . . that he lost . . ."

(HE goes into the living room.)

SHE: Where are you going?

HE: To get some fruit.

SHE: *(Painfully)* There isn't any fruit.

HE: Then I'll get a glass of water. *(In the living room HE takes the pistol out of his clothes. Loads it. Hides it someplace else. Goes into the kitchen. SHE enters the living room as HE is returning with a glass of water. SHE looks at him, wide-eyed. Showing her the glass)* Water. *(SHE runs to check behind the books. SHE doesn't find anything. Cries. Crying, SHE goes back to him, puts an arm around his waist. HE drinks a bit of water over her shoulder. . . . They go back to the bedroom arm in arm. HE locks the door behind him.)*

Blackout

YANKEE

CAST

Bill: Tall, husky, compact. Ill-cut hair, almost to the scalp in some places and long and shaggy in others. Around thirty-two years old. Speaks Spanish with a slight North American accent. When he speaks English it's the result of angry or vehement outbursts. Suddenly breaks out laughing and just as brusquely stops.
Rosa: Mestiza. Friendly features. Alberto's wife.
Alberto: Indian. Approximately the same age as Bill.
The Baby
The Lieutenant

The action takes place in Puerto Vallarta. A solitary beachfront house, on the seashore. On the first floor is a studio with doors to the street, the master bedroom, the kitchen, and the narrow stairway. On the second floor are Bill's room and a balcony. There is little furniture, barely what's absolutely necessary: in the studio are a table that Alberto uses for his desk, a lamp, a couch, several chairs; in Bill's room a cot; on the balcony two wicker chairs. The walls are impeccably white.

SCENE 1

The balcony. Bill sits in a wicker chair. It's late afternoon. During the scene the light will gradually fade into semidarkness. On the first floor the lowered venetian blinds outline the silhouette of Alberto, who is writing in the studio.

BILL: When I saw her in the marketplace, the baby in her arms . . . she chose each fruit, each vegetable with care, felt it . . . amidst the noise, the Indian sellers, the white buyers, the hurry . . . It's a curious idea, the hurry: the idea that one can get someplace else before . . . She went from stall to stall searching for the best fruit, the best vegetables, she felt them in her hand. She seemed like a Madonna to me, the baby in her arms, the Indian boy who carried the basket for her. But one's always in the same place. Here. I've been in these ruins for two hundred years . . .

Rosa enters, the Baby in her arms. She walks slowly across the balcony.

BILL: When I saw her in the marketplace . . . I couldn't help following her, you know? I followed her as if in a dream. You were an apparition . . . the Virgin of Guadeloupe.

Rosa laughs softly.

BILL: I heard the mason say he didn't want to fix your ceiling. I sold my watch and bought masonry tools.

ROSA: The ship set sail at noon today.

BILL: So what? I'm a marine? Is that what you think?

ROSA: That's what you told me, Bill.

BILL: What else did I tell you? That I was in Vietnam, for example?

ROSA: No. You didn't tell me that.

BILL: That was an unjust war, and I was never there. Period. Let's change the subject, huh?! How many years old is the baby?

ROSA: Years? *(She laughs lightly.)* He's five months old.

BILL: Who would ever think of taking care of a baby in Puerto Vallarta?

ROSA: Alberto needs to be near the ocean to write. That's why we came as soon as our son was born.

BILL: *(Suspicious)* Why does he need to be near the ocean to write?

ROSA: He says that he gets a sensation of eternity hearing it come and go. *(Pause)* Alberto's first book is full of songs to the sea. It's his most sincere book. Quite melodious. He swears that before he dies he'll return to the sea to write a farewell hymn. One of thanks as well.

BILL: Nuts. The sea's a cruel monster. I've seen it swallow a man in a single bite. Of course, from the beach it can seem like a domesticated little bug. So, your husband has never been in a storm, good. The sea inspires him, very good.

ROSA: Perhaps he'll have been in a storm before he writes his last book.

Bill looks at her incredulously. Then he looks at the Baby.

ROSA: His name's Alberto.

BILL: Ah yes, like your husband. I hope he never grows teeth.

ROSA: What? I hope they don't take too long to grow.

BILL: Then he'll bite you.

ROSA: Delicately. . . . It will be an intimate pleasure. I think.

BILL: You think. Well. Henry was born when I was five years old.

ROSA: Your brother?

BILL: Yes. I'd chosen a name for him: Ruth. I wanted a sister, you understand? I was afraid that another boy would rob me of my mother's affection. It's natural. Dr. Spock says so in all of his books. I read Dr. Spock's books one by one, where he explains that this and some of my other lunacies are perfectly normal. Well, when I got to the hospital my mother was between the sheets. I went to her and kissed her forehead. Like in the movies, when a father kisses his wife's forehead after she's just given birth, you know? I bent over and kissed her, the little gentleman. The room was full of visitors, gifts, flowers. The nurse came carrying the baby, a little bundle, she gave it to my mother. "How's Ruth, Mom?" "Very well, Bill." Behind my back someone said, "The baby boy looks just like his father." Baby boy? Baby boy? I jumped through the window. I ran through the dark garden. It was night, it was drizzling, the tears . . .

ROSA: So the room was on the first floor.

BILL: Yes. But I didn't know it. Besides, I expected them to tell me that my mother was a witch for having deceived me.

ROSA: She didn't want to lose your love, Bill. What she did wasn't right . . . but it's understandable.

BILL: Humph. My love. Do you think she cared? "Your grandfather died in the invasion of Normandy," she told me. "He died defending our right to progress. And we have progressed. You never lacked for education, food, entertainment. I, on the other hand, was a poor little orphan when I was twelve. So you should go and defend our freedom. You should go! Don't expect me to love a traitor! Uncle Sam needs you!" *(As if he were surrounded by Uncle Sams pointing at him)* He's pointing at me from every poster! You son of a bitch, you! *(He begins to march.)* Left-right, left-right, left-right. Halt! This little Oriental is your enemy. Prepare arms! Aim! *(Imitating machine-gun fire)* Taca taca taca taca taca. How do you stop machine-gun fire? I'm asking you a question, Rosa! Taca taca taca.

ROSA: I don't know.

BILL: You can't stop it. Period. Let's change the subject. No, it's not so easy. After the first death . . . after the second . . . after the first war . . . one becomes obsessed with the topic. Vietnam becomes a net full of holes, but we've already found another piece of our inheritance to pierce full of holes. It's impossible to stop. "They left us a net full of holes as our inheritance," it's an Aztec poem. "Now there's no place to flee from our solitude." When I got home Henry had hair down to here, like Jesus, and a look. "Doesn't it make you angry to have been so vilely deceived?" he asked me. "You were sent to Vietnam as a guard dog for the multinationals." We know that now, brother. Peace and love, brother. We, the whites, are fucked. Period. The fishermen and peasants of Puerto Vallarta . . . lots of dollars now that we've turned their paradise into a tourist attraction, huh? But nothing can pay for the dignity we whites have robbed from them. We've turned them into oarsmen, waiters, male and female whores. We've quickly filled the holes of their inheritance with drugs and syphilis. End of paragraph! Did I wake the baby?
ROSA: No. He's sleeping.
BILL: He wouldn't have . . . died? No, right? Go check, please.

Laughing softly, Rosa goes to see to the Baby.
ROSA: Listen to him breathe. Little cherub. . . .
BILL: You love him freely. I mean, without asking anything in return, just because he exists? *(Still laughing, Rosa nods.)* When I saw you in the marketplace . . . when I saw you with the baby in your arms I felt . . . like . . .
ROSA: Like you wanted to be him.
BILL: *(Amazed)* You're a psychiatrist.
ROSA: No, how can you think that.
BILL: A witch.
ROSA: No.
BILL: But you know some way to read people's minds.
ROSA: I swear that's not true.
BILL: Then . . . you love me. Yes: you love me. "In order to love you have to be pure. Love is the union of two pure beings." I'm going to try. It shouldn't be difficult to purify myself knowing you're nearby. You love me so much that this chaos I'm living in will suddenly dissipate and I will have forgotten the . . . about myself . . . right? Your husband said that he was going to do my portrait and that would cure me, right? That's what he said, isn't it? Isn't it?

Pause

ROSA: Yes, we're going to cure you. Alberto and I.

BILL: But your husband promised. To do the portrait. Could I rest my head on your knees?

ROSA: Come, Bill.

Bill rests his head on Rosa's lap. While he talks, he falls asleep.

BILL: It's not right but understandable, right?

ROSA: Yes.

BILL: And you're going to cure me, right?

ROSA: Yes.

BILL: You alone.

ROSA: Alberto and I.

BILL: When I saw you in the marketplace I wanted to kill the baby because you don't love him freely. You love him because he's yours. Because with him you're like a goddess. If you give him his milk, you bring him to life, if you don't give him milk, you kill him.

Pause

BILL: But you're going to give him milk, right?

ROSA: When he wakes up. He's still asleep at the moment.

BILL: Right?

ROSA: Yes.

Pause

BILL: *(Falling asleep)* Right?

ROSA: Yes.

BILL: Right?

Pause

ROSA: Yes.

Blackout

SCENE 2

Stage in darkness. Heavy footsteps are heard. With a single kick Bill opens the door to his room and stands in the doorway, tenuously illuminated. Moonlight. He carries his machine gun, ready to shoot.

29

BILL: Anyone here? Anyone here?

A noise gives someone away.
    BILL: Who's there? Answer: who's there?

The sharp voice of a woman with a Vietnamese accent is heard.
    WOMAN'S VOICE: Woman . . . woman . . .
    BILL: North or South? Answer!
    WOMAN'S VOICE: Woman . . . Woman . . .
    BILL: Answer! North or South?

Suddenly disoriented by a baby's cry, Bill uncontrollably fires a burst from his machine gun. The woman's scream is heard as she falls. The crying continues, and Bill turns in a circle, firing. When he stops firing, the crying has ended.

SCENE 3

Abrupt change to dawn. Bill awakes all at once from his nightmare. Rosa comes running in with the Baby in her arms.
    BILL: I peed . . . I shat all over the sheets. (*He gets up, wrapping the sheets around him as if they were giant diapers*) Excuse me, I'm sorry, I'm very sorry. I should go. The ship sets sail at dawn.
    ROSA: Bill, wait, calm down. Your ship, the marine ship, set sail a week ago. Don't you remember? You stayed here with us to help us fix up the house. Don't you remember? You painted the walls out front, arranged the furniture, fixed the pipes.

Bill stares at her, his eyes bulging. Then he looks around. He sits on the edge of the bed, his head in his hands.
    BILL: I'm sick.
    ROSA: It was just a bad dream.
    BILL: Where's your husband?
    ROSA: Asleep.
    BILL: Did I wake you up? Is it very early? The sun hasn't come up yet.
    ROSA: It's around four in the morning. Alberto went to bed a few hours ago. He's been working since noon. He didn't hear your screams.
    BILL: I screamed? I'm sorry. I'm worse than a baby. I'm a lot of trouble, aren't I? At least a baby has the excuse . . . of being a baby.

ROSA: You're sick. Calm down.

BILL: I'm a big idiot. I realize it. It hurts me to realize it. I'm a sick person. Nobody has to put up with a sick person. It hurts me to realize it. At least if I was a complete idiot . . . but the intelligent part of me watches me doing ridiculous things, being a burden, behaving like a big idiot. The ship sailed? A week ago? I should have been on board.

ROSA: You didn't want to go back to the ship, remember?

BILL: At least on board they had to put up with me because the big idiot is a good sailor. Besides, I didn't care what they thought of me. Your husband's asleep?

ROSA: Yes.

BILL: I didn't go. I deserted, right? Now I'm a traitor.

ROSA: Yes, Bill.

BILL: If I'm a traitor, then I'm good. If I'm not a traitor, I'm bad. It's very confusing, isn't it? It's exactly the opposite of what I learned as a child. I don't believe anything they taught me anymore. My head is a net full of holes. But I still feel bad, I should go back to the ship.

ROSA: No, Bill. You're a traitor now.

BILL: Do you really believe that? I deserted, didn't I? That proves I'm a traitor, right?

ROSA: Yes, Bill. You're a traitor.

BILL: *(Happy)* I didn't go to Vietnam, right?

ROSA: You are a traitor.

BILL: Say it again. I like hearing it from your lips.

ROSA: You, Bill, are a traitor.

BILL: But I still feel bad. Rosa, I want to make a confession, tell you how bad I am.

ROSA: It's not necessary, Bill. That's all in the past. You couldn't help what you did in Vietnam. You had to survive.

BILL: *(Defiant)* I didn't go to Vietnam. I'm a traitor. I spent the war in Quebec.

ROSA: Yes, Bill.

Pause

BILL: I was too in Vietnam. But that's all over and done with. Isn't it, Rosa?

ROSA: Yes, Bill.

BILL: I want to tell you what I did in Vietnam.

ROSA: It isn't necessary, Bill.

BILL: Yes. I'm going to tell you so you can forgive me for what I did.

ROSA: I forgive you. You don't have to tell me. All I have to see is how tender and kind you are for me to say that you're a good man now. You're a good man now, Bill. What you did before isn't important.

BILL: *(Defiant)* I killed a defenseless woman and her baby.

Pause

ROSA: You're a good man, Bill.

BILL: You're very warm, very gentle. If you loved me, maybe I could be good again. I'm going to try, you know?

ROSA: You've already been very good. You helped me a lot this week. You painted the front of the house. Redid the ceiling. You're fixing the pipes.

BILL: Isn't the baby hungry? He cried.

ROSA: Your shouting scared him.

BILL: I'm very sorry.

ROSA: Go to sleep now.

BILL: I'll clean this up now, okay? *(Indicates the dirty sheets.)*

ROSA: Yes, Bill.

BILL: I love you, Rosa.

ROSA: You're a tender, gentle man.

BILL: Would you clean this up for me?

Pause

BILL: My shit disgusts you, doesn't it?

Pause

ROSA: Take care of the baby. I'll get a rag to clean the mattress.

BILL: You won't be scared if I hold him?

Pause

ROSA: No.

Pause. Rosa hands Bill the Baby. He takes him in terror.

ROSA: I'll get a rag. *(She walks toward the kitchen. Bill gains more confidence as he holds the Baby, until he cradles him with a Madonna's tenderness, silently watching as he sleeps. Blackout.)*

SCENE 4

Alberto sits at the desk in the studio, writing. It's daytime. Rosa enters from the street with the Baby and her bag in her arms. An Indian boy carrying a basket of groceries follows her.

ROSA: Hello.

ALBERTO: *(Without looking up, distractedly)* Hi.

ROSA: I thought I'd find you asleep. You wrote all night. . . . *(Rosa shows the boy where he should leave things in the kitchen. While she goes toward the bedroom to put the sleeping Baby in his crib, she says:)* Beto fell asleep on the bus. In spite of all the bumps and the noise the people were making. How I envy children. All of a sudden they get an urge to sleep and bam! They throw everything to the wind and go to sleep. *(Alberto raises his head, murmurs: "How I envy children?" Shakes his head and returns his concentration to his desk. Rosa comes back as the Indian boy comes out of the kitchen. She gives him a tip. He thanks her with an inclination of the head. Rosa strokes his hair. The boy leaves the house, closing the door behind him.)* Would you like some coffee?

ALBERTO: No. Not now.

ROSA: Something cool, then? Some juice?

Pause

ROSA: We're lucky the house is air-conditioned. Brr, it's almost cold in here. If you knew how hot it is outside. *(Pause)* How's it going?

ALBERTO: *(Without looking up from the desk)* Good. *(Pause. Rosa starts to say something but before she can, Alberto jumps in, shouting:)* What?

ROSA: What do you mean, "what"?

ALBERTO: What were you going to ask me now? I don't want coffee. I don't want anything. I want you to let me concentrate. The novel's going well. It would go even better without interruptions.

ROSA: I only wanted to tell you that no mason wanted to come out here. They all said the house is very far away from the village and they'd lose too much time.

ALBERTO: Nothing to do then.

ROSA: The ceiling's going to rot.

ALBERTO: Can't be helped.

ROSA: Fine. One of these nights it's going to fall in on us.

ALBERTO: Certainly.

ROSA: You don't care?

ALBERTO: As long as I haven't finished my novel, the sky could fall in for all I care.

ROSA: Very funny. I'm talking about the ceiling in the bedroom.

Pause. Rosa walks toward the door. Alberto looks up from the desk.

ALBERTO: Rosa . . . Rosa, come here. You've got to understand. I came here for peace and quiet. I need absolute silence in order to write. If someone had lent us a house farther away from everything, I would have gone there. I spend hours disentangling myself from the world that surrounds me in order to enter the world of my novel slowly. I disconnect myself, bit by bit. And when I finally succeed in doing so, it irritates me greatly to have to connect with the outside world again. It means that I'll have to repeat the process all over again. And I can't be in two worlds at once. What am I explaining this to you for? This isn't the first novel I've written since we've lived together.

ROSA: But we've never been so isolated.

ALBERTO: True. That's why this will be a better novel than the other two.

ROSA: I feel very lonely.

ALBERTO: I've told you to go to town, to the hotels, to entertain yourself. It's the tourist season now, all sorts of interesting people come . . .

ROSA: In a luxury hotel in Puerto Vallarta a woman alone can only be looking for an affair. The men clearly approach you to pick you up, and the women are all much too busy looking for a man to make friends with another woman.

ALBERTO: The married couples, then . . .

ROSA: Yes, yes. I'm going to go up to a couple and say, "Good evening, my name is Rosa. I'm lonely. Do you mind if I join you?" Besides, Alberto, the baby. I can't even go to the movies with the baby.

ALBERTO: I can't promise you that I'll be finished soon. You know I work until I drop every day. But these things, creative works, take time. You can't rush them. They have their own rhythm.

ROSA: "For the poet, beauty grows slowly and silently, like flowers." Alberto Icaza. I know it by heart.

Pause

ALBERTO: I think I'll finish it before the deadline for the contest. With the prize money we'll go to Europe. Imagine: wandering through Paris, forgetting all about watches and schedules, buying whatever strikes our fancy, Rosa. Why save? I've got our treasure here. *(Pointing to his head)* Our treasure, you hear? Ours: yours and mine.

ROSA: You don't know if you'll win the prize.

Pause

ROSA: You don't have to finish the novel before the deadline. Take all the time you need to write a good book. A work of art. I understand. I want you to do it. It makes me happy that you're doing it. I believe it: beauty grows slowly. I love you because you're capable of doing beautiful things. I got angry because there wasn't a mason who would help us, that's all.

ALBERTO: I have to finish it before the deadline. If I work hard I can do it, I know it.

ROSA: Don't push yourself too hard.

ALBERTO: What does that mean? We have more energy than we can use. But more than energy one needs calm to create, patience. To find the rhythm of the poetry within us in order to let it flow. The sea soothes me. *(Pause. Rosa sits in Alberto's lap. Hugs him, strokes him.)*

ROSA: What can I do to help you?

ALBERTO: Just continue being as understanding as you are.

ROSA: Nothing more?

ALBERTO: What more could you do? You can't write for me. I wish you could. Sometimes the solitude is more than I can bear.

The Baby cries.

ALBERTO: *(Between his teeth)* God dammit, the baby.

Rosa runs out to see to the Baby. Alberto concentrates on his writing. Someone knocks at the door. Rosa comes running back in to open it. Bill stands on the threshold. He wears shorts and a T-shirt, tennis sneakers. He carries a masonry trowel in one hand and a sack of cement from which various tools stick out in the other. Despite the weight of everything he's carrying he seems to do so with ease. The Baby's crying can still be heard.

BILL: I'm a mason.

Alberto and Rosa look at each other, astonished.

BILL: A baby's crying.

Pause

35

BILL: A baby's crying. Isn't it your son?

ROSA: Yes . . .

BILL: Why don't you go take care of him?

ALBERTO: Who are you?

BILL: I'm a mason. Olvera sent me. He told me you needed a mason. Isn't that true? And, since I'm an out-of-work mason . . .

ALBERTO: You're North American?

BILL: Yes. A gringo mason. Is that bad?

ALBERTO: What?

BILL: That I'm a gringo mason.

ALBERTO: No, I don't think so.

BILL: There are masons in the United States as well, aren't there?

ALBERTO: Yes, I suppose there are. But a North American mason in Puerto Vallarta is a bit strange.

BILL: I came as a tourist, but my money ran out. A baby's crying.

ROSA: It's my son.

BILL: Aren't you going to go comfort him so he'll stop crying?

ROSA: Yes, of course.

Rosa goes to attend to the Baby. His crying will gradually die down, stopping over the next few minutes.

BILL: Thank you.

ALBERTO: Thank you?

BILL: You're an artist, right? That's what your wife told Olvera. She said that since you were an artist you couldn't fix the bedroom ceiling.

ALBERTO: You speak Spanish very well.

BILL: There are gringos who speak Spanish well, aren't there?

ALBERTO: I suppose so.

BILL: I'm a gringo who speaks Spanish very well. Is that bad?

ALBERTO: On the contrary. It's very good. I only mentioned it because it seemed a bit strange to me. There aren't many North Americans who speak our language well.

BILL: But there's nothing wrong with it, right? Could you do my portrait in exchange for my work?

ALBERTO: Me?

BILL: Don't be offended. Perhaps you're an expensive artist. But it would be an act of charity to paint my portrait in exchange for my humble work.

ALBERTO: I don't paint.

BILL: You're not an artist? Your wife lied in order to convince Olvera, is that it?

ALBERTO: I'm a writer, not a painter.

Rosa returns.

ROSA: Come through here. I'll show you where the ceiling's rotted.

BILL: Maybe we could discuss my portrait later on, all right? *(To Rosa)* Your husband's going to paint me, is that okay with you?

ROSA: You're going to paint him?

ALBERTO: *(Amused)* So he says.

BILL: It really doesn't matter if you don't paint me. You can pay me in cash, although I would be very grateful if you would do my portrait.

ROSA: But my husband draws very badly.

ALBERTO: Yes, but maybe I could do a composite sketch for him. *(He laughs but, since neither Bill nor Rosa join in, stops.)* A composite sketch, do you know what that means?

BILL: A description, you mean? Do you mean that you could write a story about me?

ALBERTO: Well, yes, that's the idea. But the thing about my suggestion is that it's a play on words. A composite sketch is what the police call the sketch an artist does of a criminal based on the descriptions of the witnesses to the crime.

BILL: I'm not a criminal.

ALBERTO: I was explaining the wordplay . . .

BILL: I know what you were explaining. That's why I'm telling you that I'm not a criminal.

For a moment the three of them stand there without speaking.

ROSA: Follow me, I'll show you the ceiling.

Rosa exits; Bill follows her. Alberto, laughing to himself, goes back to the desk and sits down, arranging some papers. Rosa comes back.

SCENE 5

ROSA: Alberto. I know I'm interrupting you again, don't get upset, but . . .

ALBERTO: What's the matter?

ROSA: The mason has already started to work, but when he saw the broken pipe, he said he could fix that as well.

ALBERTO: Great.

ROSA: He also said that, since he doesn't have any money for lodging, if we let him sleep here he'd repair anything that needs fixing.

ALBERTO: Sent from heaven.

ROSA: Doesn't he seem strange to you?

ALBERTO: The gringo? Very strange.

ROSA: And his attitude. As if he were too . . . I don't know . . . friendly.

ALBERTO: He came to Puerto Vallarta as a tourist, he ran out of money, and he needs a job. He isn't a mason, of course. You can tell he's well educated. Speaks impeccable Spanish. He must be a college student and is ashamed to say so, given his situation. It's strange but understandable. Ay, Rosa: you have to learn to respect and tolerate people's little eccentricities. What difference does it make who this guy is as long as he fixes the ceiling? You must have seemed odd to Olvera yourself. Telling him all about our lives in order to convince him to come.

ROSA: Was that wrong? I thought if he understood . . .

ALBERTO: The majority of people aren't as understanding as you are. Each one takes care of his own business.

ROSA: How terrible.

ALBERTO: Why terrible? Such an attitude has it's own advantages. As long as they fulfill their obligations each person can behave the way they want to.

Rosa moves toward the door to the stairs. She stops in the doorway. Turns.

ROSA: I'm very dumb. You have to explain things to me all the time.

ALBERTO: You're innocent, that's all.

ROSA: You mean stupid.

ALBERTO: No. Innocent. You aren't corrupted, hardened. *(Going to her)* Do me a favor: don't ever change.

ROSA: Wouldn't you like me to be less dependent? I don't know what I'd do without you.

ALBERTO: If I had wanted an astute, worldly wise companion, I would have married such a woman. But I fell in love with your innocence, my sweet. *(Kisses her briefly on the lips.)* Now let me write, okay? *(Dismissing her with a pat on the rump, he closes the door behind her.)*

Blackout

Intermission

SCENE 6

Bill, Alberto, and Rosa in the studio. Alberto reads from a manuscript.

ALBERTO: "He stared at the pieces of paper flung about the floor. He started to gather them up, but as soon as he had straightened them out, he threw them down again. He stared at the sheets of paper flung about the floor. At least, he thought, if I could get to the bottom of something, whatever it was, answer all the questions . . . But every time he dug down through a compressed layer, however deeply, there was always another layer even deeper and beyond that another, and beyond that another, and another. And, nevertheless, he said, I'm sure that the bottom of whatever it is is identical to the bottom of everything else. Then he thought of the sea." That's the end of the chapter.

ROSA: It's very beautiful, Alberto.

ALBERTO: Maybe it needs another draft.

ROSA: It seemed . . . superb to me. It's the best you've ever written.

ALBERTO: I think you're right. Even so, it might be improved. Some parts seem a bit thin. The repetitions bother me. They aren't forced, but I don't know . . . maybe they're too irritating. . . . I want to irritate the reader, of course, but not so much that he throws the book in the trash. Not that much. . . . It's awful, always thinking: How will my reader react?

ROSA: You'll always have such thoughts.

ALBERTO: You spend days and days revising a text and you end up afraid that no one but you will understand it anymore. And then comes the temptation to rewrite it in a style you know people will accept.

ROSA: I know you could do it. But you'd lose all your originality.

ALBERTO: Yes, that's the price. What did you think, Bill? Did you understand anything?

BILL: Of course.

ALBERTO: Well, that does it. If a North American understands it, so will any Mexican.

ROSA: Bill speaks Spanish better than many Mexicans.

BILL: He seemed too intellectual to me.

Pause

ALBERTO: What?

BILL: The character in your novel seemed too intellectual to me.

ALBERTO: What do you mean, "too intellectual"?

BILL: I mean that your main character's preoccupations are too intellectual for the average reader to identify with them. The majority of people worry about concrete problems, not abstract dilemmas.

ALBERTO: I don't write for the majority of people. I'm not after . . .

BILL: Most people worry about how they're going to eat in the morning.

ALBERTO: Agreed. But that kind of person doesn't even know how to read.

BILL: You don't know your own country. I'm not talking about the poorest classes.

ALBERTO: The poverty-stricken.

BILL: The poverty-stricken. I'm talking about the working class, the middle class, too. How long has it been since you've gone to the market? People are in anguish over the way the price of meat goes up every week. Do you know how much a kilo of beans costs right now?

ALBERTO: Why do foreigners always accuse Third World intellectuals of not paying attention to the plight of the Third World? Could it be that they can't stand the fact that in spite of our poverty we have the most dynamic art in the world today? Just because I have poor peasant blood coursing through my veins, that doesn't mean I don't have the right to deal with the same kinds of themes that Hegel and Nietzsche dealt with. Why do I have to write an art of poverty?

BILL: I only said what I said because I thought you were worried about your readers. I know you don't have to write about the price of beans . . . but, in any case, the common people, in Mexico, or in Yugoslavia, or in the United States, don't think about such things. They ask themselves how to love, how they're going to bring up their children, they ask themselves . . .

ALBERTO: I've never heard you talk so much, Bill. You are, contrary to appearances, intelligent. I'm amazed that you don't recognize my character's worries in yourself. I'll bet that you, too, have approached the edge of consciousness where all the humdrum, concrete problems dissipate and the kinds of problems that have occupied the brotherhood of human beings across centuries and continents burst forth: "Who am I?" my character asks himself. "What am I?" "I'm a tunnel," he says, "but from where to where, and for what? What am I driving at if I truly want to lead to something that will outlive me?"

BILL: I've asked myself these questions, sir. The answers I arrived at always proved false later on. For example, I asked myself if man was good or bad and I answered that because he can love he was basically good. Then in

Vietnam I saw things that showed me that all you had to do was loosen the reins a little and people behave like beasts. I, myself, . . . I, myself, killed, the best part of me. The part that went to church every Sunday.

ALBERTO: You had to defend yourself, isn't that the case?

BILL: You don't know who you are until you are. What's the use of abstract questions? I'm a person with good intentions right now.

ALBERTO: I believe you, Bill. You've helped Rosa and . . .

BILL: Please don't mention it. Your wife has been better to me than I've been to her. You, too.

ALBERTO: Which just goes to show that a man changes depending on the circumstances.

BILL: If that's the conclusion you've come to from what I've told you about myself, okay. But then, why ask yourself questions that have nothing to do with actual contexts?

ALBERTO: My character is in a real context, Bill.

BILL: But unique. And you want others to identify with him and learn from his experience.

ALBERTO: Of course.

BILL: Your book is, and always will be, paper and ink. The experience of reading it will be the experience of reading it. Nothing more.

ALBERTO: With that kind of logic you deny the possibility of any kind of literature. Do you realize that? Including literature that deals with concrete problems.

BILL: I realize that. That's the reason that besides giving up asking myself who I am or not as a man, I've also given up reading. Alberto, you like to formulate clear answers to questions that don't have answers. I'm saying this because of what you said about a man according to his circumstances. I'm going to contradict you again: Here, in Mexico, in your own country, I've seen Indians who've been stripped of their land, humiliated, whose inheritance has become . . .

ALBERTO: You don't have to say it: a net full of holes. I heard all about what you think the whites have done to the Indians the other day. You're obsessed with it, aren't you?

BILL: Yes . . .

ALBERTO: Why?

BILL: Let me finish what I was going to say. I've seen these people maintain their sense of right and wrong in the face of the most hostile kind of situation. I was present at the interrogation of an Indian peasant, a Cora, in

San Blas. I'm sure he knew who had set fire to military headquarters. In spite of the torture he didn't open his mouth. They beat him for an hour, two hours, three hours. They ripped off his fingernails. They hung him by his feet beneath the burning sun. The only thing the Indian did was cry, silently. They finally let him go. Physically broken, but with his dignity intact.

ALBERTO: I'm aware that such terrible things happen. Nevertheless . . .

BILL: You're aware? You'd have to have been there!

ALBERTO: You've implied you know my people better than I do from the beginning.

BILL: Maybe I've spent more time with them, recently, at least. Maybe, when you're not writing inside your four walls you spend your time with intellectuals who spend all their lives writing inside four walls.

ALBERTO: What were you doing in San Blas, Bill?

BILL: What was I doing? I was going to Manzanillo for my vacation and along the way I stopped in a town where all that took place. I went by car. I was living in Mexico City.

ALBERTO: Are you sure?

BILL: Am I sure? I can give you my exact address, if you want.

ALBERTO: And what were you doing there? What did you do in Mexico City?

BILL: I worked in the U.S. Embassy.

ALBERTO: In the U.S. Embassy? That's where you lived with the people? In those marble halls with their cushy armchairs?

BILL: I lived in a working-class neighborhood, I bought my food in the marketplace, traveled to the provinces during vacation, studied Mexican history.

ALBERTO: What was your job in the U.S. Embassy?

BILL: I guarded an entrance.

ALBERTO: Don't make me laugh. A guard? With your talents?

BILL: For a while I was an office boy.

ALBERTO: Office boy? Ha. Sure you didn't work for the CIA?

BILL: You have a very active imagination.

ALBERTO: Not too active. I know how to put two and two together. You were a marine, you know a lot about my country, you were in Nayarit. No one gets to see a torture session, especially a foreigner, unless that foreigner . . .

BILL: What?

ALBERTO: You were a military advisor to the Mexican Army.

BILL: That's not true.

ALBERTO: I think it is. And if I'm wrong, it won't be by much. You were in my country training assassins.
BILL: I taught English.
ALBERTO: Go fuck yourself. You trained assassins to kill my people.

Bill runs out. Rosa gets up to follow him, but Alberto stops her in the doorway.
ALBERTO: Wait. It has to be true. This gringo . . .

Rosa exits after Bill.

SCENE 7

Bill climbs the stairs. Rosa calls to him from the foot of the stairs.
ROSA: Bill.
BILL: Doesn't he realize that the world's breaking up? Breaking up like the sea and the sky in a storm? What's the use of talking in the middle of a storm with the sea and the sky falling into each other and you in the middle? But he writes verses to the sea. *(Spits.)* Verses from his house on the coast. *(Spits.)*
ROSA: Calm down, Bill.
BILL: I don't know how he does it. I worked like a bastard not to lose the thread of the conversation. For you, Rosa. To show you I can behave myself. Seem logical.
ROSA: He treated you like an equal.
BILL: But we're not equals. I appear logical. He's sick with logic.
ROSA: I was proud of you.
BILL: Logic has nothing to do with it.
ROSA: He told you you were intelligent.
BILL: Nothing to do with it. I swear to you that I'm not a CIA agent.

Rosa smiles at him. Goes closer. Strokes his hair.
BILL: The sea's calming down. *(Spits.)* The world's a net full of holes. Every minute, the holes get a bit bigger. The whole world will end up being a single black hole. I hope he finishes his novel before it happens. *(Laughs. Rosa laughs. Bill sees her and gets angry.)*
BILL: I'm going. I'll paint the front and go. I'm not a military advisor, but if that's what he thinks, I'll go.
ROSA: Where, Bill?

Bill looks at her, bewildered. He looks as though he's about to burst into tears but composes himself and continues talking angrily.

BILL: His turn will come. He'll be writing when a guerrilla jumps through the window and cocks a gun at his temple. "Wait a minute," your husband will say. "This is the most moving part of the chapter. The protagonist is standing in front of the sea and asking himself: 'Does God exist? Doesn't God exist?'" *(Laughs.)* But the guerrilla knows that if God exists, God is too busy to answer idiotic questions. Pumm. Good-bye, good-bye, dear Alberto. There, where you fall you will finally have silence.

Laughs. Rosa laughs. Bill gets angry.

BILL: What are you laughing about? Do you think I'm saying foolish things? Doesn't your husband want peace and quiet in this crazy world? Shut up, world, the writer needs absolute silence in order to write. "Prepare arms, fire." They're giving the order everywhere. Somewhere every minute. *(Taking Rosa and putting her against the wall)* Everyone up against the wall! Prepare arms, fire! *(Mimics riddling her with bullets from a machine gun. Rosa has become alarmed by the liveliness with which Bill mimes the execution. Bill laughs and goes up to his room.)*

BILL: His turn will come. No one can save themselves. No one. The sea calms him. Imbecile. The sea. I'll paint the front and then I'll leave, Rosa. Rosa? She's gone. She went to him. God doesn't have time to answer stupid questions. *(Taking a little bottle from the pile of tools in the corner, he opens it and, seated on the ground, inhales. In the studio, Alberto thinks aloud.)*

ALBERTO: Sometimes I'm afraid the only reason I write is to let my thoughts whirl around outside me. Vigorously, in order to give them at least the weight of the paper I'm staining. Shut up already, Alberto. The voice is fleeting. *(Smiles, types.)* Ah, this scream silenced there in the throat, ripping apart the musical chords from centuries before, long before your parents' parents. Rebellious being, looking for a way to finally scream in the insomniac night, an escaped sword of repressed rage up and down the blade, a cry constrained to crystal. If you can sculpt it, will it be a diamond? Ha: illusion's prisoner, the scream crushes more, and more . . . *(His voice dies out and Bill's comes back in between his inhalations.)*

BILL: The sea calms him. He's never been in a storm. Never seen a firing squad. Ha. The bodies falling. The sea calms him. Ha. The sea's a savage mouth. A mouth full of rage. Eat him up, eat him up, eat him up. *(The light dims. It's replaced by a blue light. A Guard and a Prisoner enter like figures in a dream. Bill slowly gets to his feet while the Guard sits the Prisoner down in a chair under the lamp suspended from the ceiling and ties him up. The lamplight gradually increases until it becomes the intense light used in interrogations. The Guard leaves. Bill punches the Prisoner energetically, laughing. But his pleasure quickly dries up from weariness and the beating becomes monotonous, routine. The door opens, and the Lieutenant appears in the doorway. His long shadow falls over Bill. Bill stands at attention.)*

SCENE 8

LIEUTENANT: He hasn't talked all night?
BILL: No, sir.
LIEUTENANT: Well, keep it up.
BILL: Yes, sir.
LIEUTENANT: Until he talks.
BILL: Yes, sir. Sir . . . maybe he won't.
LIEUTENANT: Bullshit. Every man has his limit.
BILL: Yes, sir.

The Lieutenant leaves. Bill continues beating the prisoner. His blows become farther and farther apart in time, gentler and gentler, until he gives the prisoner soft little pats on the cheeks.
BILL: Talk. Please . . . Please . . . Please . . .

Light fades to black.

SCENE 9

The studio. Rosa is talking to Alberto. He shows his impatience.
ROSA: He's all broken up. Wants to leave. I begged him not to. I explained how he hurt you. You've worked hard on your novel, and he was insensitive. . . . He wants to go, Alberto, and he doesn't know where. He doesn't have any place he can call his own. Right now, even in his own country, he feels attacked. It's not fair. He went to Vietnam believing he was defending his country.
ALBERTO: Who's attacking him? You're moved. Do you think they shout "marine" at him in the street? If he lets his hair grow long no one will even suspect his past.

ROSA: But the media attacks him. He's hypersensitive, don't you see? If you really believe what you said, that you're interested in humanity independently of . . .

ALBERTO: *(Interrupting her)* I know what you're driving at. It's true: humanity interests me independently of . . . Let's stop talking abstractly. I forgive Bill, even though he doesn't like my novel.

ROSA: You forgive him? You hurt him, too.

ALBERTO: Let him stay if he wants to stay. I will even try to forget my suspicions about his activities in Mexico.

ROSA: Won't you go talk to him?

ALBERTO: Me? *(Picking up his notebook and a pen)* I have to make some notes for the next chapter. You liked what I read, didn't you? You said it was the best thing I've written. It's true. But I still might be able to make it better. Get rid of some of the harsh edges.

Rosa makes as if to go.

ALBERTO: Tell him that I say please stay. I'm grateful for all his help. The way he keeps you company, helps take care of the baby. Tell him I respect him. Tell him I went overboard with my suspicions. If he says he was nothing more than a guard at the embassy, I'll take his word for it. *(Rosa opens the door, ready to leave.)* Tell him that even though what he said about my novel hurt me, I appreciate his opinion because he's intelligent.

ROSA: Is that all?

ALBERTO: Maybe when I finish the next chapter I'll take a break. Would you like to go dancing next weekend? . . . *(Rosa leaves)* Goddamn it.

Blackout

   Alberto organizes some papers in the study. Bill enters, head hung low. Alberto listens to him without interrupting his work.

BILL: Alberto, I came to tell you . . . I couldn't before . . . you didn't let me . . . I don't think as quickly as you do. I get confused . . . I'm . . . I was a low-ranking soldier in Vietnam. The story I told you about the Coras in Nayarit . . . I've never been in Nayarit. That story I told you about a man who never betrayed anyone despite the torture . . . was never disloyal . . . it happened in Vietnam, not Mexico. Like I told you, I was a guard at the embassy in Mexico City. I took applications, carried messages . . . After Vietnam I was too broken up inside. You're right, I don't know anything about your country firsthand. I shouldn't have argued with lies.

Everything I know about the Indians, I read. I was very lonely in Mexico City, and I read quite a lot. Náhuatl poetry, have you read any Náhuatl poetry? *(Alberto drops his papers. Stares fixedly at Bill. Lights a cigarette.)*

(Shouting) You don't believe me, do you? Say it, already. "You're a liar." *(Calm now)* I'm sorry. You'll forgive me? *(Alberto remains silent. Bill can't stand his stare, lowers his eyes, continues:)* When they discovered what you called my talents at the embassy they wanted to promote me. That's when I handed in my resignation. I was working as an English teacher, in an academy. I wanted a calm life. Without worries, without failures, or successes, calm . . . Three or four hours of class a day, lunch in a fonda, reading in the afternoon, a little bit of television before bed . . . the cartoons, you know? *(He laughs like a child.)* Cartoons so I wouldn't have to think. So I could go to bed like a zombie. That's been my routine for the past few years.

ALBERTO: You are, shall we say, an invisible man.

BILL: Yes . . .

ALBERTO: Timid, disdained. No one could envy you or demand anything of you. You've escaped from the competitive world. You don't owe anything to anyone, and no one owes you anything. You don't run the risk of being attacked.

BILL: You really understand me?

ALBERTO: You came to Puerto Vallarta on a U.S. Marines ship, Bill. You, Bill, are a liar.

Pause

BILL: Wait. Let me organize my ideas. . . . That isn't true either. From the beginning your wife thought I was a marine who came on the ship, and . . . I let her think that. At first because I thought it didn't matter to her who I was as long as I fixed the ceiling and then, when I began . . . to make friends with her . . . because in order to tell her my problems it didn't matter, how can I say this? . . . it didn't matter if my dilemma was to return to the Army or the Marines, you see? What difference did it make whether I had been a marine or a buck private in Vietnam, whether or not I got to Puerto Vallarta on board ship. When I got here, it didn't make any difference. If she . . . if the two of you, understood my confusion, why did I have to be exact about my motives? Do you believe me now? After Vietnam I was in the States, at my mother's house, for half a year, and I couldn't stand it, you see? I'd returned to a country that didn't want me,

that was ashamed of me, that made fun of me . . . I realized that in order
to forget about Vietnam I had to leave there. Every day, on TV, in the
papers, in people's conversations: "Was it a just war or not?", "They told
us it was ethical, but was it?", "How much did they do that they didn't tell
us?" They talked about us, the soldiers, as if we were strangers . . . We were
the ones who had lost the war. You know what really hurts the gringos?
Losing a war. That's why they couldn't understand us. We lost, not them.
The most important thing for them is to win, to be triumphant, triumphant, ta da dum . . . *(Laughs.)* I wanted a calm life. Without successes
or failures. I came to Mexico. I didn't accept a promotion at the embassy. I
got bored. I became an invisible man. Innocuous. You said it: disdained.
Who'd want to do the portrait of a guy like me? My stories aren't interesting. They're not what novels are made of. I'm a loser. I repeat everything
ten times. I'll leave you alone now. You want to write your novel about a
guy who asks himself transcendental questions. My animal's dead. I killed
him. Didn't give him anything to eat. Left the battle. No more sacrifices
for him. Not now, not ever. I'm hollow, an empty shell without an animal
inside, and I've become numb. I'll go now. I came to Puerto Vallarta in a
truck, from Mexico City. It's a pity; if I were a marine or a CIA agent
you'd be interested in doing a composite sketch of me.

ALBERTO: I'd do a composite sketch to turn you in. I prefer you to be who
you are.

BILL: But I bore you.

ALBERTO: You don't bore me.

BILL: *(Animated)* I met the marines in a restaurant. They invited me to a
cantina. I liked them, those noisy guys, who wanted to suck all the juice
out of their time on earth. We drank. Chatted. I told them how I felt like
a foreigner in the States, an undesirable alien. And that in Mexico I was, in
fact, a foreigner. As you rightly said, an undesirable alien. They advised me
to reenlist, this time as a volunteer. The pay was good, and with a little bit
of skill I could end up serving in West Germany, with people like me. The
idea excited me. I was drunk. I even thought that my real country was the
U.S. Army outside the United States. But as I sobered up and began to
feel hungover . . . I became upset, you understand? I became upset when I
realized my alternatives. When I realized that I'm still looking for a place
to park myself where I won't make anyone uncomfortable. I walked
quickly through the streets, almost running. Stepping forcefully, stepping
as if I wanted to step into the ground, disappear. . . . Dawn broke. The

streets were full of people. I went where they went. I got to the marketplace. . . . I saw your wife, Rosa, in the crowd, the baby in her arms,
asleep, calm, warm . . . *(As if suddenly snapping out of a dream)* But I've
been able to think while I've been in your house and I've reached a decision: I'm going to enlist. Today, tonight, I'm going to town to send in my
application. I'll go back to the army, you see? It makes the most sense. I
could have gone without explaining all this to you, but . . . you've been
very good to me. You and your wife. You've let me live in your house free
of charge. You've fed me free of charge. You've given me everything for
free, freely. That's why I wanted to explain.

ALBERTO: It hasn't been for free, Bill. We haven't given you anything for free.

BILL: Yes, everything free.

ALBERTO: You earned it with your work. You don't owe us anything.

BILL: You've given me everything for free.

ALBERTO: What are you talking about? I almost feel like we've exploited
you. The food you've eaten and the room don't even begin to pay for what
you've done. Come on, man! You've worked from dawn to dusk!

BILL: It's all been free.

Rosa enters from the bedroom. Listens to the conversation.

ALBERTO: Do you know how much a mason would have charged us?

BILL: Free.

ALBERTO: Not at all. Tell me how much we owe you. *(Taking out his wallet)*

BILL: Free, everything you've given me has been free.

ALBERTO: But, Bill.

ROSA: Free, Bill. We've given it to you for free.

ALBERTO: Rosa!

ROSA: Shut up, will you? Free, Bill.

BILL: Is it really true? All free.

ROSA: Everything.

BILL: Free.

ROSA: Free.

BILL: Thank you . . . thank you very much. I'll go to town tonight.

ROSA: No, Bill, you're not going to put in that application, right, Alberto?
We're not going to let him, are we?

ALBERTO: No, of course not. I've got a great idea. You stay here with the
baby and Rosa and I will go into town, do some dancing, and mail your
letter along the way.

Bill runs out. Alberto stops Rosa, who is going after Bill.
> ALBERTO: What did I do wrong now? *(Rosa breaks away from him and follows Bill. Alberto mutters:)* For Christ's sake . . .

SCENE 10

Alberto sits at his desk and tries, in vain, to concentrate. After spending some time angrily trying to write he goes to the bedroom. Simultaneously, we see Bill and Rosa, asleep on the terrace in the positions of the Pietà—his head in her lap. The light has dimmed almost to complete darkness when Bill gets up and goes stealthily to the bedroom. He comes out carrying the Baby in his arms and, nervously, starts toward the beach. Rosa suddenly wakes up. She calls Bill's name a few times, more worried each time. She looks for him in his room, the study, and, finally, the bedroom. She realizes that the Baby is no longer in his crib. She runs, terribly agitated, toward the beach. The waves of a stormy sea are heard, gradually becoming distorted until they sound like two choruses.
> FIRST CHORUS: For your love . . .
> SECOND CHORUS: For your affection . . .
> FIRST CHORUS: For your love . . .
> SECOND CHORUS: For your affection . . .

Et cetera.

SCENE 11

Lights come up, dawn. Alberto comes out of the bedroom and begins to write. While the light's still dim he could light a lamp, which he will put out as the light grows. Rosa enters from the bedroom. You can see she's upset.
> ROSA: Alberto, the baby. He's not in his cradle.

Alberto looks up, annoyed. Speaks brusquely. His voice is thick.
> ALBERTO: Bill took him to the beach.
> ROSA: You let him take him?
> ALBERTO: At least you could say good morning. He took him so you could sleep in and so I could have some silence. I can see that hasn't lasted long. *(He gets up and goes to the kitchen. He continues talking from there, even though Rosa has gone running toward the beach.)* I'm going to make myself some coffee. Do you want a cup? *(Pause)* The chapter's going so-so. I'm having problems. The plot's gotten all balled up on me. The damn protagonist doesn't know what to do. He stands in front of the sea. He says in a

loud voice: "All my beliefs are replaceable." "One generation's beliefs are like the waves, they arrive, soak the sand, and leave. Another wave comes. And goes. And then comes another. Is there no definitive human belief?" And then he becomes aware of the fact that the sound of the sea erases his words as soon as they're in the air. The more man expresses himself, the more deeply he reflects and the more the beliefs on which he's based his existence become intelligible, the less he believes in them. The intellect dissolves everything it accomplishes. Like words in the air. Even so, it's necessary to talk. To listen to oneself. Recognize oneself. Be heard. Recognized. Of course. That's it. He has to tell someone else what he's thinking. Not the sea. The sea doesn't stop to listen. You understand? Now. Now things are becoming clear. Your coffee's ready, Rosa. Two lumps of sugar? I'll write it now, Rosa. *(He comes out with two cups of coffee.)* Drink it when you come out of the bedroom. I've left it on my desk. Rosa? Did you fall asleep? *(He sticks his head in the bedroom.)* Rosa, dear? *(Goes upstairs. Shouts:)* You left me talking to myself! *(Opens the door to Bill's room.)* Shit! *(Opens the other door.)* Christ! *(Kicks the door.)* I can't stand talking to myself. I can't stand it when my words go up in thin air! Do you hear me, Rosa? *(His voice can be heard bouncing around the empty house.)* Christ! *(He angrily goes downstairs, so angrily that he bumps into a piece of furniture as he comes in. Kicks it. Kicks the wastebasket. Kicks the desk. The coffee spills. He runs to save his manuscript. Finally he sits down to write.)* Here's someone who really listens. This piece of paper. It remembers everything, word for word. *(Alberto concentrates. Some time passes, the light gets brighter—noon light—in order to suggest that several hours have passed. Bill and Rosa can be heard arriving in the distance, laughing.)*

SCENE 12

Rosa, with the Baby in her arms, and Bill enter, laughing. They quickly quiet down as they approach the spot where Alberto is working. They walk on tiptoe so as not to disturb him. They seem to be scared of being seen. Alberto notices them out of the corner of his eye.

ALBERTO: Why so happy?

Rosa and Bill stop, surprised.

ROSA: We were talking about the castle. Bill made a sand castle.
ALBERTO: You don't say.
ROSA: A beautiful castle. With towers and everything. A door made of

sticks. A wall and a moat around the wall. For defense against the enemy, you know?

ALBERTO: How marvelous.

ROSA: And he made a garden with palm leaves inside the wall.

ALBERTO: Palm leaves!

ROSA: I told him he should be an architect.

ALBERTO: Without a doubt, without a doubt. Would you like to be an architect, Bill? I mean, when you grow up? *(Pause)* It was a joke. Sorry if I offended you.

Bill lowers his head. He exits, head hung low, and goes up to his room. Rosa looks at Alberto reproachfully. She goes toward the door.

ALBERTO: Rosa, wait. I want to talk to you.

ROSA: What do you want?

ALBERTO: I don't like the way you're spending so much time with the gringo. The two of you are getting like children. You talk to him as if he were a child.

ROSA: Don't you realize he is like a child? He's learning how to play, how to enjoy life. *(Exits.)*

SCENE 13

Alberto follows Rosa to the stairs.

ALBERTO: Rosa.

ROSA: What is it?

ALBERTO: I finished another chapter.

ROSA: Good.

ALBERTO: Do you want me to read it to you?

ROSA: Do you want me to hear it?

ALBERTO: Me? *(Annoyed)* If you're not interested, forget it.

ROSA: Okay. *(Goes up two steps.)*

ALBERTO: Rosa.

ROSA: What?

ALBERTO: Don't you want to hear it? I think it's good.

ROSA: Do you want me to hear it?

ALBERTO: What's going on?

ROSA: God, does it cost you so much to admit that you need to read it to me?

ALBERTO: I don't need anything. The chapter's written. It doesn't matter whether you hear it or not.

ROSA: Good. *(Goes up two steps.)*

ALBERTO: Rosa! It's our novel, yours and mine.

ROSA: How strange. I don't recall having written a single line. My recollection is that I've been busy washing diapers, floors, and walls. If it weren't for Bill I'd spend months without talking to a man. Without receiving a single caress.

ALBERTO: *(Disconcerted)* You don't mean to say that you and Bill . . .

ROSA: What difference does it make to you?

ALBERTO: What do you mean, what difference does it make? If the two of you are lovers . . .

ROSA: Bill strokes me like I was his mother. He couldn't do anything more, although it would be a nice pastime for me to have a lover.

ALBERTO: Rosa . . . You know that when I'm writing I can't waste my energy on anything else. But, if you want . . .

ROSA: I'm tired. *(Goes up two steps. Bill's voice is heard from his room.)*

BILL: Rosa? Rosa . . .

ALBERTO: Rosa!

BILL: The baby . . .

ALBERTO: I forbid you to go to the gringo!

BILL: The baby is . . .

ALBERTO: It's incredible. A stranger gets more attention than I do in my own house. From my own wife.

BILL: Rosa!

The Baby's crying can be heard. Bill comes to the stairs.

BILL: He's screeching!

ALBERTO: Son of a bitch.

Rosa turns and looks at Alberto with a strangely calm expression.

ROSA: Say that again.

ALBERTO: What?

ROSA: That thing about "a bitch."

ALBERTO: It's just an expression.

BILL: What do I do? With the baby?

Rosa silently comes down the stairs.

ALBERTO: Aren't you going to see to the baby?

ROSA: Which one of the three of you? *(She laughs softly. Keeps coming down. The crying gets more intense. Just before going out toward the beach she murmurs:)* Son of a bitch, all right.

ALBERTO: Damn gringo, it's all your fault. She's had it up to here, taking care of you on top of the baby.

BILL: She said: "Which one of the three of you?" You're a baby, too.

ALBERTO: Don't talk to me about you.

BILL: I was talking about you. The baby sleeps nearly all day, wakes up, and wants his milk. You write and wake up wanting your applause.

ALBERTO: You can't . . . *(Runs up the stairs until he's standing in front of him.)* Get out of here, Bill. Get out of my house.

BILL: Let's go ask Rosa if she wants me to leave.

ALBERTO: How macho, little gringo. *(Pushing him into his room)* Listen to this. Listen well: you're not leaving here until you tell me who you are. Sit down. Now I'm really going to do your composite sketch. And it might even be for the police, understand? At least it will make Rosa realize who she's been spoiling like a snot-nosed kid.

Bill gets up from the chair.

BILL: Rosa!

ALBERTO: Sit down! *(Walking around him)* Are you a marine, Bill? An English teacher? A tourist? An employee at the embassy? A CIA agent? A psychopath? A schizophrenic? Who the hell are you, Bill?

BILL: The baby . . .

ALBERTO: The baby will shut up all by himself. Sit down!

BILL: I didn't go to Vietnam. When I got my draft notice the idea made me sick, I broke down. I couldn't disobey my mother, but I was afraid. I spent the war years in a psychiatric hospital in Quebec. It's barely a month since they let me out . . .

Alberto is disconcerted. Then he stares attentively at Bill.

ALBERTO: I don't believe anything you say anymore. I don't even believe you're crazy.

BILL: I don't know who I am. I don't remember. I don't want to remember. I'm good now. Rosa loves me. I'm her mason. Rosa's.

ALBERTO: Bill . . . *(Pointing between Bill's legs)* You just peed all over yourself in order to convince me that you're a harmless child? You're not a child

54

anymore, Bill. You have to take responsibility for what you've done. *(Laughs. Suddenly, aggressively threatening him.)* I'm going to take you to the police so they can tell me who you are.

BILL: I don't have any papers. They'll kick me out of the country. Send me back to the States. Don't take me.

ALBERTO: Yes, yes. I'm going to take you, Bill. I'm going to find out once and for all who you are.

BILL: Please. I don't want to go back.

ALBERTO: Come on. Get up. *(Bill makes a pleading gesture. A while goes by until Alberto becomes exasperated.)* Come on! Get up!

Bill closes his eyes, tenses up until he quivers. Bends over double. Suddenly leaps from his chair and, falling on one foot, with the other lets loose a kick that connects precisely with Alberto's jaw. Alberto falls backward and crashes into the wall. Slowly, he slides down the wall until he rests on the floor, inert. As Rosa's footsteps are heard coming up the stairs the rhythm returns to normal. As she comes up the stairs, little by little, talking, Bill approaches Alberto's body, embraces him, sits him in the chair, legs spread wide. Pats his cheeks, energetically at first, then lightly, impotently, thus reproducing the final image of the scene in which Bill tortured the prisoner of war.

ROSA: Bill. Alberto.

BILL: Say something. Please.

ROSA: Did the baby go to sleep?

BILL: Please . . . Please . . .

ROSA: Is he asleep?

BILL: Please.

ROSA: Bill? Alberto?

BILL: Please.

Before Rosa turns the doorknob, blackout.

PUZZLE

CAST

Jacques Mornard	Spanish Man
Colonel Salazar	Lieutenant Gomez
Natalia Sedova	Persian Ambassador
Leon Davidovich Trotsky	U.S. Ambassador
Silvia Angeloff	Russian Ambassador
Esther Cerrojo	Trotskyite Representative
Trotsky's Bodyguards	Nun
Hansen	Secretary
Cornell	Nurse
Robins	Téllez
Charlie	Reporters
Pluffea	Guards

ACT 1

Scene A

A cell in the police station. There's a loudspeaker high up in one corner. Jacques and Colonel Salazar. They are exhausted from a lengthy interrogation.

COLONEL: Why, then . . . Mr. X?

JACQUES: Jacques, Jacques Mornard.

COLONEL: Mr. X.

JACQUES: Jacques Mornard. Born in Teheran, naturalized Belgian citizen.

COLONEL: Anything else?

JACQUES: Communist.

COLONEL: Oh. *(Suddenly furious)* Why?

JACQUES: Disillusioned.

COLONEL: Mr. X!

JACQUES: Mornard.

COLONEL: Why?

JACQUES: Disillusioned. For God.

COLONEL: You don't believe in God. Why?

JACQUES: Disillusioned.

COLONEL: You don't believe in God because you are disillusioned?

JACQUES: I killed him because I'm disillusioned. Enough. Jacques, Mornard. Jacques Mornard.

The dictaphone crackles as it comes to the end of its roll.

COLONEL: That's the end of the dictaphone roll. Shall we take this opportunity to change the subject?

The Colonel unplugs the wires from the speaker built into the corner. Turns around to stare into Jacques' terrified eyes. Jacques tries to avoid his stare but seems incapable of not looking into the Colonel's eyes. They stare at each other fixedly.

COLONEL: Mr. X: on all fours.

Jacques obeys this and all subsequent orders.

COLONEL: Bark. Howl. Stand up. Half turn. Half turn. Half turn. Rest.

The Colonel plugs the speaker wires back in.

COLONEL: Put in another roll. Roll 20. August 23, 1940. A pleasant midnight to you, Mr. X.

JACQUES: *(Whispering)* Mornard.

COLONEL: *(Whispering)* Why?

Pause. Blackout.

Picture 1

Trotsky's mansion. There are two levels on the stage. Above, the study and the bedroom. A staircase descends from them to the first floor. There, the garden and the rabbit hutches. The characters are found distributed throughout the stage. They remain frozen until the plot action requires them to move. Sometimes they will act as a chorus. Natalia Sedova, Colonel Salazar, Leon Davidovich Trotsky, Charlie, Robins, Hansen, Cornell, Jacques Mornard, the Police Secretary.

Scene 1

Natalia Sedova makes her statement to Colonel Salazar. The Secretary transcribes it.

NATALIA: In the morning, waking up about seven, my husband said to me, "You know, Natalia? I feel very good. Better than I've felt in a long time. I took a double dose of sedative last night. It seems to have done me good." I responded, "Yes, I remember we noticed the sedatives helped when we were in Norway and you felt tired even more frequently than you do now. But the sedative's not what's making you feel better. A good night's sleep, no matter how you get it, is a complete rest." "That's true," he said. He opened the armored blinds in our bedroom. *(Trotsky opens the blinds in the bedroom.)* Our friends had put in the blinds after the house was attacked, three months ago or so. It was a luminous morning. An impeccable blue sky fell over the lawn in the garden. It shone like green varnish.

TROTSKY: I'm not afraid of another nighttime attack anymore, not with these blinds. Remember how the shots made holes in the window? Machine-gun blasts through here, that window, the other one. I wouldn't be here today seeing this sun if you hadn't thrown me to the ground and lain on top of me. Even so, it's almost miraculous that the crossfire didn't hit us. They didn't kill us last night, either. Even so, you're not happy. Yes, Natasha: we've been given a lucky break.

NATALIA: Death has followed us ever since we left the Kremlin. Death, personified by Stalin's henchmen. The tyrant can't stand a single voice on the planet that names his crimes and shows the people a different road. He won't rest until Leon's a cadaver. But on that forsaken morning such thoughts were far from us. Leon felt physically well, and that was all he needed in order to devote himself entirely to living. For him, devotion to life was his work.

TROTSKY: I'm going to the garden to feed the rabbits. I'll go up to the study around nine. I should finish the article on military instruction in

North America. (*Trotsky goes down to the rabbit hutches. Feeds the animals.*)
NATALIA: Hansen, one of our secretaries, arrived early. He had been away
for a few days, looking into the attack of which we had been victims a little
while ago.

*Hansen advances toward Trotsky, followed by Robins. Trotsky doesn't take his attention off
the rabbits.*

NATALIA: He brought annoying news. The Mexican Stalinists had already
insinuated in newspaper editorials that it had been a self-planned attack.
According to them, Leon Davidovich had done it in order to defame
Stalin, attract worldwide attention to himself once more, and stain the
country that had given him sanctuary and that promised to protect him.
HANSEN: The accusation has been made with a complete lack of discretion.
At a rally yesterday a Stalinist speaker said you arranged it all in order to
push President Cárdenas against the Soviet regime. I quote: "with unpar-
donable eagerness to direct Mexican politics toward Trotskyite interests."
The crowd interrupted the speech with shouts of "Trotsky, out! Trotsky,
out!" The speaker continued, inflamed, "Comrades, I thought I wouldn't
speak about the most serious charge until there was some concrete evidence to confirm the rumor, but I see now that it's essential to prevent
them. Listen: Allied with Yankee imperialism, the traitor hiding in
Coyacán is planning a coup d'état to replace the present nationalist
Mexican government with another . . ." Excuse me, the speeches were
rather long. . . . Ah, yes. I wrote the rest on the back of my notebook . . .
"with another puppet government that would give the nationalized oil
fields back to the Yankee capitalists."
TROTSKY: Me, a puppet. A puppeteer, too. Heroes and villains moved by
different wills. What tiny minds. Poor saps: A clumsy hand shakes them,
and they see themselves as daring.
HANSEN: I looked for Cárdenas. His agenda was full, but he gave me a few
minutes while he visited a recently built elementary school. That's how,
zigzagging through the group following him, through classrooms and
classrooms, I came up behind him and, trying not to seem too forward or
too humble, I gave him a brief synopsis of what had been said at the rally.
TROTSKY: And . . . ?
HANSEN: He laughed. As if I'd told him some splendid joke. When he finished laughing he asked me how the fortifications on the house were
going. I told him that this was a fortress.

ROBINS: An impregnable fortress.

TROTSKY: *(Sadly)* A medieval fortress.

HANSEN: The president told me that if the twenty policemen watching the street weren't enough, that we should talk to Colonel Salazar. Right at that moment we came out on a balcony and hundreds of children began to sing in the patio.

TROTSKY: The policemen are sufficient. What a pity I will have to postpone more interesting matters in order to respond to these base infamies. Hansen, leave the speech from the rally on my desk and come back in two hours to take my reply to the newspapers. As soon as these cottontails have been well taken care of, I'll get to work.

Hansen and Robins go to the study. Followed by Charlie, Jacques Mornard approaches Trotsky. He wears a hat and carries a raincoat over his left arm. He's smoking.

NATALIA: A little bit later, looking out the window, I realized that another visitor had arrived. It was Jacques, a young Belgian. He'd come to Mexico with Silvia Angeloff, an old friend and a frequent guest in our home, expressly to meet Leon personally. He'd probably returned today so that Leon could reread his article and suggest possible corrections again. I went down to the garden to bring my husband a hat to protect the back of his neck from the sun that was piercing him, and took the opportunity to greet the young comrade.

Natalia goes down to the rabbit hutches carrying a straw hat. Trotsky continues attending to the rabbits. With the butt of one cigarette, Jacques lights another. Smokes, puffing smoke at brief intervals.

TROTSKY: So you're going back to New York with Silvia. When?

JACQUES: Tomorrow. That's why I dared to bother you again before we'd agreed. I wanted to say good-bye.

NATALIA: To New York? If only I'd known. You could have taken something for me.

JACQUES: Good morning, madam. I'm sorry. It's been a sudden decision. Silvia should be here as well to say good-bye. Something must have kept her. *(With difficulty, he takes a box of candy out from under his raincoat and gives it to her.)*

NATALIA: Thank you, Jacques. You never come without a present. You're much too generous to be Belgian.

JACQUES: *(Very nervous)* I'm Belgian, my parents are Belgian, but I was brought up in France.

TROTSKY: Curious. You didn't act like a Frenchman two days ago either. You sat in a corner of my study, reading your article, your hat on, and without letting go of this absurd raincoat.

JACQUES: Absurd?

TROTSKY: Given this splendid sun.

NATALIA: It is strange.

JACQUES: *(Precipitously)* Not at all. The temperature here often changes from one minute to the next. Besides . . . I don't know if I've told you before: I was born in Persia. My father was the Belgian ambassador in Teheran. Of course, that doesn't explain anything about the raincoat. Or about me. Perhaps it's that I'm . . . a mélange . . . not really from anyplace . . .

NATALIA: *(Meaning it as a friendly joke)* You think very little of yourself. The same background could assure you a place at the heart of internationalism.

JACQUES: Yes, it could. . . . I wonder what's happened to Silvia? Maybe I should go look for her and come back with her tomorrow morning. That way you would be able to give me whatever it is you want me to take to New York.

NATALIA: Silvia will be here soon. Don't worry about taking anything to New York.

JACQUES: You're right: the sun is quite dreadful. *(Takes off his hat.)* I'm dying of thirst.

NATALIA: Would you like a cup of tea?

JACQUES: No, thank you. I had breakfast a little while ago. But, if it's not too much trouble, I'd be grateful for a glass of water.

NATALIA: No trouble at all. I'll bring it right away. *(Leaves.)*

TROTSKY: You're not well, Jacques.

JACQUES: No.

TROTSKY: You're pale. More than pale: you're turning green. *(Taking his wrist)* Your pulse is racing. You're sweating. Do you have a fever?

JACQUES: *(With the cigarette between his lips, puffing smoke as he talks)* It's the work. The studying. I'm preparing day and night. A party member has no time for leisure activities . . . that is, in the current circumstances. When we live the way you talk about in your books, free and equal, all our lives, at work and at rest, it'll be a pleasure. Every gesture, every action, will be art. Useful, not superfluous art. *(Swallows. Coughs.)*

TROTSKY: You're making too much smoke, Jacques.

JACQUES: *(Putting out his cigarette)* Yes, I've got a slight fever.

TROTSKY: Take care of yourself. Bad habits and too arduous a routine could kill you. The living serve the party, the more alive the better. Look: after the attack I felt weak and entrusted the rabbits to one of my secretaries. He fed them. At arbitrary hours. He cleaned the cages. Hosing them down with the animals inside. In short, he took care to carry out my instructions which, fortunately, weren't many. The rabbits turned surly. They began to fight in the corners; they've been calm for a long time now and they still react to any attempt to pet them by fleeing or scratching. *(Takes off his gloves.)* See the marks? Observe: I open the cage, stick in my hand . . . Screech, screech, screech. Conclusion: be good to yourself and you'll write clearer, more energetic, and more optimistic articles. Did you bring your article?

JACQUES: I typed it so it would be easier to . . . strike things out. *(Laughs sarcastically. Trotsky goes toward the stairs to the study. Jacques follows him.)*

TROTSKY: What did you expect? Your article was confused and in places incoherent. Would you have preferred false congratulations? Jacques, a few days ago Silvi brought some artists. Good artists, so they say. They wanted to meet me. They recited praise so out of proportion that, if it hadn't been for the Mussorgsky in the background, I would have found it difficult to take. Then they started to praise Stalin. His purges. The dissident trials. They explained to me why we should support that purification. The end justifies the means, they said. Where have I heard this before?, I asked myself. Not even for Silvi, nor for Mussorgsky, could I tolerate another minute more.

JACQUES: Silvia doesn't agree with those ideas.

TROTSKY: I threw them out.

JACQUES: Silvi was very ashamed. She cried all night.

TROTSKY: I'm not a museum piece. Not yet. Silvia should know who to bring to this house.

JACQUES: I agree completely.

TROTSKY: And she sympathizes with the Trotskyite minority, those who want me to renounce the Great Russian Revolution in order to defend their "ideal Trotsky" from this Trotsky.

JACQUES: An embarrassment. I tried to dissuade her.

TROTSKY: It's understandable to want revenge, even if it's only verbal. When children get angry with the world they often scrawl obscenities until they calm down. But Trotsky is a Marxist thinker. Objective, and

Marxist sociology doesn't get mixed up with hysteria. Tell Silvi that she's still welcome. She brightens the day whenever she comes.

JACQUES: Yes. I agree completely.

TROTSKY: You know why I've said these things up until now?

JACQUES: We're in the private space you only let your secretaries into.

TROTSKY: From the foot of the stairs to the back wall of my study. *(They both laugh bitterly. They go up two steps and suddenly Trotsky turns to confront Jacques.)* Jacques . . .

JACQUES: Yes!?

TROTSKY: *(As if confiding a great secret)* They say that radioactive food is marvelous. Investigate for me. See if you can get hold of any at the market. My rabbits would be grateful for generations.

JACQUES: No. I don't know anything about food, sir.

TROTSKY: I know. That's why I said you should investigate.

Trotsky goes on ahead. Sits at his desk in the study, reads the article. Puts on his glasses. Picks up a pen. Jacques sits on the desk. Then he moves to a piece of furniture that forms a triangle with the desk on its east side. Trotsky puts the pen to the article. Strikes something out just as Jacques takes an ice pick with a broken handle out from under his raincoat. Raises it. Natalia, in another reality, continues her deposition.

NATALIA: Twelve years ago, when we left our country's capital for exile, debilitated but still too excited to close our eyes, Leon leaned over toward my seat and, in the darkness of the compartment, took my hands in his and asked, "Would it have been better to wait for death in bed in the Kremlin? I'm old. There will be those who will accuse me of having abandoned the center of the Revolution. History bathes martyrs in an immaculate light." "No," I answered. "It's better this way." The car hit a bump and we hit foreheads. Leon whispered in my ear, "I think it's better this way, too."

Trotsky looks up at Jacques.

CHORUS: With closed eyes!

Jacques delivers the blow. Trotsky howls. Slides down his seat at the same time that he grabs Mornard's hand and bites it. Jacques manages to break away. Strikes him again. Trotsky crawls away. Gets up. Laughing, Jacques follows him, the ice pick raised in his hand. Trotsky backs up, staggering, his face bloody. He throws whatever he can between himself and his assassin. When the dictaphone is thrown it turns on. Trotsky's voice is heard dictating his article on military instruction in North America. In the meantime Natalia has come into the garden, a glass of water in her hand. She drops it and runs up the stairs. With a supreme effort, Trotsky faces Jacques. Jacques backs up a step. Staggering, Trotsky is about to fall to his knees at his feet, but the impulse of his movement turns him around and he falls the other way.

NATALIA: *(Entering)* What happened? What happened?

The Bodyguards run in. Jacques is paralyzed.

TROTSKY: Jacques . . .

Jacques, the Bodyguards after him, runs into the next room. Natalia helps Trotsky. He falls in her arms.

TROTSKY: Two things, Natalia. First, don't let them kill him. They should make him talk. Second . . . always remember: I love you.

NATALIA: *(To Hansen, who's returned)* Call the doctor.

HANSEN: Charlie's gone to get him in the car.

NATALIA: Get me alcohol, bandages, ice.

TROTSKY: An ambulance.

HANSEN: It's only a superficial wound.

TROTSKY: . . . ambulance . . .

Hansen goes toward the bedroom.

TROTSKY: *(Pointing to his heart)* I know . . . here . . . that it's all over. This time . . . they've . . . done . . . it.

In the bedroom.

HANSEN: We shouldn't kill him. Tie him up. Make him talk. *(Leaves.)*

ROBINS: I'm not going to kill you. I'm just going to break all your bones and shoot you full of bullets if you don't tell me immediately who sent you. *(Pushes Jacques up against the wall. He and Cornell beat him with their fists and the butts of their revolvers.)* The G.P.U. sent you. Confess. The G.P.U., Stalin's dogs. Don't deny it. Talk. Bastard.

CORNELL: Talk.

ROBINS: Talk.

JACQUES: Kill me. I don't deserve to live. Get rid of what's left of me once and for all.

CORNELL: Stop. *(Robins obeys.)* You're not going to die without talking. *(Strikes him.)* Even if I have to cut you up bit by bit until there's nothing left but your head, you're not going to die without talking. How'd you like a manicure, Jacques? *(Takes out a pair of tweezers. Tears off a fingernail.)*

JACQUES: It wasn't the G.P.U. I swear.

ROBINS: Who, then?

JACQUES: Them.

CORNELL: Who are they?

JACQUES: They made me. They've got something with which they made me.

ROBINS: Who?

JACQUES: I don't know. *(They tear off another fingernail.)* I don't know, I swear. But they're not from the G.P.U. You can kill me if you like, but I don't know anything more. *(They tear off another fingernail.)* Please, kill me. I don't know anything more. *(They tear off another fingernail. Howling)* They've got my mother prisoner.

Blackout, except in the Secretary's area. She puts a new piece of paper into the typewriter. Puts what's been typed into a folder. Starts transcribing again.

Picture 2

The hospital. People moving. Noise. Two Stretcher Bearers carry Trotsky on a stretcher. Natalia holds his head with both hands. The Bodyguards keep back the Reporters, who press forward. Colonel Salazar leads the maltreated Jacques along. Each wounded man is put into his respective room. A Guard is left in front of each door.

COLONEL SALAZAR: *(To Jacques' Guard)* Stay inside. Watch his hands. If he holds his breath all of a sudden, knock him down. He already tried to slit his wrists in the ambulance with a dagger he'd sewn into the lining of his raincoat. And don't let him get near the window. They could shoot him.

Scene 1

Trotsky's room. After having moved him from the stretcher to the bed, one Stretcher Bearer adjusts his head delicately while the other opens his robe, takes something out of his clothes, and points it. . . . Natalia throws herself at him at the same time as he pulls the object's trigger—a flash tells us that it's a camera. But Natalia, already in the air, knocks him down. The Bodyguards point their guns at him. Colonel Salazar runs in.

COLONEL: Téllez! What the hell are you doing here?

STRETCHER BEARER (TÉLLEZ): Colonel . . . *(Getting up. Saluting)* Doing my job, as you do yours.

COLONEL: My job is, among other things, to make yours difficult. Give me the camera.

65

TÉLLEZ: In exchange for your gun.
COLONEL: The film at least.
TÉLLEZ: Your cartridges, Colonel.
COLONEL: Don't play games.
TÉLLEZ: I'm not playing.
COLONEL: Then you oblige me to . . .

Téllez runs out. The head Doctor and a Nurse take the bandages off Trotsky's head. The doctor examines him. The Nurse cleans him up. Begins to cut his hair.
TROTSKY: Natasha . . .
NATALIA: Here, Leon.
TROTSKY: Natasha, you told me . . . I needed a haircut and I told you . . . later, there's not time now, but, you see? There's a time for everything. . . . Short in the back and long in the front please, miss.
NURSE: I'll have to cut it all off, sir. I'm sorry.
TROTSKY: Well.
DOCTOR: Don't talk. It takes too much effort.
TROTSKY: *(To Natalia)* Hansen?

Hansen comes forward. Trotsky signals to him. He takes out a pen and a little notebook.
TROTSKY: I'm convinced that the IV International will triumph. Forward! *(Pause)* Nothing more.

Hansen moves back. The Nurse begins to cut off his clothes.
TROTSKY: Natasha . . .
NATALIA: Here . . .
TROTSKY: Yes: here. You've always been "here." You undress me. Alone.

Everyone leaves. The Nurse gives Natalia a change of clothes and leaves. Trotsky and Natalia alone. She cuts the clothes off him. Trotsky indicates that she should come closer.
TROTSKY: Come here. . . . I prefer . . . *(Takes her by the waist. Brings her toward him. She's now on top of his nude body. She kisses him. He kisses her in turn.)*
NATALIA: Even now you respond to me. *(Kisses him. Is kissed.)*
TROTSKY: Even now. If only eternity weren't . . .
NATALIA: Shh. *(Kisses him. Is kissed.)* And even now.
TROTSKY: Momentarily. *(Pause. Natalia gets up. Covers Trotsky with a sheet. Opens the door.)*

NATALIA: He's lost consciousness.

Scene 2

Jacques' room. Jacques' cheekbones are purple with bruises. Hair sticks out of the bandage around his head. He smokes. There's a Guard in the corner. Colonel Salazar comes in with the Secretary. She transcribes the interview in her notebook.

COLONEL: They're going to operate on your victim. There's every chance he'll survive. In your case . . . I don't know what to do with you. The hospital director doesn't want you here. He's afraid of what might happen. The penitentiary director also refuses to admit you. He alleges that he doesn't have any way of locking you up that wouldn't allow an attempt on your life. But there must, of course, be some place on the face of the earth where they'd be anxious to receive you and celebrate your great deed. Where's that, Jacques?

JACQUES: I made it very clear in my written confession that I acted alone, without anyone's help, and without anyone else's knowledge . . .

COLONEL: Ah, yes: that typewritten piece of paper you gave to the ambulance paramedics.

JACQUES: It contains a synthesis of my biography, my confession of the crime, my motives, the way I planned to carry it out, and in general corresponds to what I, in fact, did.

COLONEL: Well, then, I have nothing to investigate. You've saved me a lot of work.

JACQUES: You still have to protect my life. Until you receive orders to . . . *(Makes a gesture of slitting his throat. Laughs.)*

COLONEL: What's your opinion of the insults the crowd shouted at you as you were being transferred from the ambulance to this room? I've never seen such repugnance toward a human being in all my life.

JACQUES: I'm an assassin, aren't I?

COLONEL: Almost. I repeat: your victim has high hopes of surviving. *(Jacques makes a gesture of disbelief.)* The public generally show some compassion for an assassin. But Leon Davidovich Trotsky is a very well loved man.

JACQUES: Where are we going with this stupid chat? Of course Leon Davidovich was a very well loved man. He was a demagogue. He spoke beautifully to all the people in the world. He told them that it was their natural right to be masters of their own destiny. And the destiny he painted for them was beautiful: a paradise on earth. As I said in my con-

67

fession I myself loved him for those ideas. I idolized him. I knew pages of his writings by heart. I recited them like a monk does his prayers. Before reaching this state of devotion I was an independent man. A journalist. A person without political affiliations who believed himself capable of distinguishing right from wrong with his own eyes. It was precisely for that reason that I had chosen journalism as a profession. An activity where a man free of prejudices could get to know the political reality and influence it by publishing rational opinions. But then I met the Trotskyites. And they convinced me that in order to powerfully influence society you have to have a goal in mind and in order to lead the people there you have to act within a larger organization. *(The Colonel stays calm in the face of Jacques' passionate outburst.)*

COLONEL: According to your confession you met the Trotskyites in Paris.

JACQUES: They laughed at my independence from all doctrine. They told me, "Lad, your voice is just one voice in the general din. Leave tilting at windmills for the constipated bourgeoisie." And among the Trotskyites I met the woman I fell in love with.

COLONEL: Silvia Angeloff.

JACQUES: "Where reason strikes barriers, love conquers in fury." Silvia told me that I should sacrifice my individualistic position in order to join the party. When I put my objections to her opinion up against Silvi's passion, they seemed like egoism. That's how I sacrificed my individualism. My solitary afternoons filled up with comrades. Ah, those nights in party headquarters. Outside, the confused night; inside, we passed around a bottle of vodka, each assuring the other that we possessed the true knowledge. Oh, how fortunate we were: all Knowledge was within our reach, as close as the bookstore, ordered, silent, in pocket editions. One day a comrade offered to sponsor a trip for me to meet our leader personally. Can you imagine what a monk would feel if they gave him a ticket to see God? I accepted immediately. But why am I telling you what I already wrote in my confession?

COLONEL: Why did you travel with a false passport?

JACQUES: There's a war on the other side of the ocean, have you heard about it, detective? In France they're rounding up civilians. With my own papers I would have been stopped at the border and sent to the army. Not to be incorporated into their ranks, by the way, but to be put in front of a firing squad for desertion.

COLONEL: Who is Jack Frank? Jack Frank is the name on your fake passport.

JACQUES: I don't know. They gave me the passport a day before I left.

COLONEL: Why did you wait several months once you were in Mexico before visiting the leader?

JACQUES: Those were my orders. I was to wait until I was called into his presence.

COLONEL: Why?

JACQUES: I don't know.

COLONEL: Did you know what Leon Davidovich wanted from you?

JACQUES: Colonel: When God calls, you don't ask, "What's the old guy want?" If I'd known that this lengthy wait would have ended in an encounter where God would show me his Devil's tail . . . My blood ran cold when he told me what he wanted me to do.

COLONEL: Go to Russia and be a saboteur.

JACQUES: Saboteur. Terrorist. I was to disrupt the work in factories. Sow panic. Buy spies. Propagate immoral ideas in the army. Finally, and above all, I should assassinate Stalin. Nothing more nor less: I was to be the instrument of his personal revenge. His petty revenge. "How could I get close to Stalin?" I asked. "We have a whole network of saboteurs in Russia," he answered. "How do you maintain this network?" I asked, bewildered. He told me about the poverty of the Trotskyite organization. Some centers couldn't even publish a newspaper, something indispensable for a political group. We have allies, he told me. Rich allies. That's when I understood where all the money came from that maintained the prophet's house like a prince's fortress. I also understood the reason the U.S. Consul visited Leon Davidovich's study. Everything was a battle for power between two tyrants. Two men squabbled over the main office in the Kremlin, and between them the devotees of one and the other believed they were fighting to get to the threshold of paradise. And all my hero's words? All the words that had become so praiseworthy fighting under his tutelage? Words. What an innocent I was. (Exhaling smoke as he talks.) Words less solid than smoke.

I contained my rage. I wanted to know just how far this cynical Jew, this trader in life and death, could go. I told him that it was impossible for me to carry out his wishes because going to Russia would mean being separated from Silvia and I love that woman more than I love myself. "Well, you'll have to leave her behind," he responded. In the tone of someone who gives an order that brooks no reply. I couldn't stand it any longer. I left his house bewildered. For a week I wandered around like a lunatic. Crossing the city quickly, heading nowhere, until I was exhausted and then pacing round and round in my hotel room at night. Understand: Imagine yourself in my place for just an instant. I was a man without a piece of earth to call my own, nameless, disinherited, all my beliefs recently torn from me. With only a woman as my piece of earth, my name, my inheritance, and even my tomb. And the person who had so recently made me renounce everything that belonged to me now wanted to take the only thing I had left in the world. I thought about killing myself. Cut off this insufferable disillusionment with a single stroke. But suddenly an idea came to me. I'd become a Trotskyite because I hated totalitarianism. I could be faithful to that clear intention to the end. To get rid of the tyrant in power or the tyrant who wanted to supplant him was the same thing.

COLONEL: You are, then, a martyr for democracy.

JACQUES: Those are your words, not mine.

COLONEL: Where did you type up your confession? Why did you date it and sign it in pencil? Who edited it?

JACQUES: I edited it and I signed and dated it a few minutes before the attack. I wasn't sure I was brave enough to kill the old man until then. I knew that I had almost no chance of escaping alive. And I wanted to make my motives clear so that no one else could interpret the assassination for their own political benefit.

COLONEL: But why did you sign it in pencil?

Pause

JACQUES: Sorry, professor. The next time I'll do it in pen.

COLONEL: Would you say that you carried out your act in a premeditated fashion, treacherously and for advantage?

JACQUES: Legalistic bourgeois terminology. Yes, in the end: in premeditated fashion, treacherously and for advantage.

COLONEL: But thanks only to an iron will.

JACQUES: What?

COLONEL: Because your crime is, ultimately, a crime of passion. You killed him because you were disillusioned. And for a woman's love.

JACQUES: You're making fun of my purity. In a world where those most esteemed are the most ambitious, those who govern with their heads and calculate every move, I, Jacques Mornard, let myself be carried away by my heart and acted out of love and disillusionment. The disillusionment that oppressed my swindled stomach—do you know that that's what the materialists call it?—and the love that made me swell.

70

COLONEL: Come with me. Let's go see your love. She's in the next room.

JACQUES: Silvia? For God's sake.

Scene 3

A hospital room. Silvia is lying on a bed. She cries convulsively. The Colonel, the Secretary, and Jacques enter.

JACQUES: Why have you brought me here, Colonel? What kind of circus are you trying to create? Get me out of here.

COLONEL: If you really love her, comfort her.

JACQUES: Colonel, Colonel . . .

SILVIA: Who's there?

COLONEL: Go to her. She's barely aware of what's going on around her.

SILVIA: Is that you? Jacques? Assassin! Are you still alive? Let me tear your eyes out!

The Colonel steps between them.

JACQUES: Silvia . . . understand. That man destroyed my life. I changed my thinking for his ideas, I betrayed my country for his promised land. I was prepared to forget my own name and take whatever name he gave me. And he took my hand and crumpled it up like a blank piece of paper. He asked me to become a saboteur. Don't you see?

SILVIA: Lies, all lies. He took you into his house graciously. You, an admirer of the sixth rank. A neophyte.

JACQUES: He wanted to destroy you as well. Separate us. He said that when he had a mission like the one he'd imposed on me a man shouldn't be tied to anyone.

SILVIA: Lies.

JACQUES: He said that you weren't worth a second glance in any case. He called you a troublemaker. Just another one of the little rabble. He asked how you dared to deviate even a millimeter from his opinions. You, an intellectual midget. That's what he called you.

SILVIA: Shut up. Pure lies. I'm not going to listen to you.

She covers her ears.

COLONEL: Listen to him, miss. He swears he acted out of love for you.

SILVIA: Out of love. Him, out of love? He's incapable of love. Assassin! Dog!

71

JACQUES: The show's over, Colonel. Kindly return me to my doghouse now.
COLONEL: Miss, listen to him. He deserves it. After all, you have been lovers for years.

Silvia calms down abruptly. Smoothes her hair and skirt.

SILVIA: He seduced me in order to use me. His plan was meticulous. He would be able to introduce himself into Leon's house as my boyfriend. I brought him right to his victim. I wish I'd never been born. I was just a vehicle for you, isn't that right, Jacques?
JACQUES: You kill me with every word, Silvi.
SILVIA: Don't call me Silvi, Mornard! You had this obsession to be someone. This obsession that wouldn't let you close your eyes at night and choked you in the middle of your dreams. You, a poor devil, thought only of leaving a foot-print in the earth. From the moment I met you that's all you thought about. Your only passion. "Sometimes," you told me once, "I feel like I'll pass away like a gust of wind between leafless trees." So, instead of doing something useful you plunged yourself into the torment of being less than a gust. Well, you've managed to become someone: the most infamous man in the world.
JACQUES: And the most unhappy, Silvi.
SILVIA: Colonel, don't let him call me Silvi or I'll scratch him!
JACQUES: As you wish.
SILVIA: What were you thinking about at night when we . . . What you had to do? What you had to do to possess me so that I'd make it easy for you to carry out the despicable little act you'd been plotting. Bastard. Dog, dog.
COLONEL: Then you believe that Jacques thought about carrying out the assassination years ago.
SILVIA: Yes. Although it would be more accurate to say that they'd bought him to assassinate Leon years ago. Hasn't he told you he's a G.P.U. agent?
JACQUES: Silvia, Silvia . . . Isn't it obvious? They've filled you with lies about me.
SILVIA: I know how to put two and two together. Now I understand where all that money came from that you threw around. Now I know why, in the building in Mexico City where you told me you worked, in the office where you told me you worked, there wasn't anyone who recognized your name. And all your weekend visits outside the city. Your constant coldness. Your cold looks. Your icy hands. Your death-filled kisses. And to think that I blamed myself because I couldn't wake the life in you. To think that I reproached myself because you never smiled or hummed a song.

JACQUES: *(Standing)* The melodrama's over. Colonel, my cell, if you please?

SILVIA: Deny that you're a G.P.U. dog!

COLONEL: Jacques?

JACQUES: This woman has gone completely crazy. I don't recognize her.

SILVIA: To think that I could have carried your child in my womb!

She tries to vomit. Jacques has a fit of anguish. Throws himself against the walls.

JACQUES: Get me out of here! Get me out! My God! My God!

SILVIA: *(Laughing)* Go to your kennel! Go to your kennel!

COLONEL: That's enough! That's enough! Silence! *(Pause)* I understand that this meeting is painful for both of you. Let's finish it calmly. The sooner the better.

SILVIA: It's painful for me. As for him . . . How can a dead man feel pain?

COLONEL: Let's avoid, wherever we can . . .

SILVIA: Yes. I won't insult him anymore. I'll calm down. Colonel: I'd like to make a statement. An objective declaration that will clear up the enigma of this case.

COLONEL: Go ahead.

SILVIA: Are you getting this down, miss? "This man is a traitor to love. To faith. To everything precious in life. He is the prototype of human evil." That's it. If you ask me about anything else, Colonel, we'll only cover the same ground.

Jacques smiles. Takes out a cigarette. Lights it. The Colonel clears his throat.

COLONEL: Where did Jacques go on these weekend visits?

SILVIA: To company headquarters, on the outskirts of the city, that was all he told me. If you know where the G.P.U. has it's headquarters, you'll know where.

COLONEL: Secret organizations usually have secret headquarters.

JACQUES: Inventions. I spent weekends with her, studying party texts.

SILVIA: Another lie.

COLONEL: Where did Jacques buy the ice pick?

JACQUES: In Switzerland.

SILVIA: No. He didn't buy it in Europe. I know his things. I packed his bags all these years. He must have gotten it here, in Mexico.

COLONEL: Jacques?

Jacques shrugs.

73

JACQUES: She's all mixed up. Delirious. How seriously can you take what a woman who uses glasses as thick as bottles did or didn't see? Don't be bashful, show him your binoculars.

SILVIA: Woof.

JACQUES: Bowwow.

COLONEL: Jacques also says his mother in Brussels gave him the money he spent these past few months, including your transoceanic trip, and that he gave you what was left over: three thousand dollars.

SILVIA: He did give me that amount. But his mother didn't give him the money. Unless his mother's Stalin's secret police.

COLONEL: Nevertheless, you didn't even suspect he was an agent until today.

SILVIA: He tricked me. He tricked me like everyone else. He's a great actor.

COLONEL: Don't get upset about what I'm going to ask you now. Think about it, and don't let loose any more insults. What's your opinion of your lover?

Silvia chokes. Hits her chest. Spits.

COLONEL: Jacques. Do you have anything to say to your lover?

JACQUES: I'd like to . . . go to sleep, Colonel.

The Colonel leads Jacques out.

Scene 4

The lower level is packed with Reporters sleeping or standing watch. Trotsky still lies unconscious on the bed in his room. Seated by his side, Natalia takes his pulse. The Nurse is in the corner. Natalia starts. Cries silently. Gets up. Goes to the door and opens it halfway. Whispers in Hansen's ear. Hansen looks at his watch and then turns to the Reporters.

HANSEN: Gentlemen . . . at 19:25 today, August 21, 1940, Leon Davidovich Trotsky died.

Scene 5

The Reporters throw themselves at the public telephones. They fight over them. In the confusion two become inoperable. Bits and pieces of their phone calls are heard in different languages. Those in Spanish stand out.

FIRST REPORTER: At 19:25 today, August 21, 1940, Leon Davidovich Trotsky died. That's it. What more can you say about a man's death?

WOMAN: Gone. *(Moans)* Gone.

SECOND REPORTER: THE BLOW WAS FATAL. Make it eight columns across, with big, fat letters.

THIRD REPORTER: HE DIED. Believe me, that's enough. Yes, eight columns across. A big headline.

FIRST REPORTER: Today, August 21, 1940, et cetera, et cetera, et cetera, up until "died," but filling the whole first page, chief.

A Reporter looks in vain for a phone to grab. A Russian beats him to it.

FOURTH REPORTER: He can't even fuck anymore, comrade. Where's your spirit of solidarity? *(Laughter)*

WOMAN: Gone. *(Moans)* Gone. *(Moans)* Gone.

FIFTH REPORTER: How much did his brain weigh? How should I know? About a kilo and a half? Great. Who told you that? Well, no, they haven't announced it officially yet, what do you think?

FIRST REPORTER: Yes, yes. The whole page. I insist.

FIFTH REPORTER: Wait until they've done the autopsy. Yes, I'll get you the information. And the heart, uh-huh. About a kilo and a half as well? Just imagine the size of his liver. That's normal? Ah.

WOMAN: Gone *(Moans)* Gone.

SIXTH REPORTER: We'll have to see if interviews will be granted. It seems a bit premature to me right now since . . .

WOMAN: Gone. *(Moans.)*

FIRST REPORTER: What's she saying?

SECOND REPORTER: Gon. Gon. It sounds like a bell.

THIRD REPORTER: It means "he's gone" in English.

FOURTH REPORTER: If she's said it already and doesn't have anything else to say she should give up the phone, shouldn't she? *(Going toward her)* It seems to me that . . . *(Putting his ear to the outside of the receiver)* She's not talking to anybody. *(Thinks about it. Takes the receiver. Dials the telephone. The Woman advances to the edge of the stage, very slowly.)*

WOMAN: Gone. *(Moans.)* Gone.

THIRD REPORTER: *(Into the telephone)* and this continues to be purgatory. Yes, as a subtitle.

WOMAN: Gone. *(Moans.)*

THIRD REPORTER: Yellow journalism? If that's what our reality is like, than that's how its heralds should report it. That's what I say.

SIXTH REPORTER: We'll have to see if they'll allow pictures to be taken.

WOMAN: Gone. *(Moans.)*

Dark stage except for the Secretary's area. She puts another page into the typewriter. Puts what she's typed into a folder. Begins transcribing again. Fade to black.

Picture 3

The hospital. Single spot on the Woman at the edge of the stage.
WOMAN: Gone. *(Moans.)* Gone.

General light. The din of the Reporters. A phone rings on the upper level. Everything stops while Lieutenant Giménez takes the call.
GIMÉNEZ: . . . Yes. *(To a Guard)* Call for the Colonel.

The Guard tells Salazar, and he goes to the phone.
COLONEL: . . . Unfortunately, general. Given the circumstances, the most effective. At the police station, isolated, under my responsibility. . . . Thank you for your confidence. *(Hangs up. In the face of the insistent Reporters—"Colonel, an interview," "Colonel, two questions"—he only answers, "Later, later." As he enters Jacques' room the tumult starts up again on the lower level.)*
FIRST REPORTER: Colonel Salazar has taken charge of the case.
THIRD REPORTER: Sa-la-zar.
SECOND REPORTER: Colonel Salazar is directing the investigation. We've got clippings on the cases he's solved in the archives.
FIFTH REPORTER: A brilliant history.
FIRST REPORTER: From Morelos, I think. A Zapatista.
FOURTH REPORTER: He joined the Zapatistas as a boy. When Zapata came to the capital he stayed here. *(Various characters enter.)*
FIRST REPORTER: "He joined the fight as a barefoot little Indian and ended up a decorated Colonel." That's text, as is the following: "There is no one more adept in the Revolution turned government to show the world the efficiency of our institutions."
SECOND REPORTER: The eyes of Humanity are focused on our country.
WOMAN: Gone. *(Moans.)* Gone.

The Colonel appears, leading the handcuffed Jacques.
REPORTER: A press interview.
COLONEL: I'm sorry, gentlemen. There are more pressing matters right now.

U.S. AMBASSADOR: *(Showing a shiny metallic badge)* Colonel, sir.

COLONEL: I'm listening.

U.S. AMBASSADOR: My government was surprised—most disagreeably, I should say—to discover through the press that it had become involved—maliciously I should add—in a bloody settling of accounts between Communists. Trotsky, a secret agent of the U.S. government, how ridiculous.

COLONEL: Those are the assassin's words, not official ones.

REPORTER: Discredit them, Mr. Ambassador.

U.S. AMBASSADOR: How?

REPORTER: Publish the names of your secret agents in the press.

U.S. AMBASSADOR: Ha, Ha, Ha.

RUSSIAN AMBASSADOR: *(Showing his card)* Comrade Colonel.

COLONEL: I'm listening.

RUSSIAN AMBASSADOR: Comrade Colonel: my government has been surprised—disagreeably, I should add—to discover through the press that it has become involved—cynically, I should point out—in a bloody settling of accounts between exiled counterrevolutionaries. Jacques Mornard, a Soviet secret agent, what calumny.

REPORTER: Discredit the calumny.

RUSSIAN AMBASSADOR: How?

REPORTER: Publish the names of your secret agents in the press.

RUSSIAN AMBASSADOR: Ha, Ha, Ha.

TROTSKYITE REPRESENTATIVE: *(Showing a shiny badge.)* Colonel.

COLONEL: I'm still listening.

TROTSKYITE REPRESENTATIVE: Colonel: Jacques, an agent of the dissident Trotskyite wing. What an insult to your intelligence. He wasn't a Trotskyite. It's undeniable that he was one of Stalin's henchmen.

RUSSIAN AMBASSADOR: Trotskyite.

TROTSKYITE REPRESENTATIVE: Or U.S.

JACQUES: Jacques Mornard.

SOMEONE: An anarchist.

A ROMANTIC: The last romantic!

NUN: A sinner among sinners.

U.S. AMBASSADOR: Whoever he is, please understand, Colonel, friend: if any suspicion affecting my government's dignity is published, our enemies will believe it, our allies will reject it. Do you know any man whose political inclinations are based on certainties? Not in this century, Colonel.

REPORTER: So full of lies.

RUSSIAN AMBASSADOR: Think about it, comrade.

TROTSKYITE REPRESENTATIVE: Reconsider.

LIEUTENANT GIMÉNEZ: Colonel: another letter. "Comrade: Remember that the party knows how to reward and how to punish. A comrade."

COLONEL: File it with the other anonymous ones. Gentlemen: No one carries any greater weight with me than anyone else when it's a question of finding the truth.

PSYCHOANALYST: Does it matter if Jacques Mornard is a red, blue, or black agent? Does it really matter if he's called what he calls himself or what others call him, or what just he and his mother call him? No. He was destined to be the assassin of a public figure. The germ of his crime can be found in his humiliating childhood. That's what's important.

COLONEL: If you can't bring me someone who doesn't have an ax to grind, don't bring me anyone else, Lieutenant.

The Lieutenant brings a child and his father forward.

CHILD: My piolet!

The Colonel shows him the ice pick.

COLONEL: Is this it?

CHILD: Give it to me. Roberts stole it from me.

FATHER: That's right, Colonel. The accused came to my seaside resort several times. He registered under the name of Herbert Roberts, from Atlanta. He always came with some beautiful woman. High society, judging by the jewels and the outfits. I met four different women whom he alternated with one another. They spent the weekend sunbathing, swimming, and horseback riding through the countryside. Mr. Roberts had two Arabian chargers in the stables. He's a splendid rider. Last weekend he watched my son climb a mound of rocks from his balcony, and I suppose he took it when the boy climbed down and left his piolet in the pasture.

PSYCHOANALYST: *(Taking the ice pick)* The sight of a boy scaling a rock must have made an impression on Jacques' subconscious. It was a living representation of his unconscious desire to scale the height of his father. His natural father was, necessarily, a distant figure. Only present in the intellectual sphere, absent in his affections. Just the way Trotsky was to him. Upon choosing the piolet Jacques completed both his conscious and unconscious plans. This instrument would kill with one blow and without noise. With that blow he became equal to his father and made him pay for having abandoned him.

CHILD: My piolet!

TROTSKYITE REPRESENTATIVE: *(Taking the ice pick)* In summary, doctor. Everything remained in the family. *(Changing to a ferocious tone)* The piolet was chosen because it synthesizes the markings of those who ordered the assassination. It's a hammer with the blade of a sickle. A sickle turned into a hammer beating. Hammer and sickle reunited in an artifact that is no longer useful for labor but only to wound.

CHILD: It's a piolet and it's mine.

COLONEL: *(Recapturing the ice pick)* I'm sorry, son. The court will want to see it.

CHILD: But it's mine.

FATHER: Andresito, remember that the gentleman is a policeman and he's right. *(Goes, taking the child with him.)*

CHILD: What did we come here for, then?

FATHER: To do our duty as responsible citizens.

CHILD: What?

FATHER: I'll explain it to you on the way home.

PSYCHOANALYST: *(Breaking the handle)* Jacques symbolically castrated the Father.

NUN: He was an angry man, God forgive him. He who lives by the sword, dies by the sword. God absolves him.

TERRORIST: Long live Death! Remember, Mercader?

NUN: Holy Lord Our God!

PSYCHOANALYST: One hand of man: the life instinct. The other hand: the death instinct.

THE ROMANTIC AND THE TERRORIST: Long live Death!

PSYCHOANALYST: In the center, the head, arbiter of the eternal conflict.

NUN: Babel!

Pause. Then all in unison and without letting anyone else interrupt, repeat their speeches to the audience, trying to persuade them and discredit everyone else. This should go from the Trotskyite Representative: ". . . undeniable that he was one of Stalin's henchmen," to the Nun: "A sinner among sinners." Then jumping to Lieutenant Giménez: "Another letter . . ." and following. The chatter ends as suddenly as it begins. Pause. The door to Trotsky's room opens slowly, halfway. From afar a popular song is heard.

He came here from very far away seeking refuge
and here a cruel hand killed him.
Put flowers on his corpse, ay,
give him flowers and songs.

A gigantic skull and skeleton, caricatures of Trotsky's features, are carried to burial from Trotsky's room. The Woman goes to the lip of the stage, swaying like a pendulum, saying, between moans:

Gone.
All of us go sooner or later
but some of us leave more pain when we go.
Put flowers on his corpse, ay,
Give him flowers and songs.

On the road to his tomb
there is a village of bitter mouths.
From its appearance make skulls of sugar,
bones of sweet milk,
blood of honey water.
Ay, put flowers and songs
on his corpse,
flowers and songs,
flowers and
songs
for this immense death . . .
flowers . . .
and
songs . . .

Gone.

ACT 2

The police station. Two levels. The Colonel's office and the Secretary's office are on the upper level. There is a dictaphone in each of them. In the Colonel's office there is, as well, an intercom system connected to Jacques' cell on the lower level. A speaker and a small bed in the cell. A staircase connects the two levels. There is a patio down below.

Scene 1

Night, the cell. Jacques, totally covered by his sheet, sleeps fitfully. The Colonel reviews his notes in his office. Turns on the intercom and the recording system, turns out the light. Goes down to Jacques' cell. Turns on an intense light. Uncovers Jacques. Little by little, he wakes up.

COLONEL: I brought you the newspaper.

JACQUES: I was dreaming. . . . You . . . the same little beady eyes, a black bird. *(Shakes his head)* It was chasing me. A sparrow hawk, I think.

COLONEL: A sparrow hawk. Did it catch you?

JACQUES: *(Totally awake)* No way. I was a long-distance champion.

The Colonel hands him the newspaper.

JACQUES: No, thank you. I prefer my nightmares to those of the world.

COLONEL: Leaf through it. Stop on every page. *(Throwing it at him)* Don't skip a single one, understand? *(Into the speaker)* Roll 21. August 24, 1940. I have the confessed assassin, the murder weapon, the crime classified. The criminal's autobiography and his statement as to his motives. Both of these texts, unfortunately, are full of unconfirmable facts and others that are more than likely false.

Jacques laughs. The Colonel turns to look at him.

JACQUES: *(Explaining his laughter)* Ramona gets crueler with that stupid Pancho every day.

COLONEL: *(Into the speaker)* Who is this man? Who formulated the plan he carried out? These are the essential questions to answer.

JACQUES: *(Without looking up from the newspaper)* I'm Jacques Mornard. The plan was formulated in my own head, every morning. Out of disillusionment, as we said yesterday.

COLONEL: That summarizes the previous twenty rolls. Mr. X: Why did you start to read the newspaper from the back?

JACQUES: To get to the funnies sooner. *(Laughs)* How short the funny pages are. No. You know why I read it backwards? Because I know the criteria journalists use.

COLONEL: Keep thinking aloud.

Jacques continues flipping through the newspaper.

JACQUES: The value of money goes down. Prices rise. Hemlines lower and necklines rise, an unmistakable sign of difficult times. Ugly women are finally photographed. New tank models. Great advances in aviation. Progress, full speed ahead: effort is the watchword. Bombardments. Deaths. Subterranean refuges. Deaths. Deaths. It isn't Sunday today. War is worse than the medieval plague: it's invading all of Europe and could cross the ocean in a second. Progress, yes . . . *(Looking at the front page. Standing up.)* And Jacques Mornard is still on the front page. Another thing: the reporter who wrote this beneath my picture is an imbecile. After photographing me all beat up in the hospital he asked me if Trotsky's secretaries had done that to me and I answered: if my temples are purple it's because spring's passed, and if my nose is running it's a summer cold. As for this lock of hair sticking out of my bandages, don't you know it's the latest thing in Paris? He very subtly comments that I show signs of madness.

COLONEL: The psychiatrist who examined you diagnosed you as a psychopath. A psychopath, according to what he told me, is someone on the edge of psychosis, of, full-blown madness, shall we say.

JACQUES: Tell the psychiatrist for me that as soon as I saw him applying his complicated tests, I diagnosed him as a chronic, irredeemable psychiatrist and . . .

COLONEL: That's enough.

JACQUES: And that I didn't need ten years in the university to make up nicknames and I made them up . . .

COLONEL: Enough.

JACQUES: Quickly and with originality.

COLONEL: Finished? Let's get back to you.

JACQUES: Enchanted. *(Looking at his picture in the newspaper.)* I look like a clown. That's the way they like it. I become an example for them.

COLONEL: An example.

JACQUES: I come along as the great buffoon in a world full of disciplined lunatics. It's humiliating. Are you listening?

COLONEL: I'm listening to you. I'm looking at you. I smell you. I've got you in my dreams. Shut up. I know lies when I hear them. And I cut them off. Because I want the truth.

JACQUES: The truth. The truth of the matter is the following: the majority of human beings work like asses so they can enjoy themselves on Sundays like cattle. Then there are those who realize what's going on and out of pity or contempt become cattlemen. But, since the cattle feel an indomitable spirit within themselves on Sundays, they feel great discomfort when they turn back into asses on Monday. In order to remedy this situation deals come and go between the cattle and the cattlemen. They change cattlemen, they change the routes the asses take, the cattle let off steam in new ways. Now the cattlemen have invented a new deal with the beasts. It's called national pride.

The Colonel raises his hand, Jacques shuts up.

COLONEL: Listen: are you making a speech?

JACQUES: I was in the preamble. I'll tell you who I am in what follows. If you let me finish.

COLONEL: What for? You're the man who dreamed he was an ass and woke up. I've heard the same thesis in five different versions.

JACQUES: You learn quickly, professor.

COLONEL: So, you're part of a speech. I see other regions besides your mouth. I feel them. Seriously.

JACQUES: But you agree that Humanity is divided between cattle and cattlemen.

COLONEL: I'm not arguing. But I want the truth and that is.

JACQUES: Is what?

COLONEL: Is. If it is, it is.

JACQUES: You're jealous of my broad thinking, and I don't blame you. *(Laughs sarcastically.)*

COLONEL: Look: a whole body doesn't fit in my hand, all of Humanity doesn't fit in my mind. That's the way I understand it. Listen: I'm asking you for simple things. Facts. Facts, Mr. X. One by one.

JACQUES: Dates. Addresses. Passport numbers, identity card numbers. Names. You want to reduce me to statistics. You've already reduced me to an X. Your work is over. Put me in a file now, and I'll go to bed.

COLONEL: I've got dates, addresses, numbers. The ones you've given me and those others have given me about you. They don't match. They cancel each other out.

JACQUES: As any choirboy could tell you, that frequently happens when you work with numbers.

COLONEL: I try to match you to your numbers, and the result is . . . you're an unidentified person. Mr. X, for short. Your train of thought is always coherent. Your biography changes.

JACQUES: Perhaps I don't have space for precise facts in my mind.

COLONEL: . . .

JACQUES: All right. You know a lie when you see one. What do you want? My identity? Just because a cultivated bourgeois believes that a man's identity depends upon which prick was stuck up which ass nine months before he was born, Jacques Mornard doesn't have to agree. But maybe the reactionary disease will satisfy you. I was born. That's a fact. Earlier or later, out of time, that's another fact. Because I was hungry and the company was irritating. I grew up hating. They called me a petty thief. A punk. A gigolo. Elegant environments reconciled me a bit with people. They made me effeminate. So as not to keep being a piece of meat used and then thrown away by refined little girls, and in order not to abandon the elegance, I became a journalist, wrote the social pages. I lived by night, when the asses bray, all was well. Then, through a friend with surrealistic tastes, I met Silvi. She stubbornly redeemed me from frivolity. She told me that there wasn't anything hateful in me: it was society that was evil. I fell in love with Silvi. *(The Colonel raises his hand.)* All right. I tried to seem in love with Silvi. In any case I'd never loved. With her support I became an apprentice to the redeemer of the world. And finding him an unredeemed ambitious man, I redeemed him with a single blow. I swear to you: he deceived us. Wrote marvels and plotted atrocities.

COLONEL: Trotsky believed. You only had to listen to him for a day to understand that. He believed.

JACQUES: I didn't know you were a Trotskyite. That explains many things, comrade.

COLONEL: You failed to mention a profession in your history.

JACQUES: Several. Life is too long.

COLONEL: I'm interested in who and where you were taught the profession of being Jacques Mornard.

JACQUES: Yes, Jacques Mornard's a profession. Salazar's another, and Trotsky another. The only difference is that you, the ones with Transcendental Convictions, bet your lives for them even though you lose and lose and lose, while I win and win.

COLONEL: Talk to me about the profession of Jacques Mornard. Tell me, for example, who taught you these insults against everyone, governments and governed.

JACQUES: The redeemer of the world. You know, comrade: he said that this all had to end. He talked about a society without cattlemen. Didn't he? A good carrot for the asses, eh?

COLONEL: And a threat for the cattlemen. That's why they sent you. Who?

JACQUES: Try to . . . I swear that he was an unredeemed, ambitious man. He wanted the biggest herd for his own: all of Humanity, nothing more. That's why I broke his head. The beast guessed it, and that's why I'm still on the front page. Our guide said that facts are irrefutable. Here I am. He's a cadaver. Let's admit it, comrade.

COLONEL: Where do they have your mother prisoner?

JACQUES: . . . We were talking about Trotskyism . . .

COLONEL: I haven't had the opportunity to learn much about the subject.

JACQUES: You haven't read Trotsky, comrade?

COLONEL: I know a few facts about Trotsky and I talked to him a few times, about practical matters. That's more than I need to know what I told you, that he believed fiercely. If you read him, you read him like you read that paper: backwards. Where's she imprisoned? Your mother.

JACQUES: My mother . . . is an old woman living on an elegant country estate in the Belgian provinces. A prisoner, perhaps, unfortunately, of nostalgia for a world in which the nobility was well thought of.

COLONEL: Yesterday she was a Spanish guerrilla.

JACQUES: . . . That's what a decrepit old man said.

COLONEL: But four days ago they kept her prisoner in order to make you carry out the crime.

JACQUES: If I hadn't said that, the redeemer's bodyguards would still be beating me.

COLONEL: And today I'm supposed to believe she's an old woman living on a country estate.

JACQUES: *(Shaking the newspaper)* Didn't I tell you that I'm the model for these sons of bitches who are killing each other: I've got three mothers.

COLONEL: . . .

JACQUES: Here's the truth: you're a detective and I'm Mr. X. File me. I'm going to sleep.

The Colonel unplugs the speaker wires. Jacques gets scared.

JACQUES: Again? What for, if you don't record it?

COLONEL: Do you know the consequences of your crime?

JACQUES: No.

COLONEL: Do they matter to you?

JACQUES: No. I'm tired of telling you I did it for myself.

COLONEL: You talked about Humanity.

JACQUES: In a civilized fashion. Take those bird of prey eyes off of me.

COLONEL: Could you know anything about Humanity? You?

JACQUES: Go to hell. Take your eyes off me.

COLONEL: I've got you up the ass.

JACQUES: . . .

COLONEL: This, what you are, is all you know about Humanity. And you're something suffering.

JACQUES: Go to hell, I said.

COLONEL: Hard on the outside, trembling inside. Something tyrannized by others' words.

JACQUES: I've read it all, yes.

COLONEL: They made you read it. You can't do anything by yourself, nothing that requires application, nothing of consequence. Not even kill, not even kill yourself. You can only take orders.

JACQUES: What truth do you want me to tell you?

COLONEL: Tell me where you were trained to be Jacques Mornard.

JACQUES: Where do you want me to say?

COLONEL: They ordered you not to say where you were trained. Is that it?

JACQUES: No one trained me.

COLONEL: They ordered you to deny they existed. Your trainers. To deny that you yourself exist. To deny. That's the willpower you learned: to deny.

JACQUES: No.

COLONEL: Are you sure?

JACQUES: No. I mean yes. Let me go.

COLONEL: Calm down. Fighting is against orders here. And with orders I'm going to break them. Mr. X: on the floor. On all fours. On your feet. Mark time in place. What a relief to get orders, eh? Stop. Half turn. Half turn. Half turn. Half turn. A sarcasm.

JACQUES: . . .

COLONEL: Ah, a sarcasm requires a certain amount of liberty. Choose something real and destroy it. Breathe deeply. Relax your buttocks. I'm sure you can do it. A sarcasm!

JACQUES: You have me up the ass . . . because my acidic shit . . .

COLONEL: Stick to reality. Your shit is acidic.

JACQUES: You love my acidic shit, vile sparrow hawk.

COLONEL: Rest.

JACQUES: I didn't finish with the reality. You love it, vile, domesticated sparrow hawk disguised as an urban kestrel fly mosquito . . .

COLONEL: Rest!

Jacques throws himself on his bed, sobbing.

COLONEL: Don't cry.

JACQUES: I'm not crying. It's exhaustion.

COLONEL: But that was my order: don't cry. In order to give orders one has to give only those orders that one could obey oneself. I can't give you orders either, to be honest. But I'm going to take all the filth they filled you with out of you. And a clean man is honest because he's honest and that's it. Cigarette? *(Jacques accepts the cigarette.)* They must be confused by the fact that you're still alive. They count on the fact that there's someone who believes. That's what can't be taped. I'll break your myth of the great buffoon into a thousand pieces and I'll add mine of the sparrow hawk. Understand? You understand.

JACQUES: Could you give me a light?

COLONEL: I don't have a light for you.

JACQUES: What are you trying to do? Drive me crazy?

COLONEL: Let's leave it at the fact that only you can know your evil intentions.

The Colonel goes to plug in the speaker wires.

JACQUES: Excuse me: you are a marshmallow. *(Begins to sing softly:)* There was a bastard and a boob, the bastard swallowed the boob but since the boob was made of cotton, a bad stomachache showed who was the bigger bas—

While Mornard sings, the Colonel takes out a letter, removes it from its envelope, and opens it. Jacques shuts up.

COLONEL: Recognize the stamp? They give advice perfectly. Official business. I'll just read a few parts. *(Reading very quickly)* "The assassination in question has produced such a universal sensation that it's on the front page of all the newspapers, relegating news of the horrendous European war to second place. World attention is focused on the Mexican authorities in hopes that they will be able to shed some light on what happened. Due to our own justifiable pride and in the name of justice and the country's prestige, we are ready to resort to any means necessary to uncover the truth. . . . We have carefully reviewed the material from your investigation, Colonel, and we agree with you that the accused's arguments are absurd. . . . They aren't worthy of either the mind or the reasoning of a child. . . . You have treated him with great consideration, using persuasion and deliberation.

It's painful to suggest tactics of another sort, however . . . Given that the prisoner has the truth inside him . . . you are at liberty . . . to rip it out of him at whatever price, at any cost, since Mexico will otherwise look very bad in world opinion." . . . *(The Colonel hands the letter to Jacques.)* I'll leave it here so you can read, and reread, the whole thing.

JACQUES: Take it with you. And the filthy newspaper.

COLONEL: No. End of interrogation.

The Colonel leaves. The Guard closes the cell. It's morning. While the Colonel climbs the stairs.

Scene 2

Jacques, alone

JACQUES: I'm invincible. Life doesn't matter to me. No: I still have one weakness: this. *(Beats his body. Extends his arms. Surprised, he looks at his reddened palms.)* This. Defeat it. . . .

Giménez, who has recently arrived, catches up with the Colonel on the stairs.

COLONEL: Up with the roosters, Giménez?

GIMÉNEZ: I want to learn the whole process close up.

They continue up the stairs. In the cell:

JACQUES: Defeat it. . . . *(Suddenly furious, he bites his right wrist. The Guard, alarmed, opens the cell and forcibly tries to free Jacques from himself, succeeds.)* Ass. I'm your redeemer. *(The Guard leaves without taking his eyes off him, afraid. Closes the cell door behind him.)*

JACQUES: Give me a light. Give me a light! For my cigarette, ass.

GUARD: *(In a very low voice)* I don't have permission to have anything to do with you. I'm not even supposed to tell you that.

Jacques laughs hysterically. Starts to kick the walls and the floor, making a ruckus. In his office the Colonel and Giménez listen attentively to what's going on in the cell.

GIMÉNEZ: I better go down and give him a sedative.

COLONEL: Leave him alone. This laughter is almost tears.

Jacques' outbursts begin to die down, become farther and farther apart and more and more high pitched.

GIMÉNEZ: He's crying.
COLONEL: *(Slowly turning off the transmitter)* Leave him alone. It's going to be a long one.

Jacques retreats into a corner and cries silently. The newspaper is scattered about on the floor.

Scene 3

GIMÉNEZ: Colonel: you can't solve it?

The Colonel stares at him fixedly. Leans his elbows on his desk. The Secretary enters the neighboring office.
COLONEL: *(High-pitched voice)* Study my notes. . . . You'll know the little . . . that I know . . . for certain.
SECRETARY: *(Entering)* Good morning . . . You don't know when to stop, Colonel. You didn't sleep last night, either. *(Giménez laughs. The Colonel remains with his elbows on his desk.)* I'd better get you some coffee. Then you can sleep.
COLONEL: Yes. Don't let anyone disturb him.

The Secretary lowers the venetian blinds.
GIMÉNEZ: Not even the doctor? But without the treatment we'll lose him. I'm repeating your own words.
COLONEL: From yesterday. Take these notes. Study them. He's curing himself.

Giménez and the Secretary exit to the neighboring office. She puts a piece of paper in the typewriter, a dictaphone roll in the player. Turns it on. Transcribes.
THE COLONEL'S VOICE ON THE DICTAPHONE: Roll number 12. August 22, 1940, night. The visitor agreed to enter the cell incognito . . .

The sound of the transcription being typed fades, while the light dims into nocturnal darkness.

Scene 4

Night. The Visitor is led in by a Guard. He carries a light bulb with him, wears a turban. The cell Guard lets him into the cell. Jacques, asleep, slowly wakes up. The Visitor talks softly, like a character in a dream.

VISITOR: *[Trans. note: All of the Visitor's lines are in Persian.]* Good evening, Mr. X.

JACQUES: Eh? *(Rubs his eyes. Sits up on his cot.)*

VISITOR: So, you were born in the imperial capital. My language should sound familiar to you. The accent at least?

JACQUES: Eh? Who are you?

VISITOR: Someone born beneath the same sky you were. Even though I suspect that I will seem a figure out of a dream to you.

JACQUES: Don't you speak Spanish?

VISITOR: *(Laughing)* Or, better yet: a figure from a nightmare. Of course, I'm used to being treated like a fantastical presence.

JACQUES: Sprechen sie Deutsch? Parlez-vous français? English?

VISITOR: *(Laughing to himself)* My country's name evokes prodigious demons, wise monkeys, flying carpets, castles of smoke in Western minds . . .

THE COLONEL'S VOICE ON THE LOUDSPEAKER: Thank you, Mr. Persian Ambassador. Jacques wasn't born in Teheran. End of the first meeting on roll 16.

VISITOR: I'm sorry. I'm sorry you've never been in Persia. For a man with your imagination it would have been a rare pleasure. Well. . . good night, Mr. X.

The Ambassador leaves, followed by the Guard, taking the light with him.

Scene 5

Jacques' cell. The same night. In the darkness Jacques whispers at the Guard who has been smoking a cigarette.

JACQUES: Could you give me a cigarette? The Colonel isn't listening. Just one. Don't you have any feelings? A drag. Please. Damn stick soldier. *(Walking in circles in his cell.)* Please. *(He stops suddenly. Doubles over in pain, pressing his stomach.)*

GUARD: *(Indifferent)* Your stomach again?

JACQUES: The butt . . . *(The Guard tosses the cigarette butt on the corridor floor. Steps on it. Another Guard arrives. They salute each other. The first Guard leaves. The second one takes his place.)*

JACQUES: Do you have any cigarettes?

The Guard doesn't answer. Footsteps can be heard dragging along the corridor. A Man arrives in front of the bars. He is small. A small beard on his chin and gray locks in his hair. He wears a green beret, carries a cane. Looks at Jacques. The click of the dictaphone is heard as the needle hits the roll. During the scene dawn arrives.

THE COLONEL'S VOICE ON THE LOUDSPEAKER: Roll 16. August 22, 1940.

MAN: Could I see him in better light?

COLONEL: Guard: put him under the lamp. *(The Guard enters the cell, turns on the hanging lamp, puts Jacques beneath its intense light. The Man continues to look at him.)*

JACQUES: Who are you?

MAN: It's him. I recognized his picture in the papers and now, up close, there's no doubt. Joaquín Mercader. I saw him several times in the trenches at Toledo during those bloody days when we had the nationalists under siege. He was with the communists like me, uh-huh.

JACQUES: *(Going close to the bars)* You arthritic old man, you're inventing.

MAN: I knew his mother, too. A very brave, fanatical communist. Eyes black as frying pans, gypsy breasts, a ballerina's elegance, and a shrewd aim. What a woman. Many of us found her attractive, and she took several of us. Soledad Mercader, uh-huh. She was in Toledo, too. When the siege was broken I fell prisoner and I lost their trail. I found Soledad years later in a bar in Madrid. It was a time when we all drank too much. The defeat, the world war, the ideological confusion: Trotsky in exile and Stalin in power making pacts with the Nazis. She bought me a glass of good cognac. She had lots of money. She worked for the G.P.U.

JACQUES: You're making it all up!

COLONEL'S VOICE ON THE SPEAKER: Shut up, Joaquín Mercader.

JACQUES: Jacques Mornard.

COLONEL'S VOICE ON THE SPEAKER: Born in Persia when your father was Belgian consul, huh? Shut up. Go on, Señor Urdabillán.

MAN: She invited me to collaborate with the G.P.U., uh-huh. I . . . I was dying from hunger and sadness and my wife dead, garroted. Dying from my little children in who knows what kind of orphanage or mountain of bones and from my friends under the warm earth now at peace, uh-huh. I told her: you're all right, Soledad, you haven't lost any flesh of your flesh. I walk through the streets and I feel my children walking behind me, Julia's footsteps beside me. I'm always just about to recognize my brothers in the faces of the people passing. I'm like someone searching for Nothing between the phantoms. . . .

91

JACQUES: Should I applaud, or would that ruin your inspiration?

MAN: I no longer know what we bathed Toledo in blood for. No one could pick up so many skulls, Soledad. I ramble, wander from memory to memory and amidst those memories I hear a voice as big as the sky asking "what was it all for?" And now I don't want any more violent memories where that same voice asks "what was it all for?" If I hadn't lost Julia, perhaps I would accept the offer to become Stalin's spy. Uh-huh. For her I would make the effort to earn some money, but for myself alone . . . what for? Uh-huh.

JACQUES: Uh-huh what, you nihilistic son of a . . .

COLONEL: Shut up, Mercader.

MAN: Uh-huh. She told me that she was going to Russia and her son Joaquín was going to take up her post in the G.P.U. Joaquín . . . *(Falls to his knees. Grabs one of Jacques' legs. He pulls away.)*

COLONEL: What's going on?

MAN: I wanted to look at the scar on Joaquín's left leg, but he wouldn't let me. So, Soledad's in Russia and her son's here. *(Laughing happily)* I bake bread, Colonel! At the crack of dawn I take hundreds of loaves out of the oven and by midday they're all gone. Uh-huh.

COLONEL: Thank you, Señor Urdabillán. End of confrontation number 2, still on tape 16.

MAN: *(Going)* I don't know why we bathed Toledo in blood. No one could pick up so many skulls . . .

Scene 6

The Guard turns off the hanging lamp. Daylight has broken.

SECOND GUARD: Put your shoes on. *(Jacques looks at him, surprised.)* We're taking a walk. *(Jacques gets up. They go from the cell to the hallway.)*

JACQUES: A bit of fresh air at last. *(Picking up the pace.)* And sun. *(Picking up the pace.)* Sun!

Just as they reach the threshold the doorway is covered by Pluffea's corpulent figure. He's about fifty, jovial, good-looking.

PLUFFEA: *(Opening his arms)* Tarkoff! Salvador Tarkoff! Spacite! Tarkoff!

Jacques has the impulse to run into his embrace, but he only lifts his arms a little, then stops himself. Turns. At the other end of the corridor is the Colonel. Pluffea embraces him anyway, kissing him on both cheeks.

PLUFFEA: Tarkoff. Priatno vstretitsia! Skolkoliet′! Skasalavnie w sórokom godú 1935 Pommilu Tijuana? Smotrich Joroshó.

JACQUES: I don't know you, sir.

PLUFFEA: Poshemú niet?

JACQUES: And I don't speak Russian.

COLONEL: How do you know it's Russian if you don't speak it?

PLUFFEA: Eh?

JACQUES: I recognize the sound.

COLONEL: Russian, Czech, Yugoslavian, I don't speak any of them, and to me they all sound the same.

JACQUES: To you. Russian reminds me of broken-down locomotives. It's unmistakable.

PLUFFEA: *(With a Russian accent)* So, you renounce the mother tongue, Tarkoff? Bad, that's bad. When we crossed the Nevada desert, him at the wheel of my good old Oldsmobile, we talked for hours and hours in our language. We talked of the motherland, of the forests, the immense snowy steppes. Imagine it, Colonel: the hot sun, in the midst of sand and more sand, going at one hundred kilometers an hour, drinking vodka and Tarkoff here singing: Volga Volga; Volga Volga. He made me cry. We had good times together, Tarkoff. Almost three years.

COLONEL: The precise date, please.

PLUFFEA: From 1935 to the end of 1937.

JACQUES: *(Imitating the Spanish Man)* Exactly when Toledo was bathed in blood, uh-huh.

COLONEL: *(To the Guard)* Raise his left pants leg. *(The Guard obeys. The Colonel squats down.)*

PLUFFEA: Ah, you're looking for the scar? *(Squatting, he lifts the pants leg even more, until it's above the knee.)* Here's the run in the stocking. That's what I called his wound. I always joked with him about it, telling him, "There's a run in your stocking, take it off, señorita." He answered me, "What you wouldn't give to have these prince's legs, mujik."

JACQUES: I'm an angel. I can be in two places at once. Right now I'm also in Acapulco. Stand up, children. *(Laughs his peculiar laugh. The others get up.)*

COLONEL: *(To the Guard, ill-humoredly)* Lock him up.

JACQUES: And the walk?

The Guard conducts Jacques back to his cell.

COLONEL: *(Somewhat violently to Pluffea)* If he was your friend why did you come to unmask him?

PLUFFEA: I told you, Colonel. I got out of bed one day and there wasn't any Tarkoff, any merchandise, or any red Oldsmobile.

COLONEL: I've investigated. You're an agent for some power.

PLUFFEA: Me?

COLONEL: They've sent you to confuse the case. Who do you work for?

PLUFFEA: For Mexicana Aviation. I'm a pilot. I showed you my credentials. For me political matters are like the airways. While they're calm, they don't matter to me. When they get rough, the only thing to do is fight them cleverly. Sometimes they are friends. The airways. Political matters . . . when? And, finally, if you didn't like the favor I did for you, I'll go. No one raises their voice to Pluffea.

COLONEL: Guard! I'm going to lock you up for false testimony.

PLUFFEA: That's Tarkoff! With a . . . What Pluffea says is the truth. *(To the Guard)* Touch me and I'll put you through the wall, you piece of shit. *(To the Colonel)* Do you really think you can lock up Pluffea?

COLONEL: I can't?

PLUFFEA: You can. You goddamn shitty policeman. You can. For putting my left boot in front of my right or my right in front of my left. But you need better reasons than that to jail a man for more than seventy-two hours in this country. *(To the Guard)* You touch me, dwarf, and I'll break your face. *(To the Colonel)* That's why I live here.

(The Colonel stares at him fixedly. Extends his hand.)

COLONEL: Forgive me.

(Pluffea takes his hand and pulls him to him. Kisses him on one cheek and then the other.)

PLUFFEA: A policeman who asks for forgiveness. What a crazy world this is. And I love it. I love it.

COLONEL: I'll accompany you to the police station. *(They walk down the hall.)*

PLUFFEA: You didn't investigate me, Colonel. And if you do you won't find anything shady. I watch my step. Never go out of bounds where it could cost me. I leave each place I enter without a mark. I was put in jail once for selling contraband and I swore to myself that I'd never return and run the risk of losing the sky. Flying. That's my greatest joy. Zum. No, I'll never risk it. *(They cross the threshold out of the hall.)*

Scene 7

The light brightens until it's midday. The tapping of the typewriter can be clearly heard. It is, once again, the morning of August 25. The Secretary finishes making the necessary preparations to transcribe another roll. Giménez continues studying the notes. Dr. Esther Cerrojo, a young, attractive woman with brown hair comes across the station patio. In his undershirt, the Colonel raises the venetian blinds in his office. He watches her, obviously enchanted. Then he quickly puts on his shirt, tie, and jacket.

ESTHER CERROJO: *(To the Secretary, handing her a card)* I would like to see Colonel . . .

The Colonel opens the door to his office.

COLONEL: Dr. Cerrojo, welcome. Please come in. *(They go into the office. Sit down.)*

ESTHER CERROJO: What a pleasant surprise that you remember my name, Colonel. We haven't seen each other since that lecture years ago.

COLONEL: Ah, you asked me a very interesting question. And, as you may have noticed, I also know that you got your doctorate. Congratulations, as well, for your post in the penitentiary. You've taken off like a rocket.

ESTHER CERROJO: How do you know so much about me?

COLONEL: I have a network of alert senses and an alarmingly exact memory. How can I help you?

ESTHER CERROJO: I'm interested in Jacques Mornard.

COLONEL: It would be strange if you were interested in anyone else. I'm at the disposal of your curiosity.

During all this a young man has climbed to the second floor. He knocks on the office door.

ESTHER CERROJO: It must be my secretary. He had a bit of trouble finding a parking space.

COLONEL: Come in. *(The Secretary enters and sits down in the chair Salazar offers him. He opens his notebook and prepares to transcribe.)*

ESTHER CERROJO: *(Handing the Colonel some documents)* It has do with an official inquiry.

COLONEL: *(After inspecting the papers.)* Isn't it unusual for a delegate of the Social Prevention section of the penitentiary to defend a prisoner? *(Esther Cerrojo shrugs her shoulders)* And that the same person would be a declared Stalinist sympathizer?

ESTHER CERROJO: That's not illegal.

COLONEL: But it is indecent. I'm asking, just the same.

ESTHER CERROJO: Colonel: when you first interrogated Jacques what state did you find him in?

COLONEL: A bit beaten up.

ESTHER CERROJO: A bit beaten up? Or terribly beaten up? Confused, and so anxious that it was feared he would commit suicide.

COLONEL: He was as I have described.

ESTHER CERROJO: And did you let him calm himself or did you immediately confront him with his lover who was in the midst of an attack of hysteria?

COLONEL: They were both excited, but they had their wits about them.

ESTHER CERROJO: Jacques' hands trembled. For a man like him, with perhaps excessive self-control, isn't that a sign of panic?

COLONEL: I didn't think so.

ESTHER CERROJO: Jacques' other statements were taken when he was already here in the police station. Was he drugged before those interrogations?

COLONEL: He was given sedatives to calm his nerves. And stimulants for his paralyzed intestine. Who gave you information concerning his stay here?

ESTHER CERROJO: We can conclude, then, that Jacques' statements have always been taken when he was in a state that you manipulated.

COLONEL: No. I repeat: he was only given medicine.

ESTHER CERROJO: What are we but flesh, blood, and bone? You inject a substance into an organism, and its ideas change. Has he been permitted to regain his psychic and physical condition, or has his sleep been continually interrupted?

COLONEL: His sleep has been interrupted from time to time. An interrogation is more successful when the prisoner's defenses are down.

ESTHER CERROJO: What other forms of torture has he undergone?

COLONEL: He hasn't been tortured.

ESTHER CERROJO: Electroshock?

COLONEL: No.

ESTHER CERROJO: Of what value are the statements of a man who is kept in a state of constant terror? *(Pause)* How many times has Jacques been submitted to interrogations directed by officials from foreign governments?

COLONEL: What?

ESTHER CERROJO: Does your memory fail you? He has been interrogated by, at the least, Persian, Belgian, and U.S. government officials.

COLONEL: The Persian ambassador questioned Jacques at my request, in order to determine whether or not Jacques was born in Teheran. A secretary from the Belgian embassy also came at my request in order to determine if Jacques' French was Belgian. In both cases Jacques had lied. Finally, the supposed "U.S. official" is Trotsky's widow's lawyer. He has no governmental position.

ESTHER CERROJO: But Jacques was interrogated by officials from capitalist bloc countries. Colonel: who was the witness who described the assassin's visit to the victim's house? Wasn't it Natalia Sedova? How old is this lady?

COLONEL: I don't know. I would say around sixty.

ESTHER CERROJO: An elderly woman, then. An elderly woman capable of giving an impartial account?

COLONEL: She is the victim's widow, but . . .

ESTHER CERROJO: Wouldn't you say that she is an elderly, rather histrionic woman, given to heroic posturing?

COLONEL: She is a heroic woman. Since when does a witness's firmness make them suspect, young lady? Let's get something straight. Natalia Sedova's statement hasn't been contradicted on a single point by those of any of the other witnesses.

ESTHER CERROJO: Statements from Trotsky's secretaries, his sworn followers. Finally: who wrote Mornard's biography and confession?

COLONEL: He insists he did. Others involved in the case think the G.P.U. did. You tell me. Perhaps I did. Or maybe, more likely, doctor, the same people who've put you in such a difficult position. To be one thing by vocation and the opposite out of loyalty to your comrades. Making you, as a person, nothing. (Pause) Do you remember what you asked me at that lecture? No? You raised your hand and said, "Colonel, our system of justice conceives of a man as being responsible for his actions and, therefore, susceptible to being guilty for them."

ESTHER CERROJO: "With what we know now about the permeability of our consciousness, and the unconscious determination of the will, isn't the idea of Justice laughable? Isn't Justice, in practice, institutionalized violence that the State permits itself to exercise?"

COLONEL: You left me bewildered.

ESTHER CERROJO: You answered, stammering . . .

COLONEL: Something worth forgetting.

ESTHER CERROJO: "It's a complicated situation."

COLONEL: That was it. Damn the pride that made me accept that invitation to give a lecture. I get lost in theory as if it were fog.

ESTHER CERROJO: But you are Justice's right hand.

COLONEL: In my heart I know what's right and wrong. To put that into words . . . no, I don't know . . .

ESTHER CERROJO: *(Laughing)* In your heart?

COLONEL: Besides, the other lawyers answered you.

ESTHER CERROJO: One sophism after another. Yes, they answered me. Bourgeois Law finds its justification in a verbose series of beautiful, florid innocences. But in practice it's violent. In the end every State is built upon violence, Colonel. All one has to decide is whom you want on top and whom to hang.

COLONEL: And . . . there's no way to tell . . . right from wrong?

ESTHER CERROJO: History shows us that in the end.

COLONEL: Wait, let me try to understand. Those who win were right and those who were beaten, well . . . they deserved it. Is that it?

ESTHER CERROJO: More or less.

COLONEL: No, no. I believe one can be right and lose. Lose in everyone else's eyes but never in your own because you know what's right even in defeat, and knowing what's right isn't anything philosophic, it's like knowing when a watermelon's sweet, not rotten. *(Pause)* You believe you're right because you think you're with those who are right. And that's because they've left you without the ability to ask questions. Comrade, they told you, from this day forward questions are forbidden. We are going to give you the only possible answer. Comrade, consider every uncertainty a weakness and all dissent a sickness—like the flu, cancer, or madness. What a pity: to have all your talent and be a slave. No longer to see with such young eyes. Your eyes are hard, do you feel it? You don't look: you stick your head out into reality in order to harvest proofs that will fit your party's beliefs. Or in order to see what has to be taken from where and put where in order to continue supporting them. *(Esther Cerrojo is bored by the Colonel's words. She smiles at him complacently.)*

ESTHER CERROJO: You don't say. In regard to Jacques' alleged confession . . . *(The Colonel opens a desk drawer and takes out a slender bundle wrapped in gauze. Places it between them.)* What's that?

COLONEL: Take a look. You'll find it interesting. *(Carefully, so as not to touch it, the Doctor unwraps a thin handle.)*

98

ESTHER CERROJO: What is it?

COLONEL: The latest thing in blades. Push the button, you need to see how it works. *(The Doctor accepts the challenge. A thin blade springs from the handle.)* In the ambulance your defendant took that out of his rolled-up raincoat and, with a rapid, well-practiced, precise gesture, opened it and tried to cut his own throat.

ESTHER CERROJO: He was desperate.

COLONEL: Geniuses. Those who thought up the plan. The enemy would disappear and, along with him, the hero would who killed him. All that would remain would be a confession. That they themselves had written. False. What do they care about? Anything? Themselves, I hope. I really hope so.

ESTHER CERROJO: *(Leaving the dagger on the desk.)* There's no brand name. We're not here to express our own opinions, Colonel.

COLONEL: Then what are we here for? Tell me: everything I'm saying suddenly sounds worn out.

ESTHER CERROJO: We are functionaries whose roles have been established by Penal Law. *(The Colonel stares at her and she looks away in order to ask her scribe for something. He gives her some documents.)* You will find one order to allow me to talk with Jacques and another so that I can take him to Trotsky's mansion on Saturday. The defense will carry out a reconstruction of the crime.

COLONEL: What crime? The only thing that happened was that Trotsky, while he was reading Mornard's article, distractedly took the ice pick from beneath Mornard's raincoat and, thinking it was a brush, fftt! Stuck it in his own head.

ESTHER CERROJO: Should I edit out that comment and the others unrelated to the case?

COLONEL: Do what you like.

ESTHER CERROJO: I will send you the transcript this afternoon. If you have no objections, please do me the favor of signing it.

COLONEL: The guard will let you through to see Mornard with this note. Tomorrow, that is.

ESTHER CERROJO: Thank you. Until tomorrow, then, Colonel. Colonel? *The Colonel doesn't respond. Esther Cerrojo and her scribe leave. The Colonel covers his face with his hands.*

Scene 8

Using the gauze, carefully, so as not to touch it, the Colonel shuts the knife, wraps it up, and puts it away in his desk drawer. Turns on the microphone that transmits his voice to the cell.

COLONEL: Jacques Mornard. Stick your head out between the bars of your cell and look at the woman leaving. She came to chat with me about many things. She's a Communist Party member. For reasons she didn't want to make clear to me, she left no doubt that you are a G.P.U. agent.

Jacques Mornard. That's not the name your mother gave you. It doesn't matter. It's no stranger than calling yourself Leandro Salazar. Now's the time to denounce them. Get them out of your head. Free yourself. *(Pause)*

JACQUES: What are you talking about? Say what you like, discover what you can discover about me, I'll grow old in this cell. Isn't that right, Frankenstein of frankness?

COLONEL: There are men in cells who are still free. *(Pause)*

JACQUES: I know a man quite well who could come and go as he pleased from one end of the planet to the other and chose to take a stroll in the cells.

COLONEL: There are men who were free nailed to a cross.

JACQUES: Yes, I've heard that. But they tell you so many things. According to their chatter the Word made man and since then he can't shut his trap. I've heard preachers from the most diverse doctrines. Their blah blah blah blahs repeated in wailing for miles or in café conversations. Ah: I know about catastrophes unleashed by blah blahs and about a single blah that inspired the tallest, most sublime cathedrals. That were later destroyed. Now I confess, down to my marrow, nothing ever moved me. Keep on building and tearing down, faster, more efficient each time, building and tearing down. To hell with all you men of faith. When I nailed that ice pick into his skull, I separated myself from everyone else with a single gash. I withdrew from the air itself. I turned into Jacques Mornard. The one who hears the indefatigable blah blah in the distance and no longer worries about penetrating it. Will any blah blah blah penetrate him? Impossible. Because I'm Jacques Mornard I'm untouchable. Everything I do or say I'll do as Jacques Mornard and I'm not going to wreck my idol for any little colonel. Jacques Mornard: unique, infallible, in glory or misery, very far from what I was or could be, for always, in spite of the universe, until the universe explodes. Jacques Mornard: written in fire. *(Pause)*

COLONEL: And there are other men who rot with hate under a clear sky, prisoners of their own ribs. And that's obvious to you. *(Pause)*

JACQUES: Blah. *(Pause. The colonel turns off the microphone. Blackout.)*

ACT 3

Picture 1

Trotsky's mansion. In a similar fashion to that of the beginning of act 1, the characters are dispersed throughout the stage, frozen in position. Natalia Sedova and Hansen have been replaced by other people. Lt. Giménez replaces Trotsky. Policemen, Reporters, Colonel Salazar, and Esther Cerrojo are all present. The study door and shutters are sealed. The Secretary puts a sheet of paper into the typewriter. Types.

Scene 1

The police search all those present. Hansen, Robins, Cornell, and Charlie all protest on being relieved of their weapons. Lt. Giménez breaks the seals on the study door. Then the seals on the window. The sound of the typewriter will serve as cadence for the call and response between the chorus and the characters. The chorus is now made up of the Reporters who never cease their search for compelling images.

CHORUS: Here he comes. Poor devil. He's trembling all over. Does he even know where he is?

FICTITIOUS NATALIA: He's been drugged.

FICTITIOUS HANSEN: He's been tortured.

Jacques staggers forward between everyone, his head down. The camera "flashes" bring him out of his haze for a moment as if they were fleeting, terrible apparitions.

CHORUS: And if he's like this because he knows where he is?

FIRST REPORTER: Jacques turned out to be a coward.

CHORUS: Is he made of steel or straw? He looks like a boxer beaten before he's even entered the ring. *(In a growing whisper)* Salazar, Salazar, Salazar.

SECOND REPORTER: Here he comes.

CHORUS: He's a strong man but not an executioner. Look at his background.

THIRD REPORTER: It really would be something if the assassination of a public figure could bring him down to nothing in just a few days.

CHORUS: Salazar? He's fearless. The other one's stumbling about. He's unmoved. Why do think that is?

TÉLLEZ: That's what I call a man.

CHORUS: Who?

TÉLLEZ: Salazar.

CHORUS: And the other one? Is calling him a criminal enough?

TÉLLEZ: A great actor. *(Approaching Salazar)* Jacques' pretending.

SALAZAR: As always. Téllez: this isn't official.

TÉLLEZ: Then I never asked. *(Approaching Jacques)* A great actor acting a human corpse? *(Observing him)* Bah. *(Robins comes up behind Jacques' back.)*

ROBINS: Jac! *(Jacques falls to his knees. The Guards push Robins back to his spot. With someone's help Jacques gets up laboriously. The sound of the type-writer fades.)*

SALAZAR: Quiet. All those who aren't involved in the reconstruction will leave. No pictures until we are finished, please. *(Those not involved leave. The Colonel turns things over to Dr. Cerrojo.)*

ESTHER CERROJO: Let's start.

Lt. Giménez puts on Trotsky's glasses, which had been lying on the desk. Goes downstairs to the rabbit hutches. Pretends to feed the rabbits. Someone takes Jacques to the edge of the garden, puts a hat on him, places him in front of Charlie. They go toward the rabbit hutches. Charlie purposively steps on his heels, making him stumble.

FICTITIOUS TROTSKY: Damn it! That rabbit bit me. Ah, Jacques. How are you? You're leaving tomorrow for New York with Silvia?

JACQUES: *(As if he were reciting from memory but unsure of himself.)* That's why I came to say good-bye. She should be here any minute. *(The Fictitious Hansen approaches, followed by Robins. Opens his briefcase. Hands a bundle of bills to the Fictitious Trotsky.)*

FICTITIOUS TROTSKY: In dollars? Splendid. And the marks?

FICTITIOUS HANSEN: We aren't on the Third Reich's payroll yet.

Murmurs. Whistles. Applause. Jacques starts to display more confidence in his role.

FICTITIOUS HANSEN: But we've asked them to include us, sir.

JACQUES: Are you thinking of taking U.S. money with one hand and the enemy's money with the other?

FICTITIOUS TROTSKY: Whose enemy? We don't have friends or enemies. We have a goal to reach. Along the way we find traveling companions and obstacles. At any moment the companion may fall and the obstacle rear up. Then, arm in arm with our new companion, we'll march forward over the fallen ex-companion. Pure dialectic, my good Jac.

Applause. Laughter. Disgusted exclamations. Above the din Robins's voice is heard.

ROBINS: A pistol . . .

TROTSKY: *(Handing the bundle of bills to the Fictitious Hansen.)* Leave these on my desk. As soon as I finish with these furies I'll count them. I don't think it's any more or less than it should be, but it never hurts to be careful.

The Fictitious Natalia Sedova comes down to the garden carrying the straw hat. It's stained with blood. Jac trembles when he sees it.

FICTITIOUS NATALIA: Hello, comrade. *(Closing her eyes and holding out her arms with her hands open.)*

TROTSKY: *(Embarrassed.)* Natuchele.

JACQUES: I'm sorry. I didn't bring you any surprise today.

FICTITIOUS NATALIA: And what's that sticking out of your raincoat pocket? Let me see. *(She takes it. It's a rolled-up newspaper.)* An ice pick. Going mountain climbing?

JACQUES: That's . . . well . . .

TROTSKY: *(Taking the rolled-up newspaper)* Jacques likes mountain climbing. He goes to the mountains every weekend. I asked him to bring me an ice pick to use as a paperweight.

ROBINS: *(Sadly)* A pistol . . .

JACQUES: The sun's wonderful.

NATALIA: Would you like some tea?

JACQUES: No. But I would be grateful for a cigarette.

FICTITIOUS NATALIA: I'll bring you one. *(Leaves.)*

TROTSKY: Please excuse her. Being in exile has changed her. We rarely see anyone.

JACQUES: Yes. You both look bad.

TROTSKY: Did you bring your article?

JACQUES: *(Taking it out from beneath his raincoat and handing it to him.)* It's typed so it'll be easier to strike things out. *(Laughing sarcastically)*

TROTSKY: *(going up the stairs to his study)* What did you expect? Your earlier version was bad. It contradicted the basic principles of the party. I can't allow those principles to be disputed.

JACQUES: It's my duty to question them. Where would we be if all we did was blindly follow what you've said? We'd be sterile. Unable to adapt to a continually changing reality. We'd become metaphysicians.

FICTITIOUS TROTSKY: *(Facing him)* Jac. About the next presidential election in Mexico . . . Lombaro Toledano and Avila Camacho are both obstacles. Almazán is a good traveling companion. See what you can do for him, without mentioning me, understand? *(Murmurs.)*

JACQUES: No. I'm not up to date on this country's politics.

FICTITIOUS TROTSKY: I know. That's why I told you to look into it. And Jac: take your hat off before you come into my study. *(They enter. Trotsky is already reading the article as he sits on the desk and leaves the rolled-up newspaper on top of some papers.)*

TROTSKY: *(Furiously picking up a pen)* You don't know what you're talking about. *(Striking something out)* You can't question what's already a law. I don't want another split in the party. We'll become a debate club incapable of acting as a group.

JACQUES: Let others think! You don't have a monopoly on intelligence. Wouldn't it be wonderful if we each had our own ideas and only followed what you proposed if it were obviously useful.

TROTSKY: I've already thought about what has to be done! It's your generation's duty to do it!

JACQUES: If it's so important to act, why did you flee from the eye of the hurricane? What damn sense does it make to run a revolutionary party millions of kilometers away from the only proletarian revolution on the planet?

TROTSKY: How dare you, you intellectual eunuch! *(Throws a blow at Jacques that he avoids. Moves around the desk.)*

JACQUES: Don't attack me.

TROTSKY: Idiot.

JACQUES: I'll tell them about this totalitarian attitude in New York.

TROTSKY: You're not going to New York. It's not convenient at the moment.

JACQUES: I'll tell them how you don't listen.

TROTSKY: I demand obedience. You're not going.

JACQUES: How deaf you are.

TROTSKY: I've taken enough insubordination. The continual fragmentation of the party must be avoided. You're not going.

Trotsky takes a revolver out of his desk drawer. But before he can aim it, Jacques gets the newspaper roll. He lands a strong blow on Trotsky's face. Camera flashes. Trotsky slides down the chair. Jacques, laughing, lands another blow. Téllez runs into the study, camera in hand. The other Reporters follow him.

TÉLLEZ: Let's go back to the moment of the blow, please.

They go back to the moment of the blow. The Reporters fire their triggers.

FIRST REPORTER: Again!

Flashes as the blow lands. The Bodyguards run up to the study.
SECOND REPORTER: Again, Mr. Jacques!
THIRD REPORTER: Make it look real!

Jacques lands the blow and suddenly the uproar coming from all those present is muted as we hear the increasingly loud howls of the absent Trotsky, distorting the assassin's face. Jacques knocks over the chair, terrified, and the fictitious Trotsky falls and crawls on all fours behind Jacques. The howling, unrealistically sharp, continues.
FICTITIOUS NATALIA: *(As if she were shouting, but barely audible)* What's going on? What's happening? *(Jacques is paralyzed. The Bodyguards grab him and throw him in the next room.)*
SALAZAR: Quiet.
ROBINS: Then we brought him here to question him.
SALAZAR: Quiet, I said. This is pure mimicry.

The howling continues, extremely sharply. Jacques is brought into the study again like a sleepwalker. Charlie, Robins, and Cornell rabidly beat a ghost. Hansen, furious as well, runs across the study to the stairs.
ESTHER CERROJO: *(To Trotsky's Bodyguards)* Splendid, gentlemen. You keep beating Mornard until he doesn't know who he is while Hansen runs to write his confession. *(Hansen, already on the stairs, stands stock-still. The flashes first illuminate his surprise, then his indignation.)*
THIRD REPORTER: *(To Jacques)* Are you sorry?

The howling increases.
JACQUES: What?
THIRD REPORTER: Are you sorry?
JACQUES: For what?
THIRD REPORTER: For having killed Trotsky?
JACQUES: *(Ferociously)* Are you married?
THIRD REPORTER: *(Confused)* Yes . . .
ANOTHER REPORTER TO THIRD REPORTER: Are you sorry?

Laughter. The laughter starts to drown out the howling.
JACQUES: How many times a week do you fuck your wife?
THIRD REPORTER: *(Openmouthed)*. . .

JACQUES: How many times a month? Once a year?

More laughter drowns out the howling.
> THIRD REPORTER: You have no right to stick your nose into my private life.
> JACQUES: We're in complete agreement. You have no right to stick your
> nose into my private life. None of you. Never. Gentlemen, lets reenact the
> blow slowly, so you can take a beautiful sequence of images to your editors.

Jacques slowly reproduces the moment of the blow. Flashes. The light fades until suddenly the stage is illuminated only by the flashes from the Reporters' cameras.

Scene 2

Jacques kisses Esther Cerrojo's hand amidst camera flashes. Then he says good-bye to the fake Hansen, Natalia Sedova, and Trotsky (Giménez). He is escorted to the mansion gate by Reporters and Guards. A Guard returns their firearms to the Bodyguards. They clean them. Salazar is at the back, almost hidden. Téllez stops Giménez, who's leaving with the group.
> TÉLLEZ: Giménez, wait. I saw Salazar's face while you acted your part. He
> was hurt.
> GIMÉNEZ: That's too bad. But I already had one father, and he was enough.
> I buried him. See you later.
> TÉLLEZ: Wait a minute, chameleon. Today you were red. Tomorrow?
> GIMÉNEZ: Red as today's teacher. Tomorrow I'll follow the next one. See you.
> TÉLLEZ: Calm down. Maybe you've learned all there is to know about right
> and wrong. Why dig any deeper? Tell me, are you ever going to show your
> true colors?
> GIMÉNEZ: You listen to me, Téllez. I'll tell you what it's all about. When
> I'm on top you'll see my true colors, if you're still around.
> TÉLLEZ: Get out of here, then.
> GIMÉNEZ: You better realize something, old man. There are no more
> utopias. They were fantastic. But there were a lot of them, and they were
> all fantastic.
> TÉLLEZ: Hurry up, get out of here, run. *(Giménez leaves hurriedly.)* You
> stink.

During the previous dialogue Trotsky's secretaries have been loading their guns. Charlie picks up the rabbit cages in the distance—that is, offstage. The secretaries aim their guns. Salazar slowly comes forward from where he was partly hidden, unnoticed.

HANSEN: Open the first one, Charlie! *(The Guards aim and fire.)*
ROBINS: Three out of three. Good, good, good.
CORNELL: Let them get away from the cages before firing. Eh? It'll make it more emotional.
HANSEN: Agreed. Open another, Charlie!

The Bodyguards follow their prize with their eyes. Robins and Cornell fire. Hansen doesn't yet. He slowly turns, following his prize toward where the Colonel is. For a moment it looks like he's aiming at him. Then he turns away, fires.
CORNELL: Well done, Hansen.
HANSEN: I don't hold any grudge against you, Colonel. You're nothing more than the master of ceremonies for a carnival of scoundrels. This one's for the Colonel. It's on the house.
CORNELL: Another one, Charlie!

The Colonel takes his time. Fluidly he draws his gun and fires, turns on his heels and fires, turns on his heels and fires, turns and then follows his prize for a long time.
ROBINS: What a pity. The last one escaped. No, look, there, in the high grass, do you see it? That little white stain against the dry grass.
COLONEL: No. I won't return to what I was. *(Holsters his gun. Hansen stares attentively at the Colonel. Keeps staring at him while he leaves, meditatively. The other secretaries exchange questioning looks.)*
HANSEN: All those left together, Charlie! *(While the Colonel leaves, the secretaries follow their prizes. A moment passes, then each one fires two, three, then four times. Blackout.)*

Scene B (this scene is optional)

Three different realities: In an upper corner, Pluffea the pilot. Dreaming in another, the Spanish baker. Below, in the center, the Psychoanalyst.
PLUFFEA: Sometimes, when I'm alone and very high up in the air, I stop the motor and glide. And gliding through the curves in the air I feel like I'm climbing. Like I'm slowly climbing. I go up, and up, and could fall through the sky forever.
PSYCHOANALYST: But you know that you'll fall to earth, I hope.
PLUFFEA: One of these days, the day I feel that: Pluffea, it's the day, I'm going to flip the plane on its back, put on the automatic pilot, and really go falling through the sky . . . falling . . .

SPANISH MAN: Falling, through the transparent sky . . .

PLUFFEA: I'll cross the stratosphere . . . and I'll go on . . .

SPANISH MAN: A burst of red, green, and purple . . .

PLUFFEA: . . . falling . . .

SPANISH MAN: A beautiful tomb for a flyer.

PLUFFEA: *(Slipping into the darkness)* . . . falling . . .

PSYCHOANALYST: *(Shaking his head in disapproval. Pointing at Pluffea.)* Masochist. *(Pointing at the Spanish Man.)* Schizoid sadist.

SPANISH MAN: *(Slipping into the darkness)* Uh-huh. A beautiful tomb . . . a deep tomb . . .

PSYCHOANALYST: *(Putting his forefinger to his forehead)* Or could this be transference? Too much religious education? *(Slipping into the darkness)* Who warned me suicide was a sin? My mother? How old was I? I remember I wanted to slit my wrists in order to find out if beyond the grave there was . . . what? I was in dad's bathroom. I'd climbed up on a small bench and was looking at myself in the mirror and . . . the razor blade . . . what did I do then? I wound a curl between my eyes, or did I cut it?! Or . . . Oh heavens. . . .

Picture 2

The police station.

Scene 1

Jacques' cell. There's no one inside. There's a fruit basket and flower arrangements. Wine and whisky bottles. Boxes. Outside the cell a Guard plays solitaire. A bundle of clothing can be seen burning in the patio in the distance. The Colonel enters.

COLONEL: Guard!

GUARD: *(Standing at attention)* Colonel!

COLONEL: Where's the prisoner?

GUARD: In the showers.

COLONEL: By whose orders? I gave orders that nothing was to be done with him without my permission. You weren't even supposed to talk to him.

GUARD: He wanted to bathe, you weren't here, and a little while ago your secretary said, "All right, let him do what he wants." We thought things had changed. The flowers came for him. Food. Liquor. Packs of cigarettes.

COLONEL: What's burning in the patio?

GUARD: His old clothes. They brought him new ones. Very fancy, Colonel. And look: a mirror with lights around it like they say the movie stars use.

COLONEL: Nothing has changed here. Mr. X is still incommunicado and under my complete authority. Take all this up to my office. The way you're all impressed by these gifts is incredible.

GUARD: *(Standing at attention)* Yes, Colonel. Colonel: it wasn't just the gifts. It was mainly the message from the penitentiary.

COLONEL: What message?

GUARD: That they're coming for him this afternoon.

COLONEL: Carry out my orders. Did Mr. X give you those cards?

GUARD: He said he didn't like games he could lose.

COLONEL: Burn them.

The Guard salutes. Sadly burns the cards. The Colonel hurriedly goes up to the office level.

COLONEL: Miss Alvarez.

SECRETARY: Yes, Colonel?

COLONEL: Since when do you give instructions about the prisoners?

SECRETARY: Dr. Cerrojo called and asked that Mr. Jacques be given a bath.

COLONEL: Mr. X!

SECRETARY: When the Guard came looking for you to ask your permission I'd just received the order. I'm sorry, but . . .

COLONEL: And did Dr. Cerrojo say when the people from the penitentiary would be coming for him?

SECRETARY: At six, on the dot.

COLONEL: *(Looking at his watch)* In two hours. That's what she thinks. Get me the General . . .

SECRETARY: The General called, Colonel. You didn't give me a chance to tell you. He said that the doctor's orders should be carried out.

COLONEL: Get him, I said. *(Goes into his office.)*

Scene 2

The office telephone rings. Salazar waits for it to ring again before picking up the receiver.

COLONEL: I still haven't got the truth out of him, General. That's why you gave him to me, remember? Uh-huh. Uh-huh. Uh-huh. No, how can I agree? I said "uh-huh" because all these political reasons are very well for-mulated but irrelevant in this case. Uh-huh. Leave him with me for two weeks. Torture? In comparison to what we know how to do he's had a few pinches, that's all. But they say we've gotten more civilized since then. Ten days.

It's insane. Mornard or Tarkoff or Mercader or Roberts or however they sign him in at the penitentiary will have a pretty good life there. Even if I manage to verify his real name before they take him. He'll have a special cell. Books. Visitors. Consolation. Be a trusty soon, I imagine. All the privileges his protectors can give him within the letter of the law. He'll get the maximum sentence because the nature of the crime and the advantage to be gained are undeniable and premeditation easy to see. He'll serve twenty years and then he'll be out on the street.

The theory he killed him in self-defense? Very imaginative, isn't it? They'll have to hypnotize the judges for them to take it seriously.

Uh-huh. Listen: This broken man's fate doesn't matter. What matters is the truth. *(Pause)* If the truth doesn't matter, well . . . what's left for honest men? They'll have to fight their institutions as if they were crazy giants. Cheats and swindlers will rule their kingdom. There'll be treachery and deception everywhere. Distrust will squeeze out all hopes. Good-bye to the dream of a people united by one conscience and a common goal. Truth is one: it unifies. Lies are infinitely multiple.

No. I'm not intransigent like Zapata. I'm as I am. And I thought powder, blood, and wails were a road we'd suffered too much. I believed that with peace, we'd all be able to purify ourselves. I want to go on believing that, that's why I'm arguing.

No, I don't want to see things from another point of view for even an instant because I'd have to forget who I am and start to invent who it would be better for me to be. How tiring, how exhausting this all is.

Yes, I'm listening to you, if you like I'll repeat what you say to me. Listen to me, General, listen to me. Me, General? *(The Guard enters with Jacques' presents and puts them on the desk in such a way that Salazar becomes hidden.)* It had occurred to me that I'd been promoted because I'd decided to retire, but it seems I was so absorbed in criminal cases I didn't realize that what I'd predicted—an age of swindlers in the police station—was already in progress. *(Slowly circling the desk.)* Christ: just my fate to be so stupid. You can have my stripes for ten days with the prisoner. Five. Two. Shit.

Yes, I'm still here. But in my mind I flew far away. To the south. To a little ranch nestled in the mountains, with a picket fence and on it a silent sparrow hawk. Very silent, casting its shadow over the black earth. And I felt a shout unleashed inside . . .

As a boy it was a war call, a shout of brotherhood, faith. Land . . . and . . . Liberty. That empty dream. Now. An echo. Spent. And why not, if the person babbling about it is the thick-lipped old man looking at me courageously from the mirror? *(He turns on the mirror lights. Turns them off. To the Guard.)* What do you have there?

GUARD: Personal letters for Mr. Mornard. *(The Colonel takes them. Smells them.)*

COLONEL: Perfumed letters. Love letters. No need to say: I'm destined to be an idiot.

Yes, I'm still here, General. But not for long. I want . . . to retire. That's it. No I tell you, this broken man doesn't matter much. It's just that, if I felt I owed some debt to society, I think that after so many years of . . . so many years of work . . . I've paid it, that's all. And I miss the simple pleasures of . . . the deep, fragrant earth. The freedom of the open sky. Yes, I'm stammering. The emotion. A difficult decision. No, it's difficult to say, that's all. My successor? Choose him yourself. I'm serious. You seem to be able to adapt yourself to whichever way the wind blows.

Seriously? Was I all that? *(Sadly)* Stop, or I'll start believing you. *(Looking for rolling paper and tobacco amidst the presents. Without losing track of the phone call he takes out his pistol and removes a cartridge. Opens it. Rolls a cigarette, mixing the tobacco and the gunpowder together.)* Better to pay tribute to . . . Listen: for me it'll be enough to know who I am when I leave this life. Uh-huh. Uh-huh. I'll visit you there. Uh-huh. Until then. We'll chat, of course. *(Hangs up)* Blah, blah, blah.

Scene 3

Jacques is escorted by four Guards through the patio and toward his cell. He is recently bathed, refreshed. He wears a white suit, a sky-blue silk shirt, a black tie, and a red carnation in his lapel.

SECRETARY: They're bringing Mr. X to his cell, Colonel.

The Colonel puts the cigarette in his jacket pocket. Takes the dagger wrapped in gauze from his desk and puts it in his pocket as well. Hurries to meet Jacques on the lower level. When he sees him coming down the stairs, Jacques puts on a pair of dark glasses. The four Guards come to attention in front of the Colonel.

FIRST GUARD: He told me to bring him to the showers, Colonel.

SECOND GUARD: He was the one who gave me the order.

THIRD GUARD: Your secretary told me to do it, Colonel.

FOURTH GUARD: They brought him to me at the showers.

COLONEL: Mr. X. How handsome you look.

JACQUES: I can't say the same for you, my esteemed Colonel Y.

COLONEL: Then why not look me in the eyes? You can take off your dark glasses. Seriously.

JACQUES: Maybe. The sparrow hawk doesn't chase me in my dreams anymore.

COLONEL: Are you sure he chased you? He took the same road, that's all. But you're very fearful and very conceited. The same road for a while, nothing more.

JACQUES: Last night he turned away and gained altitude, the sly fellow.

COLONEL: He left for another dream.

JACQUES: Is that it? *(Slowly taking off his glasses)* He left. *(Laughing sarcastically)* There's a little spark still flashing in those eyes, a spark of rage. The prize is gone, and there's no way to catch it. *(Laughing joyfully)* That little spark is very beautiful. Take care of it for me; it makes me happy.

COLONEL: Such haughtiness doesn't suit you, Mr. X. Try something more anxious, more distressed. That's what will move the public at your trial.

JACQUES: They're so stupid it won't be long before I'm the judge and they're all Trotsky's assassins.

COLONEL: I'm going to miss your sarcastic comments.

JACQUES: Which ones? *(With a fluid gesture the Colonel takes the wrapped-up dagger from his pocket and throws it. Jacques catches it instinctively.)* What's this? *(Cautiously unwrapping it)*

COLONEL: The knife you tried to cut your throat with after the assassination.

JACQUES: Yes. *(Pushes the button in the handle, and blade jumps out. Looks at it, puzzled.)* What's this all about?

COLONEL: When will you stop being so suspicious? I took it from you; I'm returning it.

JACQUES: It's not just your eyes, your brain's become dull. After all that's happened I don't have any use for this dagger. It's yours.

COLONEL: You could use it as a letter opener, for example.

JACQUES: I insist: it's yours. As a small token of thanks for your gymnastic lessons. I exercise this *(referring to his body)* three times a day. You taught me other things as well, professor. *(Lets the dagger fall to the ground.)*

COLONEL: And you me. You got the sparrow hawk out of the cells for me. Let's take a walk. I want to settle accounts with you. Get on your good side, that is. You wanted to see the patio; I'll show it to you. *(They walk.)*

JACQUES: They tell me the penitentiary isn't so gray.

COLONEL: There's no comparison. It's a garden. There's a greenhouse and an orchard. A soccer field. Listen, if you got yourself a mare, you could let her run free.

JACQUES: You're exaggerating. I'm going to a penitentiary, not a country estate.

COLONEL: With your connections . . .

JACQUES: Well, supposing they'd be silly enough to humor me, I don't know, it would depress me to trot amidst the poorer beasts in the herd. I'm a martyr to democracy. Remember your own words?

COLONEL: I haven't forgotten a thing. Nevertheless, I do believe it'll be better for you than twenty years of vacation. You'll feel liberated from all the world's temptations. All of those deep emotions whose temptations you only knew how to run from while in the world: faith, love, truth, power.

JACQUES: Incredible. Salazar the Wise and Silvi the Naive united in a sentence the synthesis of which is "Blah." Well, what will happen to me, Colonel?

COLONEL: For the moment you'll stop running in your dreams.

JACQUES: The sparrow hawk's gone.

COLONEL: And the long-distance championship race is over. They tell me cell walls are very difficult to sleep in. Whether you open or close your eyes, there they are. *(Pause)* I knew a prisoner who was always laughing, he laughed and laughed. I asked him, "Why?" "And why not?" He said to me. "You know something? Light is made up of little dots of color. A diminutive confetti that I watch float by. That's where I go every holiday." "And the prisoners?" I asked him. "Oh, they're beautiful things. Of course, you've got to be careful. If one of them stares at you it's because they've confused you with an old lover or an old enemy. Then, discreetly, you turn around and quickly leave." He made little masks carved out of avocado pits. They got so valuable he paid his bail. He didn't have any family or friends outside. Like you, right?

JACQUES: . . .

COLONEL: I remember what he told me: "Here in jail I learned patience. We'll see if I don't get confused outside."

JACQUES: If I beat the cleverest of them, I'll beat the stupid walls of a cell.

COLONEL: You'll learn to enjoy what happens in spite of our desires: the light, the silence, the moon . . .

113

JACQUES: They can't beat me.

COLONEL: The rain . . . and lots of other things difficult to say simply. . . . But you'll have to free your will. You'll have to stop fighting.

JACQUES: Jacques Mornard doesn't fight: he wins.

COLONEL: Win without fighting. To fight is already to lose. You made it, but I didn't give you credit. On the other hand, I learned from you. I'm telling you: you were born with such power that you'll defeat Nature itself. *(Jacques laughs ferociously.)* I'm telling you: someone who hates so much is just a step away from Heaven's Gates.

JACQUES: Talk to me in Spanish. I don't understand code.

COLONEL: I suspect that one of these days you'll wake up singing.

JACQUES: Oh yes, a nightingale in his cement cage. *(Jacques tries a warble.)* When it happens I'll write you. And Silvi. At least it will get her ulcer going.

COLONEL: Let me know when you don't sing out of tune and the melody sounds strange even to you. If that happens . . .

JACQUES: Out of tune? *(Tries out another warble.)*

COLONEL: Speaking of music: there's a law that comes from fugue, the fugitive law. Why did you stop? Are you familiar with it?

JACQUES: The . . . the law . . . . the law used in some compo . . . sitions? Bach fugues, for example, Handel . . . Musors . . .

COLONEL: Don't play dumb. I'm talking about the first thing that crossed your mind. The fugitive law is when you try to escape and I riddle you with bullets. Guards! *(The Guards approach.)*

JACQUES: *(To the Guards)* I'm not . . . trying . . . to escape.

COLONEL: Well, that's your version of events. Ours is that—*(Consulting his wristwatch)*—is that it's now an hour and forty-five minutes later. The van from the penitentiary has just arrived to take you there, and I'm in a well-known restaurant in the city eating pinchón. Escorted by a guard you are crossing the patio toward the van. . . . Suddenly, from who knows where, you pull out the dagger—it will probably be surmised that it was hidden in the basket of red roses they sent you—and you stab the guard with it. Fortunately, without any grave consequences—Which one of you, boys? Who should it be?

ALL FOUR GUARDS: Me.

FIRST GUARD: *(Running to where the dagger fell)* He sliced me across my stomach.

COLONEL: Don't touch it! It has Jacques' fingerprints on it. We'll cut you later without touching the handle. They say that after you attacked him, you ran toward the wall. Unquestionably, we thought you were going to scale it. But this brave man had yelled for help and these other brave men came running into the patio. Stunned, they see you escaping. Do you see him? *(Jacques backs up a step.)*

SECOND GUARD: How fast he's going.

THIRD GUARD: Incredible.

COLONEL: You'll have to chase him going backward for a bit, understand what I mean? *(The Guards trot backward.)*

FIRST GUARD: For the experts in ballistics.

COLONEL: That's right. A bit prematurely you decided that you wouldn't be able to catch him and stopped dead. Ready to shoot him? *(The Guards cock their guns. Aim. It looks like a typical firing squad.)* Stay like that. *(He goes to Jacques. Jacques tries to say something.)* Shut up, Jacques Mornard. I warned you that we had to settle some personal accounts.

JACQUES: You said you wanted to get on my good side.

COLONEL: I tried. But if I tell a man he could master Nature itself and he laughs ferociously, it's more than I can take. He's more conceited than I could ever dream. Too small.

JACQUES: You were making fun of me, and I laughed in order not to cry for you. I beat you, Salazar the Wise. I'm an infallible poison.

COLONEL: Yes, too small.

JACQUES: You made me take pity. Take it away, quickly. How it hurts. Quickly. I'm beginning to hurt all over.

COLONEL: I'm glad.

JACQUES: Ha, ha, ha.

COLONEL: Perverse times when telling the truth sounds sarcastic.

JACQUES: And if I told you now?

COLONEL: Who cares where you came from, little man. It's where you're going that matters.

JACQUES: Through the gates of heaven, huh? Blow me far away. Do it already.

COLONEL: That's it, do you want your dark glasses? *(Jacques shakes his head.)* Any last message you want to give me? No. Is there some special place on the planet where you'd like to be buried? No. Shall we cremate you and toss your ashes wherever? All the same to you. A last request, please. Relax, think about it. There must be something you're pining for in the last moment of your life. *(Jacques doesn't answer, stares at the guns aimed at him.)* I see. *(Taking the cigarette from his pocket. Sticking it between Jacques' quivering lips.)* Well then: this tribunal, consisting of you and me, having found you guilty of disillusionment, sentences Jacques Mornard to fall dead on top of his own shadow under the unappealable warning that he's the one falling, not the universe.

JACQUES: A light, my good pupil.

COLONEL: A light, of course, excuse me, since I don't smoke . . . *(The Colonel lights a match. Without taking his eyes off the guns, Jacques smokes avidly.)*

Pause

COLONEL: Are your guns cocked? *(Pause)* Aim.

The cigarette blows up in Jacques' mouth. He falls flat on his face. The Colonel breaks out laughing. The Guards are completely surprised.

SECOND GUARD: Did you fire?

THIRD GUARD: No. Did you?

FOURTH GUARD: No way, man.

SECOND GUARD: Well, then?

THIRD GUARD: The cigarette, stupid. It blew up in his face.

FOURTH GUARD: Christ. He must have shit his pants.

COLONEL: *(Still laughing)* Take him to his cell. *(The Guards pick Jacques up off the ground. He's rigid. His eyes are very wide in the middle of his scorched face. His white suit is stained. They carry him.)*

COLONEL: You there, come here.

The first Guard approaches him while the Colonel unhooks the shield he wears on his lapel.

FIRST GUARD: *(Coming to attention)* Yes, Colonel?

COLONEL: I've worn this on my lapel for many years. *(Handing it to him)* For having offered to slice your gut.

FIRST GUARD: I'd have done more. You're my Colonel. Thank you, Colonel. *(Saluting)* Is it an eagle or a vulture?

COLONEL: A city boy, eh? Something in between. A thin eagle.

FIRST GUARD: Does it do anything more than glitter?

COLONEL: It doesn't fly.

FIRST GUARD: It seems . . . heavy.

COLONEL: Yes, it's gold. Okay, get out of here. *(The Guard starts to salute, but the Colonel interrupts him.)* No. You'd better stay here and keep watch until a new chief comes or I return, resuscitated. Or the truth everyone knows so well disappears like a word that's been dropped from the dictionary, or it rains stars. Sit down, if you want. Understood?

FIRST GUARD: But . . . is this a joke or . . . ?

COLONEL: *(Energetically)* Not at all. Stay here with your gun ready and cover the rear guard for me in case anything unexpected happens. Until I give you another order!

FIRST GUARD: *(Saluting)* Yes, Colonel.

With his gun ready the Guard keeps watch. The Colonel walks toward the back of the patio. Jacques is deposited in his cell and locked in. The Colonel leaves. Slowly, nodding, Jacques comes out of his stupor. The Guard, not really knowing what he's looking for, keeps watch. He aims his gun at any movement the audience makes. Fade to black.

HERESY

To Abraham
who entered my secret niche of idols
and broke them.

To Abraham
who showed me reality
like an incalculable temple.

To Abraham
for the third time.

CAST

Luis de Carbajal the Elder
Isabel de Carbajal
Luis de Carbajal the Younger
Rafael Rodríguez Matos
Francisca de Carbajal
Viviana de Carbajal
Brother Agustín
Felipe Núñez

Jesús Baltazar
Doña Guiomar de Carbajal
Jorge Almeida
Old Man
Rabbi
Julia
Inquisitors, Guards,
    Dominicans

NOTES

Except for the first seven, all the characters are incidental. The play could be easily mounted with eleven actors doubling roles.

The events and personalities described take their inspiration from those that Luis de Carbajal the Younger noted in his autobiography. They can also be inferred from documents found in the National Archive relating to the trials that the Holy Inquisition carried out against the members of the Carbajal family. The first volume of Alfonso Toro's "La Familia Carbajal" greatly abridged the search for anecdotal material, summarizing the greater part of it and indicating the primary sources already mentioned. This text doesn't pretend to reproduce the period. The stage set shouldn't attempt faithful realism. The use of theatrical convention and, above all, the mixture of past with present are taken for granted.

The action occurs in New Spain between 1578 and 1590.

Translator's Note: The *cante hondo* is a musical form from southern Spain, typically accompanied by flamenco dance or hand clapping, or both. Both song and dance are a visceral expression of feeling, and the hand clapping *(palmadas)* is both an extension of that feeling and a means of keeping time percussively. It may vary in beat and syncopation, with each person usually clapping differently to produce a highly involved rhythmic pattern.

Picture 1

Scene 1

Torture chamber. Semidarkness. An Inquisitor. Two Executioners. A Man tied to a stake.

INQUISITOR: Your secret name.

MAN: Hilario de Carbajal.

INQUISITOR: Your secret name, I said.

MAN: . . .

INQUISITOR: Give it to him.

They whip the man.

INQUISITOR: Your creed.

MAN: . . .

INQUISITOR: Take pity on yourself and help us avoid this torture as well. Your creed!

MAN: . . .

INQUISITOR: Give it to him.

They whip him.

INQUISITOR: We know you follow a forbidden faith. We know you write your name from right to left. Singer of a dead tongue, we know you and your mistaken ambition of Paradise, but we must hear you confess. . . . Finding you guilty and sentencing you isn't enough. You have to repent. Speak. Let Satan out. Let him escape: Evil has no power before me: the true God protects me. *(Nothing happens.)* First tell us the names of your accomplices, my son. Then your sin will leave you more easily . . .

MAN: I won't betray my tongue.

INQUISITOR: Give it to him!

They whip him.

MAN: . . .

INQUISITOR: Your creed, pig!

MAN: . . .

They whip him.

INQUISITOR: Your secret name!

FIRST EXECUTIONER: He's out of breath.

INQUISITOR: Your secret name!

MAN: Mmmaann.

INQUISITOR: What? What? What? What's he jabbering?

SECOND EXECUTIONER: Mmmaann.

FIRST EXECUTIONER: Man, he said.

SECOND EXECUTIONER: Man!

INQUISITOR: He says his secret name is man! Ave María Purísima! We have before us a poet writing not with pen and paper but with flesh and blood! *(The Inquisitor goes and sits down in a corner. Routinely)* Cut off his tongue.

CHORUS: Aaaaaaaaaaaaah! Iiiiiiiiiiiiiiiiiii!

Pause

INQUISITOR: Now, I'll ask you again: your secret name?

The man produces an unintelligible guttural sound. The Executioners laugh.

INQUISITOR: *(Gently)* Give it to him.

The Executioners raise their whips: blackout.

Scene 2

Darkness. Dungeon.

LUIS DE CARBAJAL THE YOUNGER: *(As if it were an intense cante hondo)*

Ay, how much will my parents have sinned
for me to be born amongst men who imprison love
How much will my parents have sinned, ay,
for faith to have made me a martyr.

Scene 3

Shadows of three Inquisitors stretch across the floor until they darken the boots of Luis de Carbajal the Elder. Don Luis sits gallantly, his right hand holding some documents that he consults from time to time and his other hand resting on his embossed gold belt buckle. He is fifty years old, with long gray hair and beard, wearing the garb of a powerful, intense man. At times he appears exasperated, like someone obliged to give accounts and who feels offended at having to do so.

LUIS DE CARBAJAL THE ELDER: *(Gruffly)* My baptismal name is Don Luis de Carbajal y de la Cueva. *(Clearing his throat; attempting to calm the indignation in his voice)* I came into the world fifty-one years ago, in 1539, there on the other side of the ocean, of course, in the village of Magodorio, on the Portuguese border. But when I was very little my father took me to Salamanca where I immediately learned Spanish and how to write. And, of course, the Christian prayers that have been my daily solace since that time. A few blond hairs had barely appeared on my chin when it occurred to me to get married. And I got married. To Doña Guiomar de Rivera, daughter of Miguel Núñez, an agent who contracted Negroes in Santo Domingo. That is how I came to have both a house and a business at a very young age. By the end of two or three years we were ruined. A bad deal with wheat. So, I embarked for the New World. Alone. That is to say: without my wife. I went as admiral of the fleet His Catholic Majesty ordered formed on the island of Palma. *(Rising from his seat, his eyes shining)* At the head of that fleet, as is known around the world, I entered the port of Jamaica in small vessels,—our general, whose name I prefer to forget, had stayed behind on his ship—and I demolished the three ships of John Hawkins's corsairs, who had taken the port in order to sack it. . . . For myself, señores, I didn't take even a maravedí, despite the fact that as admiral I didn't receive any salary, only the pleasure of my small command

and the immense opportunity to shine among men for some heroic deed. Yes, I shone: my name became a way of saying daring and honor. Here is the letter in which the viceroy at the time, Viceroy Don Martínez Enríquez, whom God has at his right hand, expresses his esteem for me in sonorous adjectives. I won't read it: I'll leave it here in case your curiosity or mistrust requires it. In order to continue my tale, it is enough to say that in the final paragraph he names me mayor of Tampico. *(Don Luis pauses, satisfied.)*

Scene 4

Felipe Núñez gives his declaration before the tribunal.

FELIPE NÚÑEZ: Since I was ten years old. *(Drumming the fingers of one hand)* I embarked for New Spain with Don Luis and never served any other master. *(Biting his tongue)* Everything I know and everything I own I owe to him. None of it illicit. *(Drumming the fingers of his other hand)* I was with him during bad times and good times, when he was nobody and when they called him a hero and his position as mayor of Tampico allowed us to live in luxury. Mayor of Tampico: it's easy to say and almost sounds enviable. But I swear that being mayor of Tampico was like being sentenced. It meant constantly keeping one eye on the sea, watching for a pirate attack, and the other eye on the mountains, awaiting an avalanche of painted Indians who ate people. And all to protect some blue bloods who readied their wagons and fled, screeching like sissies at any sign of danger . . . only to return when we, Don Luis and his handful of soldiers, had freed the port. But then luck returned and expanded our future. By order of the Viceroy Enríquez we were hunting some lazy Indians on the other side of the mountain, when I, who was carrying the compass and the maps, was astonished to realize that I didn't recognize anything around me. I put spur to horse, passed Don Luis, stopped the animal, and jumped to the ground, kneeling down like this. *(He kneels.)*

Scene 5

In another area, Don Luis de Carbajal the Elder slowly gets to his feet.

DON LUIS DE CARBAJAL THE ELDER: I dismounted. My loyal Felipe Núñez had tears in his eyes. What's the matter, Felipe?

FELIPE NÚÑEZ: It seems that the lands we are now on do not appear on any map or list. I beseech your grace not to throw away your right of discovery.

Nor to risk becoming governor by putting it in the viceroy's hands. Don't you want more than words of praise for all your efforts? I beg you, then, to take possession at once of this kingdom whose borders can't be seen by the naked eye.

DON LUIS DE CARBAJAL THE ELDER: *(After a brief meditation, in a very loud voice that produces echoes)* I, Don Luis de Carbajal y de la Cueva, take possession of the New Kingdom of León, as these parts shall be called from this day forward and forever. *(He sits down, satisfied. Felipe Núñez gets up.)* We must go to Spain and have this ratified by His Imperial Majesty himself.

FELIPE NÚÑEZ: Of course.

DON LUIS DE CARBAJAL THE ELDER: And ask for colonists to populate this kingdom . . .

FELIPE NÚÑEZ: Of course.

DON LUIS DE CARBAJAL THE ELDER: And title both while I live, and in perpetuity so that I will be able to name a son . . . or lacking a son, someone of my blood, as my successor. Because I'll be fucked if for pacifying this nest of Chichimecas I get nothing but a little cell in my old age.

Felipe Núñez is hurt. He turns toward us, a sad grimace on his face.

FELIPE NÚÑEZ: Of course.

Scene 6

FELIPE NÚÑEZ: *(Indignant)* Yes, yes, of course all those emigrating to the New World were to be fully investigated. It never even occurred to us to do it any other way. We had to free the colonies from any contamination by Jews, Mohammedans, apostates or schismatics, polygamists, sorcerers, wizards, conjurers, succubi, or incubi.

Another part of the interrogation room is illuminated. In it:

DOÑA ISABEL DE CARBAJAL: But my uncle chose the colonists one by one. They were all his relatives. Close or distant. And it was and is widely known that Don Luis is a sincere Catholic.

FELIPE NÚÑEZ: We were surprised, but we accepted exemption from investigation as an honor conferred upon us by His Majesty.

DOÑA ISABEL DE CARBAJAL: Philip the Second made public his absolute confidence in my uncle.

FELIPE NÚÑEZ: The sea urged us on, it called to us, roaring. It was good sailing during those months.

INQUISITOR: Who were you hiding, Don Luis? Tell us: why did you set sail for the colonies without the prescribed investigation?

DON LUIS DE CARBAJAL THE ELDER: Philip the Second was spending his days fasting and doing penance. I was desperate. I had no idea when it would occur to him to sign the papers that the civil authorities had barely initiated to give me permission to sail. I slipped into the palace basements, where it was said that, after flagellating himself, the Imperial Catholic King walked, uttering sighs and moans. Note how helping oneself a little, God takes care of the rest—I came across his pallid Majesty in a dark corridor . . . I said to him: Your Grace, permit me to sail now, and His Grace looked at me strangely. He stared at me a long time, as if he were looking at me from the other end of the universe, and said, "You are the third man I have seen in the last three days; in nine days hoist your sails." *(He breaks out in laughter.)*

FELIPE NÚÑEZ: The king knew Don Luis hurried only for the glory of Catholic Spain.

Don Luis laughs joyfully.

Scene 7

The ship. While a sail is being lowered to the stage, several porters cross in front of Don Luis carrying chests and trunks.

FIRST PORTER: Saws!

SECOND PORTER: Nails!

DON LUIS DE CARBAJAL THE ELDER: *(Writing on a piece of paper)* Saws, nails.

THIRD PORTER: *(From offstage)* Yokes, harnesses!

DON LUIS DE CARBAJAL THE ELDER: Yokes, harnesses. Saddles in the hold. Barrels of red wine! Barrels of olive oil!

FOURTH PORTER: *(From offstage)* Four pigs!

DON LUIS DE CARBAJAL THE ELDER: *(Taking it down)* Four pigs and one red dog. *(To the audience)* You keep these lists first as a record of what was loaded. Then just in case. And, finally, out of tenderness.

WOMAN: *(Crossing with boxes)* The dishes.

DON LUIS DE CARBAJAL THE ELDER: Ah, yes: the dishes. *(He writes them down, along with the following provisions.)*

FIRST PORTER: *(Crossing)* Nutmeg. Yeast.

WOMAN: *(From offstage)* Seedlings!

FOURTH PORTER: *(From far away)* Thirty cases of Portuguese sherry.

DON LUIS DE CARBAJAL THE ELDER: My god! It was as if we were emptying the contents of the Old World into a single ship! And the list of colonists . . . Yes, I have it here. All of them related to me in one way or another. *(Don Luis enters his cabin. Felipe Núñez remains on deck.)*

DON LUIS DE CARBAJAL THE ELDER: In my cabin I read the names, and Felipe Núñez called them out on deck. *(Reading)* Juan de Saucedo. *(In a low voice)* Carpenter. *(On the list, to one side of the name he puts a check and then the profession. He will do the same with the other passengers he names.)*

FELIPE NÚÑEZ: *(Calling out)* Juan de Saucedo!

VOICE: Here I am, with my wife and my son!

DON LUIS DE CARBAJAL THE ELDER: Juan Nava. Tailor.

FELIPE NÚÑEZ: Juan Nava!

VOICE: Juan Nava, Ana Nava, Juanito Nava!

DON LUIS DE CARBAJAL THE ELDER: Pedro Sánchez, navigator.

FELIPE NÚÑEZ: Pedro Sánchez!

VOICE: Pedro's on the port side!

Doña Guiomar crosses. Hiding herself from view, she goes toward the cabins.

DON LUIS DE CARBAJAL THE ELDER: Rodríguez Matos! Rodríguez Matos!

RODRÍGUEZ MATOS: *(Sticking out his head)* Rodríguez Matos.

DOÑA FRANCISCA: His wife Francisca.

LUIS DE CARBAJAL THE YOUNGER: His son Luis.

VIVIANA: Viviana.

RODRÍGUEZ MATOS: My daughter.

DON LUIS DE CARBAJAL THE ELDER: Tell the boy to come here.

FELIPE NÚÑEZ: Hey, Luis; your uncle's calling you. He wants you in his cabin. *(Luis is about twenty years old, but his leanness on the one hand and his dreamy air on the other make us feel at times as if he's younger or livelier. He walks slowly across the bridge: it is as if he were made out of the same air that gently blows.)*

DON LUIS DE CARBAJAL THE ELDER: How does he look, Núñez? Carries himself well? There's the mark of nobility in him. He's the son of a merchant but can't calculate. Won't think about numbers. . . . They say he plays guitar, writes verses for the musicians. I hope he doesn't turn out to be a poet, for Christ's sake! No, knock on wood.

FELIPE NÚÑEZ: He looks rather frayed to me.

DON LUIS DE CARBAJAL THE ELDER: We'll dress him up like a little duke soon enough.

Felipe Núñez steps aside for Luis as if for a great noble, but he has the bitter look on his face that we've seen before. Luis goes down into the cabin.

DON LUIS DE CARBAJAL THE ELDER: Sit down, son. Keep me company for a while while I take care of these obligations. Good for you to learn about those who will be your subjects. And many others who will come to the New Kingdom of León. You'll protect them, and they will pay you tribute. But we'll have to make it known without a doubt. . . . Come here, Núñez. *(Felipe comes down into the cabin. Don Luis needs him as witness to what follows. To his nephew:)* What would you think of renouncing your father's name and calling yourself from now on Don Luis de Carbajal the Younger? *(Luis stretches his legs, smiles. Rodríguez Matos and his family leave the scene unnoticed.)*

LUIS DE CARBAJAL THE YOUNGER: What's in a name? *(His smile is so sweet that the older man is disconcerted.)*

DON LUIS DE CARBAJAL THE ELDER: Yes, what's in a name? . . . *(He turns to consult Felipe but finds him absorbed in thought, twisted with anger.)* Well . . . *(Reviewing his list; reading in Felipe's ear)* Doña Isabel de Carbajal. My niece. Widow. *(Felipe wakes up at the mention of Doña Isabel and her denomination.)* Hey, Felipe Núñez? I said: Doña Isabel de Carbajal, the one Felipe likes so much. Call her. *(Felipe goes out on deck.)*

FELIPE NÚÑEZ: *(Calling out)* Doña Isabel de Carbajal, graceful as a swan.

DON LUIS DE CARBAJAL THE ELDER: Olé.

Doña Isabel comes out of a cabin. She's a woman of thirty, well formed, proud. Her full lips trace a complaisant smile. She goes out on deck, her right hand on her waist.

DOÑA ISABEL: Doña Isabel!

FELIPE NÚÑEZ: *(Lowering his voice)* Olé. *(But he immediately turns his face, his teeth chattering, as if he'd received a slap.)*

Doña Guiomar, who had been hidden, crosses rapidly to Isabel and reveals herself.

DOÑA GUIOMAR: *(Hissing)* Isabel.

DOÑA ISABEL: Doña Guiomar!

DOÑA GUIOMAR: Quiet. Let's go into the cabin. *(They go into the cabin.)*

Scene 8

DOÑA GUIOMAR: Close everything up. Close it up, I say. *(Isabel closes the door and the window.)*

DOÑA ISABEL: Doña Guiomar! Are you sailing? Thank God. They had told us you wouldn't. Now your husband Don Luis won't have to live like a widower. How wonderful, Doña Guiomar.

DOÑA GUIOMAR: Shh. Lock the door. Lock it. *(Isabel obeys. This whole dialogue is rushed and hushed.)*

DOÑA GUIOMAR: I'm not sailing. I came here disguised to talk with you. Do you know why I'm not Don Luis's wife? Because, although we were both born Jews, he pretends to be more Catholic than the Pope. And that is nothing more than blasphemy, sin, and the road to hell. *(Pause)*

DOÑA ISABEL: You are a Jew, señora?

DOÑA GUIOMAR: I knew your mother, Isabel. Intimately.

DOÑA ISABEL: Do you hate your husband so much that after abandoning him you want to destroy him? Accusing him of protecting the daughter of Jews? Don't pull me into the fire, señora. Know that before I was born, my parents converted to the Catholic faith. As did the other Carbajals, including the parents of Don Luis. So, your trap closes without any prisoner. It's no sin to be a convert.

DOÑA GUIOMAR: No, no sin. There are dark times when the true law has to survive in secret. It has to be guarded. Nurtured like a little flame between the right hand and the heart, so the wind lashing the earth doesn't snuff it out. Only the purest of the chosen people can take such care and be so constant. The impure soon give in. They are poor, crazy people in the end: born with open eyes, they gouge them out walking among the blind. *(Pause)*

DOÑA GUIOMAR: Keep the Sabbath, Passover, the fasts.

DOÑA ISABEL: Of course.

DOÑA GUIOMAR: Men speak their prayers at the top of their voice, women breathe them sweetly. They are the heroes and the rabbis; for them are the battlefields and the regions of knowledge; we make the ordinary marvelous, Isabel: our mission is to make beds and tables sacred places.

DOÑA ISABEL: You inspire me, señora. Go on.

DOÑA GUIOMAR: A widow has the leisure to put into delicate words what the family woman puts into acts, plainly. When you need faith, remember your mother's daily labors. The essence of all our religion is in her tenuous smile while making a bed. What can you tell me about worshipping images?

DOÑA ISABEL: Worship something manmade? It is idolatry.

DOÑA GUIOMAR: But praying to Saint Anthony to get a fiancé isn't dangerous.

DOÑA ISABEL: Not to any saint. Nor to Jesus Christ nor to his mother. They were all made of flesh. Putting the soul into something you can touch traps it there. Only God himself can save it from perishing.

DOÑA GUIOMAR: And what is the Mass, Isabel?

DOÑA ISABEL: Air, señora, air.

DOÑA GUIOMAR: Praised be God who has put you in my place, next to my husband. Don't you understand? You're going with Don Luis to watch over his heart. Listen to me. You have to be the one who returns him to God. Wait for some sorrow, a time when he breaks down and then, gently but surely, lead him back to the law of Moses, the only useful one in saving the spirit. Promise me, woman.

DOÑA ISABEL: I will do it, señora.

Doña Guiomar unwraps a book from her kerchief as she speaks:

DOÑA GUIOMAR: Forget about what the priests tell you: that you, because you don't wear the habit, can't read the Bible yourself. Read it, each morning, alone. A thousand religions will flower from this trunk and fall withered; but these words that contain the universe will remain. Here. Take my Bible.

DOÑA ISABEL: I have my grandmother's. These hidden here in the bottom of my trunk are those of Doña Francisca and her husband Rodríguez Matos. Be happy, Doña Guiomar. Yes, them as well.

DOÑA GUIOMAR: Praised be the God of Israel: we are like sands in the sea. But . . . doesn't Doña Francisca have a son who's a monk in New Spain?

DOÑA ISABEL: A mistake. *(Doña Guiomar laughs heartily but interrupts herself.)*

DOÑA GUIOMAR: Careful. I hear footsteps.

DOÑA ISABEL: . . . No, señora.

DOÑA GUIOMAR: A little light, daughter. We are going to embroider flowers. *(Isabel understands the hidden significance of what she's said. She opens the door and the window while Doña Guiomar takes two embroidery cloths, each with its own needle, from her bag. She gives one to Doña Isabel. They both embroider. Doña Guiomar intones a religious song in a low voice, and the other follows her. Gradually their voices die away. But the slight movement of their lips gives away that both of them are still singing in their hearts.)*

Scene 9

Dungeon. Luis de Carbajal the Younger bends and raises and bends his torso, in the usual movement of Jews when they pray. With a low voice he continues the prayer that Doña Isabel and Doña Guiomar intoned in the scene before. He's in rags. Luis notices a light in the peephole on the door. He changes his position in order to find its origin. It is a star.

LUIS: The first star of the Sabbath! Be quiet, sorrow, the Saturday queen descends even to the dungeons. Oh, queen of light, if there's no bread, wine, or glory to give thanks with, at least let me have their memory.

In another area, a few centimeters from the ground, three candles in a candelabra deposited in a box are being lit. The front and top of the box have been removed. It is Doña Francisca, the mother of Luis, who lights them murmuring the prayer that consecrates them: Baruch atá Hashem Eloheinu Melej Haolam . . . Now you can barely make out Doña Isabel, Rodríguez Matos, and Viviana in the tenuous light. They are at a small table covered with a white cloth.

LUIS: My mother's prayer in a whisper . . . Everything is done secretly. Even though the hacienda is surrounded by cultivated fields and the road passes by up on the saddle of the hill. . . . Maybe some servant hasn't understood the Carbajals want him resting on Saturday or, understanding, has become a danger. . . . Some passing horseman glimpses the light or recognizes the Hebrew tongue floating in the night. . . . Like a dangerous serpent the Hebrew tongue undulates in the sacred night . . .

Rodríguez Matos bends over in order to fill, beneath the table, five cups with dark wine. Raising his cup before drinking the consecrated wine:

RODRÍGUEZ MATOS: Baruj atá Hashem Eloheinu melej haolum haboré peri haguefen. *(Passes out the cups. They all say: "Amen" and drink. But Rodríguez Matos still has one extra cup in his hand and a bitter expression on his face.)*

DOÑA FRANCISCA: Luis won't be long. He had to stay with his uncle in the mayor's office.

RODRÍGUEZ MATOS: Working even . . . on the Sabbath, the day of rest. Or is he in the cantina? Why not, now that he's playing the Catholic prince? *(Rodríguez Matos takes a braided bread out of a sack. He cuts it and distributes the slices. Before biting into it he blesses it.)*

RODRÍGUEZ MATOS: Baruj atá Hashem Eloheinu melej haolam, hamotzi lehem min haaretz.

ALL: *(Except the father)* Amen. *(Luis leaves the dungeon. He enters the area where the dinner is dimly lit. Takes a cup.)*

LUIS: *(Toasting)* L'Chaim to life!

RODRÍGUEZ MATOS: Shh. Silence. You look washed out.

LUIS: Used up, which isn't the same thing. I was galloping up the mountain when I found a tiger cub and jumped down to get the better of him.

RODRÍGUEZ MATOS: *(Indignant)* The motive?

DOÑA FRANCISCA: Tiger cub or tiger? Tell the truth, Luis.

LUIS: Tiger cub, mother, a little cat.

RODRÍGUEZ MATOS: The motive, I asked.

DOÑA ISABEL: *(Ruffling Luis's hair)* To play with one of God's creatures. You know Luis . . .

VIVIANA: How lovely: Luis and a tiger cub playing.

RODRÍGUEZ MATOS: Lovely indeed.

LUIS: But I've come to toast: L'Chaim!

RODRÍGUEZ MATOS: Lower your voice! What are you trying to do? Warn your uncle's soldiers? *(Luis passes the cup in offering to all those present.)*

LUIS: *(With all his soul)* To life!!!

RODRÍGUEZ MATOS: Shut up!!! *(Doña Francisca puts her head out the window. Looks around.)*

LUIS: I'm cursed with an immense thirst, father. And blessed by the same thirst. Because our God, king of the universe, lives: there is water galore. *(Pouring the wine over his face)*

DOÑA FRANCISCA: Not a soul sits . . .

LUIS: L'Chaim!!! *(All, their cups raised, respond, although Rodríguez Matos looks as if he's been beaten.)*

ALL: L'Chaim!!! *(They remain with their cups in the air for an instant. Another one. Then, slowly, all goes dark.)*

Entre Act

CHORUS: The short history of Jesús Baltazar. A business proposition that for him ended in ashes.

JESÚS BALTAZAR: Pity, pity

a man who can't tell Good from Bad.
I went to serve in the Carbajal household
for a miserable salary, shelter and bread.
Walking there one afternoon,
I saw a book under a blackberry bush.

Rodríguez Matos enters.

RODRÍGUEZ MATOS: Aha. So you are reading, Jesús Baltazar. Show me what you are reading.

JESÚS BALTAZAR: This isn't my book, boss. I found it.

RODRÍGUEZ MATOS: Uh-huh. Of course it isn't yours.

JESÚS BALTAZAR: It's a . . .

RODRÍGUEZ MATOS: Give it to me. It's mine.

JESÚS BALTAZAR: A Jewish thing.

Rodríguez Matos takes the book. He takes a few steps. Returns.

RODRÍGUEZ MATOS: What do you know about Jews, Jesús?

JESÚS BALTAZAR: Nothing. That they killed God. And for that now, sixteen centuries later, the Holy Inquisition kills them.

RODRÍGUEZ MATOS: I am from Benavente and a nobleman, and I don't want to hear anything spoken about Jews on my estate.

JESÚS BALTAZAR: All right.

Rodríguez Matos takes a few steps. Returns.

RODRÍGUEZ MATOS: You are suspicious of me, Jesús Baltazar. Well then: it's true. I am Jewish. How can one be a Christian if Christ hasn't come down to Earth? Inventions of people who came and left their teachings behind. The Bible you've been reading makes it very clear, Jesús Baltazar. When Christ arrives, misery on earth will end. The lion and the lamb will sleep together. Food will be plenty. There will be no rivalry nor mistrust amongst God's creatures. Well, and? Let's be frank with one another, Jesús Baltazar. Is this world Paradise? If only it were!

JESÚS BALTAZAR: To me, this whole confession seemed wrong, but to keep up appearances, I replied: "It's all right, Don."

RODRÍGUEZ MATOS: It's all right?

JESÚS BALTAZAR: Your sister-in-law Isabel has already noticed that I'm a Jew. It's all right, I say.

Rodríguez Matos observes him suspiciously. Little by little he gets animated.

RODRÍGUEZ MATOS: Well, look, now that I'm close to you, you do seem Jewish . . .

JESÚS BALTAZAR: And look at my profile. *(He shows it.)*

RODRÍGUEZ MATOS: You look like a rabbi! *(Opening his arms)* Brother!

JESÚS BALTAZAR: *(Falling into his arms)* Brother!

Rodríguez Matos breaks away. Takes a few steps but returns.

RODRÍGUEZ MATOS: This isn't right. It isn't right that you live so badly, brother. Go to the capital of the kingdom. I'll give you two thousand in gold to start your own business. Go tomorrow.

JESÚS BALTAZAR: How about three thousand?

RODRÍGUEZ MATOS: Agreed. But get out of here tonight. *(He gives him the money.)*

JESÚS BALTAZAR: All right. *(Rodríguez Matos leaves.)*

> How was I to know
> that five years later
> Doña Isabel de Carbajal would
> name me as a brother of the faith
> before the Holy Tribunal.
> I don't know anything.
> Not a thing.
> All I know about this book that now
> condemns me is the covers.
> Have pity!

CHORUS: Pity, pity,
> for a man who, in questions of
> Good and Evil has no ability.
> The short history of Jesús Baltazar
> who became a Jew as good business
> and for being Jewish ended up ashes.

Picture 2

Scene 1

Living room in the Carbajal home. Doña Isabel embroiders. Doña Francisca enters, followed a little later by Don Luis de Carbajal the Elder. He enters with stained clothing and a taciturn expression. Doña Isabel kisses them both on the cheek.

DOÑA FRANCISCA: Sit down, Luis. Give him a sherry, Isabel. I found him wandering about in the pine grove. He must have been there all night long. I'll bring you a change of clothes, Luis.

DON LUIS DE CARBAJAL THE ELDER: Leave me alone. The dew stained me. It's dry already.

DOÑA ISABEL: Here's your sherry.

DOÑA FRANCISCA: If you want to talk to your sister, I'll be in the kitchen.

DON LUIS DE CARBAJAL THE ELDER: When will you learn to hire servants, damn it. *(Doña Francisca leaves, unoffended.)*

DOÑA ISABEL: Your eyes are red.

DON LUIS: I cried to imitate the dew falling on the fields. Enough rhetoric: cheers. *(He drinks his sherry in one gulp.)* I have two pieces of news. Since one of them concerns you very personally, I'll tell them to you first. Some good news and some bad.

DOÑA ISABEL: Tell me.

DON LUIS: Felipe Núñez has asked me for your hand.

DOÑA ISABEL: *(Indignant)* Now tell me the good news.

DON LUIS: You've been in mourning for a long time, Isabel. Forget the one that died already. Felipe Núñez never tires of pursuing you and is what they call a man. I swear he'll be able to give you satisfaction—I speak plainly with you like this because you're not a virgin—; besides he's rich and formal.

DOÑA ISABEL: Don't go on. I hate that farmhand. It horrifies me that he looks at me with his watery eyes and . . .

DON LUIS: *(Interrupting her)* Fine. I'll tell him that you still love your dead husband so as not to hurt him, and that will put an end to it.

DOÑA ISABEL: Tell him as well that I'm offended when he brings singers to my window.

DON LUIS: I'll tell him. *(Pause)* The other news, the bad news, is that my wife Doña Guiomar, died in Salamanca. . . . But maybe that should be the good news, since I'll finally be free to marry again. No. I'll never remarry now. . . . It's like a bullet blew a hole in my chest to know she's gone. Even though we were only together a couple of years, there was an invisible thread that bound us together. One that crossed the mountains and the sea. Curse the moment that thread bound us together affectionately. And curse this one when it broke and left me spinning and spinning like a top. In truth, everything I did I did for her. To impress her. Suddenly, with her below ground, nothing makes sense. *(Don Luis becomes lost in thought.)*

DOÑA ISABEL: What will you do to ease your pain, uncle?

DON LUIS: Pay for a few Masses, I suppose. *(He takes a rosary out of his vest.)* I've prayed. I prayed during the night in the pine grove, but then I forgot and the memories came. I should pray now, I suppose. God save you, Mary, you are full of grace, God is with you. . . . These holy words cure me a little but only while they are in my mind. As if they were a brief shower that soaks me but leaves me in the stream and I'm still burning up. God said, "I am with you, blessed are you among . . ."

DOÑA ISABEL: *(Who has been calculating when to intervene, interrupts him.)* There isn't any Christ.

Don Luis scrutinizes her. He gives her a powerful slap.

DOÑA ISABEL: There still isn't any Christ.

Don Luis gets up. He slaps her each time she repeats that.

DOÑA ISABEL: There isn't any Christ. There isn't any Christ.

DON LUIS: *(Grabbing her by the hair)* Doña Guiomar should be sizzling in hell for having taught you this evil.

DOÑA ISABEL: She didn't teach me this truth. My father, my mother, and my soul taught it to me daily. Do you remember King David, full of goodness and wisdom?

DON LUIS: *(Letting her go, astonished)* What a calamity of a woman! Why are you talking about King David here?

DOÑA ISABEL: Because by being the perfect servant of God and his law, David was very rich. And the law I am talking about is that of Moses, not of the false prophet Jesus.

DON LUIS: Better you were never born, Jewess.

DOÑA ISABEL: Don't lie, Don Luis: you too were born Jewish.

DON LUIS: I was born human. That's all I know for certain. All the rest has been attributed to me by others. I was born like everyone else with hands and feet and desires to live and make my mark. And if doing that means I have to pray to Jesus, to Jesus I'll pray. And if the devil was the god governments ordered, I'd pray to the devil. In the end I'm generous and brave in all my deeds, and this is the life I know and that's important to me. Or haven't I been generous to you, Isabel?

DOÑA ISABEL: But your soul, uncle. Save your soul.

DON LUIS: My soul. Point it out to me, and I'll save it. Can I see it? I can't see it. I can't hear it. What's it smell like? Do you want me to lose my entire fortune? Mine and many others. Who have I hurt? A few Chichimecas. Amen. *(Doña Isabel is about to reply, but Don Luis is ahead of her.)*

DON LUIS: Now, listen to me: according to the Holy Inquisition you are in mortal sin. So am I unless I inform upon you to my confessor and they arrest you. There's no way out for a Jew, Isabel. Ever since they were kicked out of old Jerusalem Jews don't have a place to call home. No king

to protect them, no God to lower his hand and say "This is my son."
Being Jewish is a pointless kind of stubbornness, daughter. It means you're
a stranger everywhere, if not everyone's enemy. Be smart: convert.

DOÑA ISABEL: We will wander the earth, uncle, until the Messiah comes; then
we, the chosen people of God . . . *(Don Luis interrupts her with a loud guffaw.)*

DON LUIS: The chosen people of God! What divine arrogance! Divine stu-
pidity! Chosen as the scapegoat for everyone else, perhaps.

DOÑA ISABEL: As the example of fidelity.

DON LUIS: Miserable creatures inventing paradoxes so they can keep
dreaming! Go convert, Isabel.

DOÑA ISABEL: I am baptized. I go to Mass. God pardons me because it's all
done in order to be able to love him secretly in the only law, the law for
which I am ready to live and for which I am ready to die.

DON LUIS: *(Desperate)* Then, what? Do I risk the New Kingdom of León
for your cause or do I turn you in? Answer me! Should I turn you in? Aie,
I see a kind of pleasure in your eyes . . . perverse . . . I bet you yearn to
burn at the stake with the crowd behind you yelling: Jew, Jew . . .

DOÑA ISABEL: *(Raising her voice until she sings)* Listen Israel: my God our
God is the only . . .

DON LUIS: *(Beating her)* Christ! Christ! Christ!

Doña Francisca comes to her aid. Then Rodríguez Matos and Luis the Younger. Viviana.

DOÑA FRANCISCA: What's all the shouting about? Oh: you've hit her.

DON LUIS: Your niece has told me something atrocious: that I am deceived
by following Christ's law.

*Don Luis observes the reactions of those present. Doña Francisca in turn consults her chil-
dren with a look.*

DOÑA FRANCISCA: She says so to do you good.

DON LUIS: *(Stuttering)* No! It can't be. A worse disgrace couldn't fall on me.
That Isabel and then you. You? All of you? Accomplices . . . *(He throws
himself on top of Rodríguez Matos. He bends him back over a table and takes
out a knife that he is to pass through his throat.)* Traitor. In Spain I
asked you if you were a Jew, and you told me that everyone in your household was a devout Christian.

RODRÍGUEZ MATOS: Isabel just goes crazy, Don Luis. From time to time
these evil spirits enter her. The demons of her parents who really were Jews
possess her. It's happened since she was a child. Isn't that right, Isabel?

DOÑA ISABEL: Yes, my mother and father enter me and fill me with shame. They bring me to the edge of the cliff: "Jump," they whisper in my ears. "Let go of the world and win eternal glory."
RODRÍGUEZ MATOS: *(Plaintively)* But you realize that all this is madness, Isabel.

Doña Isabel realizes that she should lie.
DOÑA ISABEL: Yes, they call it madness, I know.
RODRÍGUEZ MATOS: And all she needs to do is to remember that in order to wake up, Don Luis.

Don Luis is doubtful but sheathes his knife. Approaches Luis the Younger.
DON LUIS: But you, Luis, don't betray me.
LUIS THE YOUNGER: I won't betray anyone because I'm busy doing nothing more than trying not to betray myself.
DON LUIS: *(Confused)* Well. But . . . you must believe in the mystery of the Holy Trinity: Father, Son, and Holy Ghost. *(Doña Isabel sarcastically kneels and begins to recite Ave Marias while Don Luis retreats step by step toward the door.)* And you must believe in the other mysteries. All those proclaimed by the Holy Mother Church in Rome. *(Viviana and Rodríguez Matos kneel and pray.)* You must believe in Salvation through adoration of the Son.
DOÑA FRANCISCA: Christ. *(She kneels and prays.)*
DON LUIS: *(Leaving)* Because whoever doesn't believe is lost. *(He leaves. Those left behind abruptly say, "Amen." Blackout.)*

Scene 2

Jorge Almeida's house. In front is a vestibule, and in back a bedroom. In the vestibule, which is quite dismal, are Luis de Carbajal the Younger, Jorge Almeida—a big man, husky, with a pockmarked and twisted face, bordered by a black beard—and a black woman, Julia, his housekeeper. In the bedroom, lying on the bed, is Rodríguez Matos, with Brother Agustín, who is receiving his last confession.
LUIS DE CARBAJAL THE YOUNGER: *(To the audience)* My father and I came to the capital of New Spain to do some cattle business. We'd barely entered the capital when my father started to tremble. His heart beat fiercely. His sweat was cold, and he could barely breathe. . . . We came right to Jorge Almeida's house, an old friend of the family. We laid out my father. He had enough breath left to call for Brother Agustín, his first born. He no longer wanted a doctor.

A little time passes. Brother Agustín comes out of the bedroom into the vestibule. He is thin, dark-skinned, his eyes are the most notable thing about him. They are big and shiny. He wears the Dominican habit.

BROTHER AGUSTÍN: He has received communion. Very devoutly. He's calling for you, brother.

Luis goes into the bedroom. Between his father's hands, against his chest, there is a crucifix. Luis can't contain his sobs.

RODRÍGUEZ MATOS: Come here. *(Luis kneels at his father's side.)* Listen Israel: my Lord our God is the only God. *(Luis's sobbing has stopped. Rodríguez Matos places his right hand on his son's head.)* Take care of and obey your mother. Don't leave your sister unprotected. Be good. *(He blesses him in the Jewish manner, placing both hands on Luis's head. But just at the end a coughing fit overpowers him, leaving him exhausted.)* I'm going now but take this body that I leave behind and wash it for me. Cut the fingernails and the hair.

LUIS: Jorge Almeida has told me privately that he knows the cleansing rites and wants to prepare you. He has also gotten hold of a tunic.

RODRÍGUEZ MATOS: With the folds that the law of Moses decrees?

LUIS: Yes.

RODRÍGUEZ MATOS: *(After a pause)* But your brother doesn't suspect.

LUIS: Of course not.

Pause. Something in the air captures the amazement of Rodríguez Matos.

RODRÍGUEZ MATOS: There are two doors. Which one do I cross? *(Pause)* Be good, son. Did I say that already? I'll take this one. *(Pause)* There are two new doors. . . . I'm afraid. . . . Did I say that already? yes: I've always been afraid. This one then, quickly. *(Pause)* Two doors. More? This one? That one? That one . . . *(Rodríguez Matos stretches, terrified.)* There are two doors . . . *(Suddenly he relaxes. Luis closes his father's eyes. Bows his head. Goes out into the vestibule.)*

LUIS: He's dead. He wants Jorge Almeida to wash his body, so that he isn't all dirty when the worms get him.

He has said all this simply, but his listeners look at him as if he has said something impious. Finally, Jorge Almeida, signaling Julia to accompany him, goes into the bedroom. They undress the corpse and begin to wash it. Jorge begins to cut the fingernails with a pair of scissors.

139

JULIA: Why do you skip fingers? You cut one, skip one, and then go back to cut the ones you skipped.

JORGE ALMEIDA: It's the way the deceased cut his nails while he lived, and I cut them that way out of respect for his whims.

JULIA: Is it some sort of superstition?

JORGE ALMEIDA: Why don't you finish the washing silently? You have your superstitions, too. Don't you cross yourself each time a black cat crosses your path? No divine law asks you to do that.

JULIA: But what if this business with the fingernails is a satanic invocation?

JORGE ALMEIDA: We will see if Satan appears.

JULIA: And if it's a pagan rite?

JORGE ALMEIDA: If you don't shut up, I'll shut you up. Close the door. *(She closes the door. The brothers are lost in thought in the vestibule. Luis is the first to speak.)*

LUIS: Are you sincere, Agustín?

AGUSTÍN: I live in order to purify my soul.

LUIS: Can one be pure in a corrupt world?

AGUSTÍN: There is an evil that comes from seeing and hearing perverse things. Therefore one shouldn't look at or listen to forbidden things.

LUIS: Is that why you live shut up in the monastery?

AGUSTÍN: That's why.

LUIS: You know, I doubt all the time. All I know is that what makes me feel good is good.

AGUSTÍN: But the pleasures of the world are fleeting. The greatest pleasure is spiritual. Once you find that, everything else is extra.

LUIS: Blessed are you who has all the replies memorized.

AGUSTÍN: They are true.

LUIS: But the question still is: are you sincere?

AGUSTÍN: While my desires may be small at times, I prefer to obey the doctrine in all things. In this way I am sincere, until I reach the place where Grace is granted me.

Pause

LUIS: I want to confess.

AGUSTÍN: Right now?

LUIS: Tomorrow?

AGUSTÍN: No. Find another confessor.

LUIS: I want to confess to you, now.

AGUSTÍN: Come see me tomorrow in the monastery. I'll bring you to someone better, someone who will be better for you.

Pause

LUIS: What did my father confess?

Pause

AGUSTÍN: Nothing that you his son couldn't hear and pardon. But nothing that I, as a cleric who should keep the secret of confession, can repeat.
LUIS: Are there sins that you would be obliged to inform your superiors about?
AGUSTÍN: There are.
LUIS: Were there any?
AGUSTÍN: No.
LUIS: And if there had been?
AGUSTÍN: There is an evil that comes from imagining evil.
LUIS: And another that comes from being blind.

Pause

AGUSTÍN: None of my father's sins oblige me to decide between my love for him and my love for the Holy Father.
LUIS: You are blessed.
AGUSTÍN: Enough discussion. Be quiet out of respect for our father.
LUIS: For you the simplest thing is to be quiet. That's what my father taught you: a gracious submission. But the inheritance he left me was conflict. "Be good," he told me as he died. But he didn't tell me how to be good, nor could anyone who died with his face so full of fright tell me that. You have to help me. Take my confession. *(He embraces him.)*
AGUSTÍN: Let me go.
LUIS: I'm begging you.
AGUSTÍN: Leave me alone. *(He frees himself from the embrace. Each one stays in his corner. Blackout.)*

Scene 3

A woman sings in the cante hondo *style.*

> Two cemeteries
> Two pairs of brothers

carry the coffin
of a single father
to its grave.

Two pairs of brothers, each carrying a coffin, enter flanking each side of the stage. They advance from the back to the front of the stage. They put down the coffins. The pair on the right cross themselves. The pair on the left rend their clothing. One brother from each pair says a prayer.

LUIS: Idgadal beitagash sheme raba.

AGUSTÍN: *(In unison)* Dust you are and to dust shall you return.

Blackout

Scene 4

The bedroom in Jorge Almeida's house. It is night. A lamp is lit. Jorge Almeida sits on the bed. Julia enters.

JULIA: I haven't shut my eyes. Thinking: was it a pagan rite or not? My soul's all eaten up with remorse. Was he Jewish, a Moor? His eyelids were purple. Well, just in case, I'm going to confession tomorrow. You should, too. Because if he were a Jew or worshipped something evil they're going to know, and when they know they're going to catch us. And I say he was the sinner, not us who go to Mass and take confession, and we didn't clean him in such a strange manner for any other reason than to please the dead. I tell you I'm going to confession so they don't condemn me. Why are you looking at me like that, as if you're afraid?

Jorge Almeida goes toward her slowly. He puts both hands on her throat.

JULIA: Holy Mary! Holy Mary!

JORGE ALMEIDA: Yes, let Holy Mary save you. Let her save you.

He strangles her. Lays her body on the bed. He sits at one end of the bed. Picks up the scissors. Mops the sweat on his face with his sleeve. Begins to cut her fingernails, skipping every other one . . .

JORGE ALMEIDA: One yes, one no; one yes, one no; one yes . . .

Blackout

Scene 5

LUIS DE CARBAJAL THE YOUNGER: *(In the style of the* cante hondo*)*

Lord, I don't care if I understand anymore:
Make me your singer
Lord, my eye is salty
and my tongue sweet
Sadness doesn't bother me
if I can sing about it
Make me your singer, Lord
Your singer, Lord, make me.

Scene 6

On the banks of the Pánuco, Viviana and Luis de Carbajal the Younger
VIVIANA: It was a sunny Sunday. I was reading to Luis on the banks of the
Pánuco.

Viviana reads a Bible, slowly, spelling.
VIVIANA: "This will be . . . my contract that you will keep between you
and . . . me . . . and your seed . . ." Abraham's?
LUIS DE CARBAJAL THE YOUNGER: Yes, the Patriarch Abraham's.
VIVIANA: "Who will be circumscribed among you . . . a complete man."
LUIS DE CARBAJAL THE YOUNGER: Circumcised.
VIVIANA: Cir-cum-cis-ed. "You will cir-cum-cise . . . the flesh of his fore-
skin and it will be a sign . . . between you and me. Circum- not again!—
Cir-cum-cised will be those born in your house and those who are bought;
and the uncircumcised man will be cut off—cut off, it says!—from my
people, my contract annulled."

Luis has listened in anguish. He stands, his back to us.
VIVIANA: "Those who have not been circum-cised will be wiped from the
book of, from the book of life."

Luis unsheathes his knife, walks toward a palm tree, spreads his legs.
VIVIANA: What are you doing?
LUIS DE CARBAJAL THE YOUNGER: Don't turn around.
VIVIANA: Oh, I know: you're peeing. I better read somewhere where there

aren't so many big words. *(She flips back a few pages. Reads.)* "And when Abraham was ninety-nine years old, Jehovah came to him and said to him: 'I am God, the all-powerful.'" *(Luis moans.)* Does it hurt? *(Luis responds with another moan.)* "Walk before me and be perfect." *(Luis shouts. Throws the knife into the ground. Laughs and cries. Viviana looks at him open-mouthed. Whispered voices are heard.)*

CHORUS: Mazal Tov. Good luck. Congratulations. *(While, little by little, the light fades)*

Scene 7

The light comes up little by little. The main room in the Carbajal household. Doña Isabel—with her head out the window—and Doña Francisca, both dressed for a party. Viviana stands on a chair in a wedding gown. Her mother is finishing the hem of her gown. In a corner Luis is softly strumming a guitar.

As the light comes up onstage, the voices of the Chorus gradually fade.

CHORUS: Mazal Tov. Good luck. Congratulations.

DOÑA ISABEL: They're coming. They're on the crest of the hill. On black chargers. They're raising the dust from the road. What a handsome bride-groom, Viviana. He's at the front. After him the rabbi and your brother Luis. Oh, two women are looking out from the Velázquez estate. They're waving white handkerchiefs. What will they say when they find out that rich gentleman is coming to marry you, tucked away in the last corner on earth.

DOÑA FRANCISCA: They'll say, "It's a miracle, a miracle."

DOÑA ISABEL: They're here, at full gallop. *(Turning to the other women)* Mazal Tov! Good luck, Viviana! But, child, it's your wedding, not a funeral.

VIVIANA: And if we don't like him?

DOÑA ISABEL: Your brother Luis picked him, and he loves you.

VIVIANA: Luis loves me, but the other fellow?

Doña Francisca and Isabel laugh loudly and clap their hands flamenco-style. There are two knocks at the door. Isabel dances over to open it.

Luis brightens up the music when Jorge Almeida, the fiancé, and the Rabbi enter.

DOÑA ISABEL: Mazal Tov!

They all repeat "mazal tov," exchanging embraces.

RABBI: Where's the chupa?

DOÑA FRANCISCA: Here it is, Rabbi.

Jorge Almeida has gone straight to his fiancee. He is about to touch her hand.
LUIS: *(In the style of a* copla.*)*

> Don't touch her, don't touch her yet
> She's still my sister
> Not your wife, not yet

JORGE ALMEIDA: But in an hour . . .
LUIS: But she's still my sister

> not your wife, not yet

DOÑA FRANCISCA: Quiet! *(Pause)* Yes: it's not just my heart. . . . Someone's galloping. . . . *(She goes to the window.)* Felipe Núñez is getting off his horse. Hide the chupa. Hide the bride.
DOÑA ISABEL: Sit down, Rabbi. Make conversation, Jorge. Talk about business, go on.

Luis plays a funereal air. Felipe Núñez enters. He keeps looking as if he expects to find something hidden.
FELIPE NÚÑEZ: Good afternoon. . . . I saw some riders arrive and I thought, I don't know, that perhaps . . .
LUIS: Here they are. Señor Moroines and Señor Almeida, from the capital.
FELIPE NÚÑEZ: Pleased to meet you.
LUIS: They came to see our cows.

Doña Francisca crosses, wagging her behind like a cow. Laughter. Felipe doesn't quite get the humor.
FELIPE NÚÑEZ: Since when do you do business without donLuis's permission?
LUIS: They've just come to look at them.
FELIPE NÚÑEZ: Just to look at them? From the capital?
DOÑA ISABEL: *(Irritated)* What did you think, Felipe? That they came to see me? The truth is they came to ask for a hand in marriage. *(Doña Isabel enjoys the congestion overtaking Felipe's face.)* Viviana's hand.

Felipe laughs nervously. Takes Isabel into a corner, where she sits on a stool.
FELIPE: *(Happy)* I thought, Isabel, I thought that you were deceiving me. That you'd given up mourning your husband and had forgotten that you'd promised me . . .

DOÑA ISABEL: *(Interrupting him)* Nothing. I haven't promised you a thing. Good-bye, Felipe Núñez.

FELIPE: Tell me what I lack or what you don't like about me. I'll tear one out or go find the other.

Isabel is distracted by a noise among those present, who are watching what's happening out of the corner of their eyes.

DOÑA ISABEL: *(To Felipe)* They can hear you.

FELIPE: Well, my voice is hoarse from wanting to cry, here, on your shoes. Worse shames would seem sweet, woman, if they were to win you. All I'm asking is that you live under my roof, that you take care of what's mine, nothing more. And with time, perhaps . . . But it wouldn't matter either if you never . . . *(Felipe, the strong soldier, is about to burst into tears. Jorge Almeida can't suppress a chuckle. Isabel turns to look at the Rabbi.)*

ISABEL: This gentleman knows me very well, Felipe. Ask him, since you don't seem to believe me when I tell you. That for me to love one man, above all others, is no longer possible; that I direct all my love toward God.

FELIPE: If this were true you'd already have gone into a convent. So why are you looking me in the face? What prevents her, gentlemen?

There is a painful pause.

LUIS: She can't give up the deserts and the donkeys.

There is laughter and a sob from Doña Francisca.

DOÑA ISABEL: I'll become a nun soon, don't rush me.

DOÑA FRANCISCA: Why don't you two talk another day, Felipe?

FELIPE: Yes, Doña Francisca. And please excuse the desperation that has made me burst in here amidst your friends. *(He goes toward the door. In the doorway he turns on his heels.)* Listen, Luisito: Don Luis is the one who should give away the hands of the Carbajal in marriage.

DOÑA FRANCISCA: It's still early. They will come to ask him for her. And if everything turns out well, the wedding will take place in the cathedral in Mexico City.

JORGE ALMEIDA: *(Proudly)* If God wills. *(Jorge Almeida makes the sign of the cross with his right hand and crosses himself. They all do the same, except the Rabbi, who makes a vague gesture, similar to what one would do to scare a fly away from one's face. Felipe fixes all of his suspicion on this gesture. Slowly, the*

Rabbi tries to make the sign of the cross, all the time beneath the gaze of Felipe and amidst the apprehension of everyone else.)

Felipe approaches him fiercely. He arranges the Rabbi's fingers so that they form the sign of the cross and stay there trembling.
FELIPE: Any other way would be blasphemous.

Felipe casts a glance around the place. Nods his head. Leaves. His galloping beast is heard. The Rabbi still has his right hand in the sign of the cross. Luis strums a festive tune on the guitar. The chupa is brought out. Doña Francisca brings the bride out from behind the curtains. She brings her to the bridegroom, who waits under the chupa, in front of the Rabbi. The bridegroom raises her veil. Puts a ring on her finger. She does the same to him. The bridegroom stamps on the ground.
ALL: Mazal Tov!

They are frozen for an instant. Another. Blackout.

Picture 3

Scene 1

Luis de Carbajal the Elder before a civil tribunal. A Lawyer at his side.
LUIS DE CARBAJAL THE ELDER: Until now I have given a very brief summary of what I achieved for the greater profit and honor of the Spanish crown before going to Spain and returning as the governor of the New Kingdom of León. Well, it's just a manner of speaking, because the so-called New Kingdom of León was nothing more than a combination of untamed nature and what had already been civilized. The towns, the sowed fields, the mines—both open and disputed, the refined metals, the Chichimeca settlements, the roads, the bridges I invented, gentlemen. Me, Don Luis de Carbajal y de la Cueva, to the benefit of many, many people and the enlargement of the fortune of Castile. After all that, of course, the pretensions of the new viceroy, Don Lorenzo Suárez de Mendoza, who had just arrived, infuriated me. His contention that several towns and mines are under his jurisdiction is a fantasy all his own. Very recent and very fleeting.

A great uproar. His Lawyer takes him by the elbow. They talk beneath the whispering of the imaginary crowd at the trial.

LAWYER: Careful, Don Luis! Curb your tongue. You are talking about the highest authority in all of New Spain.

DON LUIS DE CARBAJAL THE ELDER: Pass me those documents, Mr. Lawyer.

LAWYER: Why have you hired me, then?

DON LUIS DE CARBAJAL THE ELDER: Frankly, I don't know. Instead of supporting me with arguments, you do nothing but ask me for moderation every second. *(A few bangs of the gavel make the crowd calm down.)* Pass me those documents, I said. *(To the Judges)* In order to prove my words, I here present the royal provision dated the fourteenth of June of 1579 in Toledo by His Majesty Philip the Second, in which he authorizes me to *(Reads.)* "pacify two hundred leagues in longitude and latitude," in other words, the area of my kingdom, and to "erect in them those settlements that you deem convenient." And he adds that "during your lifetime, you will be governor of that territory, and at your death, you will have the right to name your successor."

LAWYER: Good, Don Luis.

DON LUIS DE CARBAJAL THE ELDER: The saying goes: the great always swallow the small. Contrary to popular opinion, I believe that only happens among fish and other animals. In order to stop fat gluttons we humans pass laws. Or isn't that so, your honors? Well, in any case, if your honors don't rule in my favor, I think I will go to Spain, where I know a few fish heavy enough.

Long pause

The Lawyer pulls his hair. The gavel sounds.

VOICE: The Royal Court of Mexico closes the session.

Scene 2

The Dominican monastery. Distant religious chants. The chapel. Brother Agustín kneels, praying. Luis de Carbajal the Younger enters, silently. He kneels beside his brother. Brother Agustín senses him.

BROTHER AGUSTÍN: *(Lowering his voice)* Luis, when did you arrive in the capital?

LUIS DE CARBAJAL THE YOUNGER: Today. I've come from far away to confess before my brother. I asked you by letter, but you didn't respond. Take my confession.

BROTHER AGUSTÍN: No.

LUIS DE CARBAJAL THE YOUNGER: I need it.

BROTHER AGUSTÍN: *(After crossing himself)* No. *(He leaves quickly. Luis follows him.)*

In the atrium

LUIS DE CARBAJAL THE YOUNGER: *(In a normal tone of voice)* Take my confession.

BROTHER AGUSTÍN: A hundred times no. Find another confessor.

LUIS DE CARBAJAL THE YOUNGER: No.

Slowly, hooded brothers enter. Luis kneels.

LUIS DE CARBAJAL THE YOUNGER: I was lost in the mountains. I was lost in the cloudy night. Amidst the howls of the distant jackals. The rocks were frozen, the ground muddy. I knelt, staring at the starless sky. Then I felt it. I lowered my eyes: there it was: at first just a silhouette in the dark. It seemed to me it was an Indian because his naked skin shone in the darkness. He came slowly toward me. . . . But, no, it wasn't an Indian. His face, a face the size of an arm, was red and streaked with black and yellow . . .

FIRST BROTHER: Blessed Virgin Mary.

LUIS DE CARBAJAL THE YOUNGER: But, no, it wasn't an Indian sorcerer either. It was my fear. My fear made flesh coming toward me. Great God, how can one of your creatures keep such terror in his bones? I threw myself against him, I grasped him fiercely by the waist. We fell. We rolled. I tore off his mask. What eyes: what deep wells: what a long descent through them . . . I kissed his lips, I kissed my fear. I kissed it deeply.

BROTHER AGUSTÍN: Luis: get up. Compose yourself. Forgive him, brothers.

LUIS DE CARBAJAL THE YOUNGER: Please don't forgive me. What would you be forgiving me for? No sin has been confessed here. What would you say to a blue-eyed Moor? What reason would you give him to follow Christ's law and not Mohammed's?

SECOND BROTHER: We would tell him that one is God's law and the other that of the Devil.

LUIS DE CARBAJAL THE YOUNGER: The Moor would say the same.

THIRD BROTHER: *(Menacing)* And you, what do you say?

LUIS DE CARBAJAL THE YOUNGER: I say that I need to confess before my brother and only before my brother. Because my brother loves me above all laws, including those divine. He loves me from our mother's milk. He can give me comfort, a comfort that passes between yes and no and tickles the armpits.

BROTHER AGUSTÍN: Luis, stand up. Let's go to my cell. He's upset, brothers.

The brothers leave, and still Brother Agustín can't raise up Luis.

LUIS DE CARBAJAL THE YOUNGER: What kind of a God is yours who puts you in a cell to love him well? Must be a timid God, who doesn't want you to see his creation.

BROTHER AGUSTÍN: What kind of a God is yours, Luis, who can only be worshipped among accomplices? God of the persecuted, of pariahs . . .

LUIS DE CARBAJAL THE YOUNGER: My God says he's the only one. Yours, I've heard, says he's the only one as well. Why don't we believe them? Perhaps the two are a single one. Take my confession; maybe we can understand this mystery together.

BROTHER AGUSTÍN: You haven't told me anything specific. You haven't given me the name of your God. It's better that way. Don't follow me. *(He starts to go.)*

LUIS DE CARBAJAL THE YOUNGER: Become a saint, Brother Agustín. Save yourself and lose me as a brother.

BROTHER AGUSTÍN: Good-bye, Luis. *(He leaves.)*

LUIS DE CARBAJAL THE YOUNGER: Poor little son of the bearded hierarchies in Rome. In Paradise there are no priests, Brother Agustín, no dogma, no free will. I should know who enter Paradise every day. Paradise is here, in this air, when the air becomes sweet and fine. Can it be? Can it be, Luis, you little piece of wind? Little Messiah. I am the son of God: the sun is my halo, the world my shoes: come worship me. Shh. The one who began this story said the same, and the end scares me. Shh. But I truly believe that I am he: the very same omnipotent, all-powerful . . . Or almost . . . Almost . . . I want to confess, brother! I want to confess!

Scene 3

Brother Agustín enters his cell. Closes the door. From a distance come Luis's pleas. Slowly he takes off his habit. Folds it. Puts it on the floor. He picks up a whip. Flagellates himself. His moans, then his sobs, slowly drown out his brother's pleas.

Scene 4

The atrium. Three soldiers cross. Luis hides himself. Brother Agustín's cell. Brother Agustín continues punishing himself.

FIRST VOICE: Open up! Open for the Holy Office of the Inquisition!

The soldiers enter. They grab Brother Agustín. They carry him off as he is, almost naked, the whip in his right hand.

> *Another trio crosses the stage in the other direction, exits.*

> > SECOND VOICE: *(From offstage)* Open up! Open for the Holy Office of the Inquisition!

The trio of soldiers returns, flanking Doña Francisca and Viviana, whose eyes are blind-folded. They exit.

> VOICE: *(From offstage)* Open up! Open for the Holy Office of the Inquisition!

Jorge Almeida and Luis the Younger enter running, pursued by two soldiers. Another pair of soldiers appears to block their path. Jorge Almeida manages to flee. Luis is caught and car-ried off. From the back of the stage a pair of soldiers advance toward the proscenium, clasp-ing Doña Isabel's elbows. They throw her forward.

> SOLDIER: On your knees, pig!

Doña Isabel remains on her knees. Like echoes, the order sounds from various distances.

> > On your knees, Jew!
> > On your knees, Jew!
> > On your knees!

Scene 5

A black wooden lattice descends behind Doña Isabel. The long shadows of three Inquisitors fall over Doña Isabel. She raises her face.

> DOÑA ISABEL: I know nothing. *(Pause)* I practiced the Jewish rites secretly, alone. Nobody, no one, except for my dead parents and the husband of whom I am widowed, ever accompanied me. *(Pause)* Before I left my house, when the soldiers were already calling me to the door, I turned and looked at myself in the mirror and I said good-bye to the face they call Isabel. Burn me now.

Two Executioners, their faces covered with triangular hoods, grab her by the shoulders.

Scene 6

Through the lattice, two Inquisitors and Felipe Núñez.

> FELIPE NÚÑEZ: Will they torture her?

FIRST INQUISITOR: Until she confesses her sins and those of her accomplices.

SECOND INQUISITOR: And then repents.

FELIPE NÚÑEZ: Doña Isabel will never do what she doesn't want to do.

SECOND INQUISITOR: Then she will die unrepentant in the fire.

Pause

FELIPE NÚÑEZ: Those screams . . . Blessed Virgin Mary: those screams are from my master Don Luis.

FIRST INQUISITOR: You're imagining things. Calm yourself.

SECOND INQUISITOR: And if they were his, so what?

FELIPE NÚÑEZ: What do you mean, so what? The viceroy swore that Don Luis's person would be respected. His nephews and nieces are the Jews. I am sure he was always a faithful Christian.

SECOND INQUISITOR: We shall see.

FELIPE NÚÑEZ: Then they are torturing him. But he has nothing to confess. How long will they make him suffer?

SECOND INQUISITOR: Until he confesses.

FELIPE NÚÑEZ: But he has nothing to confess!

SECOND INQUISITOR: We shall see!

Pause

FELIPE NÚÑEZ: Cursed, ambitious, villainous viceroy. So it's all been about getting the New Kingdom of León. What a fool I've been. He told me I should help free Don Luis from his corrupt relatives. He told me they put Don Luis's honor in danger. He told me . . .

FIRST INQUISITOR: He didn't lie to you. He simply couldn't keep his promise. For the Inquisition the viceroy's word is null and void.

SECOND INQUISITOR: Stop whining, hypocrite. Your left hand knew very well what your right hand was doing and hollowly waited for its reward. With all of his relatives in jail who would inherit from Don Luis? Who did you imagine? Answer. You?

FELIPE NÚÑEZ: I saw his nephews betraying him behind his back. I wanted to keep them from ruining him. My motives were for the good of my master.

SECOND INQUISITOR: Like Judas then: you turned him in with a kiss.

FELIPE NÚÑEZ: Don't mention the gospel, you're its greatest assassin.

FIRST INQUISITOR: Shh: Felipe. You've just said something that puts you in mortal sin. Go: go someplace we can't see you and won't have to judge you.

Felipe steps back, frightened.

    FELIPE NÚÑEZ: I'll talk to the viceroy. *(Leaving)* I'll threaten him. Now we'll see what I can do to correct my mistake. *(Leaves.)*

The Inquisitors sigh deeply.

Scene 7

Brother Agustín. Three shadows fall upon him.

    BROTHER AGUSTÍN: *(Crying, distractedly moving his hands, rubbing them hard as if he were washing them with furious, painstaking care)* My parents: Doña Francisca and her husband Rodríguez Matos. Them. But I've just recently suspected it. If I'd suspected or known anything earlier, I would have run and said something to my confessor, the superior of the Dominicans. And Doña Isabel. It's true she had a little print of King David in the kitchen. . . . And one day she recited a verse from the Old Testament to me from memory, the part where Joseph's brothers sell him. I told her immediately that she had sinned. That she shouldn't read the Bible. She told me I was an idiot. I don't argue with women. I thought . . . not that she was a Jewess . . . that she wasn't anything more than an impertinent reader, a curious female, that she was above all . . . And now that I put two and two together I think that the children, Luis and Viviana, necessarily, them, too, because they lived with Doña Isabel,—I saw her two or three times as a child—as I said, I think, them as well. As to the elder Luis de Carbajal . . . he never gave me any suspicion, nor do I recall any doubt about him . . . I don't say this desiring to keep Don Luis's fortune in the family. The monastery is my home and the Holy One my father. Luis the Younger . . . well, I refused to take his confession but only because I thought he was a noisy little boy and that confession with another priest would have been easier. I knew nothing about his internal torment. I thought that if anything were bothering him it was, I supposed, the feelings he must have felt toward several . . . several . . . young ladies. . . . Am I an idiot? A woman told me in confession that she'd seen a candelabra lit in her sister's house one Friday night. The candelabra was in a box, which seemed suspicious or something diabolical to her. The sister's name is Laura Garcés and her husband's name is Andrés Garcés and they have three children, two little boys and a daughter. They live on Apartado Street here in the capital. All the Dominicans, perhaps all the priests, will become doubtful about me if I'm accused, publicly, of . . . It would be a scandal . . . *(Brother Agustín bows his head.)* In Tampico, the pharmacist, one Eulatario Mendoza, had another little print of King David in the back room. And the shoemaker, also in Tampico, had the same print in his box of tools. Goodness, that little print was all over the New Kingdom of León. *(He looks out front.)* Should I make a list of all the places the little print was . . . ?

Scene 8

A small walled patio. An Old Man and Luis de Carbajal the Younger walk around, following parallel lines; they are prisoners stretching their legs. A Guard, indifferent, also walks from one side to the other, more slowly. Then after a bit:

OLD MAN: *(Upon crossing with Luis, without stopping, in a low voice)* I know you. *(Crossing with him again; in an even lower voice)* From the bordellos.

LUIS: Making love.

The Guard turns to look at them. They change their respective paths. Cross one another again.

OLD MAN: What are you here for, son?

LUIS: For being a Jew. And you?

GUARD: Silence!

OLD MAN: *(Very low)* Sodomite. *(Changes his path. After a bit)*

GUARD: Silence!

Luis changes his path. As the Guard and the Old Man cross each other

OLD MAN: And you? Why are you in jail?

The Guard stops, perplexed. Then he gets angry.

GUARD: You old imbecile, can't you see my sword, my lance, the keys to your cell on my belt?

OLD MAN: Of course, you're our guard. Excuse me. *(He changes his path.)*

GUARD: *(Laughing to himself)* Why am I in jail? What a question!

They all change direction.

OLD MAN: You're the guard, of course. But you're still in jail.

They continue walking. Change direction.

Scene 9

A cell. Don Luis de Carbajal the Elder in a corner. The door opens. Flanked by a Guard, Felipe Núñez enters. His hair is gray.

DON LUIS DE CARBAJAL THE ELDER: Felipe! Felipe? I needed you. But, how did you get so old all of a sudden?

FELIPE NÚÑEZ: I've suffered.

DON LUIS DE CARBAJAL THE ELDER: Straighten up. Comb your beard.

FELIPE NÚÑEZ: They will never get you to confess to being a Jew.

DON LUIS DE CARBAJAL THE ELDER: Because I never was.

FELIPE NÚÑEZ: Because they are going to stop torturing you.

DON LUIS DE CARBAJAL THE ELDER: They haven't started yet. You're surprised? I'm not lying to soothe you. They've promised me they'll begin tomorrow. And I've already confessed that I concealed Jews. Which I did.

FELIPE NÚÑEZ: *(Furious)* You? *(Little by little resigning himself)* It doesn't matter. I've managed to get them only to exile you from the Indies for twenty years.

DON LUIS DE CARBAJAL THE ELDER: You were always slow. And, above all, a poor calculator. In twenty years I won't be alive, and, if I am, I'll be an old bitter man. And my good name? What would happen to my good name? A penitent freed by the Inquisition won't be permitted to wear fine clothing or jewels, not even ride a horse.

FELIPE NÚÑEZ: We could go see the Pope and ask for his forgiveness.

DON LUIS DE CARBAJAL THE ELDER: I don't want to ask for forgiveness or anything else. Don't you despair, my motives are good, I'm calm. *(Pause)* Listen, the world is twisted. When there is so much talk of morality, every house is infected. When there are high courts of Justice, injustice has taken root in every heart. The world is twisted, but Don Luis de Carbajal y de la Cueva will not bend. I'm sick of myself: I've heard myself insist on my dignity too often; it all has to be torn down. What are you crying about, bastard? Give me your dagger and get out of here. I'm sure you have, as always, the thin blade in your boot.

FELIPE NÚÑEZ: No.

DON LUIS DE CARBAJAL THE ELDER: Don't let them break me. Give me the dagger.

FELIPE NÚÑEZ: I'll kill myself first.

DON LUIS DE CARBAJAL THE ELDER: You'd kill yourself to keep me from carrying out my will? You haven't learned a thing.

Felipe takes a stiletto out of his boot and sticks it in the floor. As soon as the door opens, he flees. The door closes. Don Luis picks up the dagger. The blade shines in his hand.

Scene 10

Cells. Cells. Cells without number. Prisoners. Prisoners.

    FIRST VOICE: She was naked.

    SECOND VOICE: They carried her off naked.

    THIRD VOICE: They brought her naked.

    DOÑA FRANCISCA: Is it possible? Can they shame a mother this way?

    FIRST VOICE: Wretches! Look what gets lost in these cells: She's a mother!

Doña Francisca, naked, flanked by hooded Dominicans, walks between the cells, crying with shame.

    DOÑA FRANCISCA: God have pity on your souls.

Luis de Carbajal the Younger recognizes her voice in his cell. He throws himself against the door.

    LUIS: Mother, mother. It's Luis.

    DOÑA FRANCISCA: Don't look at me, son.

    FIRST DOMINICAN: Open the door for the son, brother.

    DOÑA FRANCISCA: Don't look at me, little one, don't look at me.

    FIRST DOMINICAN: Open the son's eyes, brother.

    SECOND DOMINICAN: *(Pulling at Luis's face)* Open them!

Luis throws the Guard aside violently. Opens his eyes.

    FIRST DOMINICAN: Isn't she built, little one? Isn't she built?

    LUIS: Yes.

The Dominican shuts the door to his cell. Doña Francisca is obliged to continue on. Luis throws himself on the floor.

Scene 11

Torture chamber. In front of the rack, a table with four chairs. Seated: two Inquisitors, the Prosecutor, the Court Clerk. Doña Francisca kneeling. Two hooded Executioners.

    CLERK: *(Mechanically reading from a book)* You are warned to tell the truth, without giving us cause first to torture you with all the risk to your life that entails. Save yourself from such suffering, excuse yourself from such pains and martyrdom. For the reverence of God tell the truth and take pity upon yourself.

The Clerk writes down everything she says.

DOÑA FRANCISCA: But what truth do you want me to tell? I've told you a hundred times already that I was born a Jew and have been one devotedly and if that is a sin . . . No, no, the only sin is in this body. This body where I am humiliated and terrified. *(Pause)* I have nothing to say . . . nothing but evidence and may God take my life before I give it . . .

At a signal from the Inquisitor, the Executioners pick up Doña Francisca. They put her on the rack. They begin to lash her to it with the leather straps.

CLERK: First turn of the rack.

They carry it out. Doña Francisca opens her mouth in a mute scream. In his cell, Luis de Carbajal the Younger opens his mouth in a mute scream.

Up above, in another area of the stage, three crucified figures. An Executioner with a whip.

EXECUTIONER: *(To the first crucified figure)* Your creed?

FIRST CRUCIFIED: Jesus.

They whip him.

EXECUTIONER: *(To the second crucified figure)* Your creed!

SECOND CRUCIFIED: Jesus!

They whip him.

EXECUTIONER: *(To the third crucified figure)* Your creed!

THIRD CRUCIFIED: Jesus.

EXECUTIONER: *(Falling to his knees)* Save the son of God!

Scene 12

The torture chamber, minutes later. The rack is now vertical with Doña Francisca tied to it. The Executioners lie on the ground but in postures of standing up. The table is also vertical, the Inquisitors are seated in their chairs, but the chairs are also lying on the ground. The whole scene is disturbing, unsettling.

CLERK: *(Reading, mechanically)* You are warned once more to tell the truth,

thereby suspending, with such risk to your life, continued torment. Save
yourself from such suffering, excuse yourself from pains and martyrdom.
For the reverence of God tell the truth and take pity upon yourself.

The Clerk takes down what she says.
DOÑA FRANCISCA: I believe in Christ. I have been deceived by my parents
since I was born. I believe in the mystery of the Holy Trinity. I ask
clemency for my soul. Satan, leave my body. I believe in the mystery of the
Virgin Mary.
INQUISITOR: No, no: names, woman. We are looking for the names of the
Jews you know.

Pause
CLERK: She's biting her tongue. *(He makes a note of it.)*
INQUISITOR: Open her jaw.

An Executioner opens her jaw.
DOÑA FRANCISCA: All this is evil.
CLERK: Second round on the rack. *(He writes it down.)*

*The Executioners carry out the order. Doña Francisca screams silently in unreal slow
motion.*
*In his cell, Luis, in slow motion, silently screams. From someplace above, a circle of light
falls on the stage. But no one is there.*

Scene 13

Torture chamber. Same as the scene before.
CLERK: *(Reading mechanically)* Once again you are warned to tell the truth,
thereby suspending, with such risk to your life, continued torment. Save
yourself from such suffering, excuse yourself from pains and martyrdom.
For the reverence of God tell the truth and take pity upon yourself.

Pause
DOÑA FRANCISCA: Put me on the rack, put me on the rack. Kill me. All I
know is that I was born sad in my mother's womb.
INQUISITOR: You cannot die unconfessed. . . . You would go directly to
Hell. *(To the Clerk)* Can she take it?

The Clerk studies her. Nods.
  At a signal from the Inquisitor.
    CLERK: Fifth round on the rack. *(He writes it down.)*

The Executioners carry out the order. Doña Francisca screams silently. In an area above, a smoking potato slowly lowers and floats. Then an angel descends, a sword in its right hand. From his cell, Luis sees all this.
    LUIS: *(Stunned)* Baruj ata adonai . . .
    ANGEL: Blah, blah, blah. Praying before an angel is like carrying a fistful of salt to the sea. Come and eat potato, you're dying of hunger! Potato? What a delicacy.

Luis, in a dream, ascends, levitating.
    ANGEL: Well then: this exquisite potato is your mother. Look what they're doing to her. *(The Angel cuts the potato in half with his sword.)* Smells good! Ready to eat. Who ever said God loves potatoes less than roses? Maybe he loves them more, since the world needs more potatoes than roses. Take some potato, son. *(He gives him half.)*
    LUIS: Is there any butter?
    ANGEL: You are the butter.

Happy, Luis eats potato. The Angel does the same.
    ANGEL: It isn't true that the Lord has bad moods. Intrigues of idiots, I assure you.
Luis eats all of the potato.

Scene 14

The torture chamber. Doña Francisca on the rack. Everything is now arranged normally.
    CLERK: *(Reading mechanically)* Once again you are warned to tell the truth, thereby suspending, with such risk to your life, continued torment. Save yourself from such suffering, excuse yourself from pains and martyrdom. For the reverence of God tell the truth and take pity upon yourself.
    DOÑA FRANCISCA: The first people I heard talk about the Law of Moses were my parents. Alvaro and Beatriz de Carbajal. That was . . .

At a signal from the Inquisitor.
    CLERK: Wait. You already gave up your parents. Untie her. Give her a chair.

They carry Doña Francisca from the rack to a chair.

DOÑA FRANCISCA: *(As if absent)* Juan . . . Castellanos . . . Hernando Rodríguez . . . Francisca Ullis de Luna, Gabriel Ríos, Domingo Ríos, Manuel Morales. *(She continues, each time more quickly and without emotion while the light falls.)* Dorotea Morales, Isabel Morales, Ana López . . .

Scene 15

A corner. Doña Isabel, Luis de Carbajal the Younger, the Old Man. They wear the sanbenito, the cap and garment stigmatizing the penitent accused by the Inquisition. They wear high hoods and are chained at the wrists and ankles. Their faces covered with pink and purple marks. Somehow they remind one of sad clowns.

LUIS: After eating the potato, I returned to my cell and, feeling myself to be a totally fortunate man, stretched out on the humid ground, between those walls, walls that saw me journey from pain to divine grace.

OLD MAN: Divine grace; yeah, yeah: humility and more anecdote, singer.

LUIS: I lowered my eyelids. . . . I saw Christ.

DOÑA ISABEL: *(Crying)* After Jehovah's angel? God save me, Luis, a rabbi will excommunicate you.

LUIS: With a candle in his hand Christ walked on a hillside. It was night. After him came Jonah, also with a candle in his hand. Then Saint Francis.

OLD MAN: With a candle in his hand.

LUIS: I saw Ibn Gabirol.

OLD MAN: With a candle in his hand.

LUIS: Pythagoras.

OLD MAN: With a candle in his hand.

LUIS: Maimonides.

OLD MAN: With a candle in his hand.

LUIS: Scheherezade amidst floating candles. Li Po falling down drunk.

OLD MAN: There was a multitude.

LUIS: Mohammed, Alexander the Great, St. John the Baptist, shoulder to shoulder.

OLD MAN: And each one with a candle in his hand.

LUIS: I saw you there, graceful Isabel. You wore a red tunic burning like your passion. Your face was like white enamel.

OLD MAN: Then came other people without fame.

LUIS: Anonymous people dispersed throughout all the saints.

OLD MAN: Tell me . . . was I there?

LUIS: You were. Even I, the worst of all, was there, carrying a candle in my hand. I saw myself from far away. . . . And I was that scene and everything that happened . . .

OLD MAN: Where were we going?

LUIS: We went up the hill. Shadows among shadows. And the little red flames from the candles floated in the darkness like an innumerable caravan of fireflies. One by one we went over the horizon . . . *(Pause)* and the line of the horizon was left golden. And the golden horizon began, slowly, to expand, in a magnificent splendor . . . similar to . . . similar to any dawn. *(Pause. A Guard enters.)*

GUARD: To the stage.

Followed by the Guard the three of them leave.

Scene 16

A wooden platform. Stakes with piles of firewood at their feet. Three immense Inquisitors wearing cothurni, tunics, and miters. As they are named, the prisoners will be brought forth by the Guards and tied to a stake. They wear sanbenitos with their crimes written across them.

FIRST INQUISITOR: The merchant Manuel Diez.

SECOND INQUISITOR: Crimes.

FIRST INQUISITOR: Heretic, blasphemer, Lutheran, proselyte of ideas different from those of the Pope, Vicar of God, impenitent.

SECOND INQUISITOR: Anathema.

THIRD INQUISITOR: Death by fire.

FIRST INQUISITOR: Alberta Dominga Pascual, servant.

SECOND INQUISITOR: Crimes.

FIRST INQUISITOR: Blasphemer, employer of magic formulas to obtain husbands, prostitute, penitent.

THIRD INQUISITOR: Death by garrote. Then by fire.

FIRST INQUISITOR: Francisca de Carbajal and her children Luis de Carbajal the Younger and Viviana de Carbajal. Isabel de Carbajal.

SECOND INQUISITOR: Crimes.

FIRST INQUISITOR: Heretics, Jews, blasphemers, impenitents.

SECOND INQUISITOR: The mother, feigned penitence.

THIRD INQUISITOR: Fire. Fire. Fire. Fire.

FIRST INQUISITOR: Anathema. Anathema.

THIRD INQUISITOR: Ana and Telma: players of the game of kids sucking goats' milk.

SECOND INQUISITOR: Crimes.

THIRD INQUISITOR: Lesbians, proselytizers, simulators, incubi, fire.

FIRST, SECOND, AND THIRD INQUISITORS: Ashes. Ashes.

FIRST INQUISITOR: Jorge Almeida.

SECOND INQUISITOR: Crimes.

FIRST INQUISITOR: Jew, heretic, assassin, fugitive.

SECOND INQUISITOR: He'll be caught.

THIRD INQUISITOR: Kriptus. Kriptus.

FIRST INQUISITOR: Brother Gaspar Alejandrez Bichir; priest.

SECOND INQUISITOR: Crimes.

FIRST INQUISITOR: Solicitation of women in the confessional, freebooter, investigator of stars, occultist, maker of astronomical maps, follower of Jeremiah the Jew, alchemist, impenitent.

SECOND INQUISITOR: Death by fire.

FIRST INQUISITOR: Anathema. Anathema.

THIRD INQUISITOR: Luis de Carbajal the Elder.

SECOND INQUISITOR: Crimes.

FIRST INQUISITOR: Heretic, protector of Jews, suicide.

SECOND INQUISITOR: Exiled to the Indies for twenty years.

FIRST INQUISITOR: I said suicide.

SECOND AND THIRD INQUISITORS: Amen.

FIRST, SECOND, AND THIRD INQUISITORS: Anathema. Anathema. Anathema.

SECOND INQUISITOR: Tema de Ana Robles.

SECOND INQUISITOR: Crimes.

FIRST INQUISITOR: Heretic, thematical, barefoot, succubus, impenitent.

FIRST INQUISITOR: Anathema and Kriptus.

FIRST, SECOND, AND THIRD INQUISITORS: Fire. Kriptus. Fire!

Machine-gun fire is heard.

FIRST INQUISITOR: Rodríguez Matos.

SECOND INQUISITOR: Crimes.

FIRST INQUISITOR: Heretic, Jew, blasphemer, impenitent. Dead.

SECOND INQUISITOR: Being dead, he will be burnt in effigy.

A statue is raised at an angle.

FIRST INQUISITOR: Anatema Kriptus domini pater anatema.

FIRST, SECOND, AND THIRD INQUISITORS: We are not the ones who condemn them. They are condemned by the holy laws of the Holy Office of the Inquisition. The laws, the holy laws. No, we are not us, they don't condemn us; we are not us, we are not, no, we are not: No!

Misericordia for these souls! *(They raise three crucifixes.)* Holy Christ of Pity! *(The Inquisitors hold up the crucifixes, which the prisoners, now tied to the stakes, kiss. They leave whispering.)* Miser miseri misericordia. Miser miseri misericordia.

The stage darkens. The statues are set on fire. The stage darkens until blackout. Then the other bonfires are lit and burn rapidly.

BIBLIOGRAPHY OF WORKS BY AND ABOUT SABINA BERMAN

Compiled by Jacqueline E. Bixler

DRAMATIC WORKS

1975: *Esta no es una obra de teatro,* later titled *Un actor se repara. Teatro de Sabina Berman.* Mexico City: Editores Mexicanos Unidos, 1985 (contains both versions). Premiere 1977. Remounted in 1984 with the title *Un actor se repara.*

1978: *Suplicio del placer. Teatro de Sabina Berman.* Mexico City: Editores Mexicanos Unidos, 1985; *Berman.* Mexico City: Grupo Editorial Gaceta, 1994; *El suplicio del placer.* Mexico City: Consejo Nacional para la Cultura y las Artes, 1994. The play premiered in Mexico City in 1978 with the title *El jardín de las delicias.* It premiered again in 1986, in Mexico City and under the direction of Martha Luna, with the title *Suplicio del placer.*

1979: *Bill.* Later titled *Yankee. Teatro joven de México.* Ed. Emilio Carballido. Mexico City: Editores Mexicanos Unidos, 1979; *Teatro de Sabina Berman.* Mexico City: Editores Mexicanos Unidos, 1985. The premiere was directed by José Caballero in the Teatro Granero of Mexico City in 1980.

1981: *Rompecabezas. Más teatro joven.* Mexico City: Editores Mexicanos Unidos, 1982; *Teatro de Sabina Berman.* Mexico City: Editores Mexicanos Unidos, 1985. First titled *Un buen trabajador de piolet.* Abraham Oceransky directed the premiere in Mexico City in 1981.

1982: *La reacción.* Unpublished. Premiere, 1982.

1983: *Herejía.* Originally titled *Anatema. Teatro de Sabina Berman.* Mexico City: Editores Mexicanos Unidos, 1985. In 1992, a longer version was published with the title *En el nombre de Dios* in *Tramoya* 32 (1992): 25–57. Premiere in Mexico City in 1984 with the title *Herejía.* Repremiered with the title *En el nombre de Dios* in Mexico City's Teatro Reforma in 1996, under the direction of Rosenda Montero.

1985: *Aguila o sol. Teatro de Sabina Berman*. Mexico City: Editores Unidos Mexicanos, 1985. Premiere directed by Abraham Oceransky in Mexico City in 1985.

1988: *Muerte súbita*. Second version in 1991. *Muerte súbita*. Mexico City: Editorial Katún, 1988; *Berman*. Mexico City: Grupo Editorial Gaceta, 1994. Premiere in Mexico City in 1988, directed by Héctor Mendoza.

1990: *La grieta. Tramoya* 15 (1991): 7–40. A much shorter version was published in *Tramoya* 9 (1987): 98–113, with the title *El polvo del tiempo*. Premiere directed by Carlos Haro in the Teatro de la Conchita, Mexico City, 1996.

1992: *El pecado de tu madre*. Unpublished. Premiere directed by Elka Fediuk in Xalapa at the Universidad Veracruzana, 1992.

1993: *Entre Villa y una mujer desnuda. Berman*. Mexico City: Grupo Editorial Gaceta, 1994. Premiere directed by Sabina Berman in Mexico City's Centro Cultural Helénico, 28 Jan. 1993. Film version, 1995.

1994: *El gordo, la pájara y el narco*. In *El suplicio del placer. El gordo, la pájara y el narco*. Mexico City: Consejo Nacional para la Cultura y las Artes, 1994.

1994: *Arux*. Unpublished.

1996: *Krísis. Tramoya* 52 (1997): 51–100. Premiere directed by Sabina Berman in Teatro Telón de Asfalto, Mexico City, 1996.

1998: *Molière*. Mexico City: Plaza y Janés, 2000; *Tramoya* 58 (1999): 129–94. Premiere directed by Antonio Serrano in Mexico City's Teatro Julio Castillo, 16 Oct. 1998.

2000: *¡Feliz nuevo siglo, doktor Freud!* In *Teatro, mujer, país*. Ed. Felipe Galván. Puebla, Mexico: Editorial Tablado Iberoamericano, 2000; *Tramoya* 68 (July–Sept. 2001): 5–43. Premiered in 2000 in the Teatro Orientación, Mexico City, under the direction of Sandra Félix.

2000: *65 contratos para hacer el amor*. Unpublished.

CHILDREN'S THEATRE

La maravillosa historia del chiquito Pingüica. El arca de Noé. Mexico City: Editores Mexicanos Unidos, 1984. Premiere, 1983.
El árbol de humo. Mexico City: Ediciones Corunda, 1994.
Caracol y Colibrí. Mexico City: Consejo Nacional para la Cultura y las Artes, 1996. Premiere, 1988.

TRANSLATIONS

Tepperman, Shelley. *Between Pancho Villa and a Naked Woman. Theatre Forum* 14 (1999).
Versényi, Adam. "The Moustache." *Performing Arts Journal* 59 (May 1988).

CRITICAL STUDIES

A'Ness, Francine M. "The Production of a National Playwright: Sabina Berman, Her Audience, and the Changing Mexico City Stage." Diss. U of California at Berkeley, 2001.

Berman, Sabina. Interview with Emily Hind. "Entrevista con Sabina Berman." *Latin American Theatre Review* 33.2 (2000): 133–39.

———. Interview with Lydia M. Gil. "Entre fronteras: Entrevista con Sabina Berman." *Dactylus* 13 (1994): 29–36.

Bixler, Jacqueline E. "*Krísis,* Crisis, and the Politics of Representation." *Gestos. Teoría y Práctica del Teatro Hispánico* 13.26 (1998): 83–97.

———. "The Postmodernization of History in the Theatre of Sabina Berman." *Latin American Theatre Review* 30.2 (1997): 45–60.

———. "Power Plays and the Mexican Crisis: The Recent Theatre of Sabina Berman." *Performance, pathos, política de los sexos.* Ed. Heidrun Adler and Kati Röttger. Frankfurt-Madrid: Vervuert-Iberoamericana, 1999. 83–99.

———. "Pretexts and Anti-PRI Texts: Mexican Theatre of the 90s." *Todo ese fuego. Homenaje a Merlin Forster.* Ed. Mara L. García and Douglas Weatherford. Mexico City: Editorial Ducere, 1999. 35–47.

———. "Sabina Berman y la posmodernización de la historia." *El teatro y su crítica.* Ed. Osvaldo Pellettieri. Buenos Aires: Galerna, 1998. 83–89.

———. "El teatro de la crisis: Nueva dramaturgia mexicana." *Tradición, modernidad y posmodernidad.* Ed. Osvaldo Pellettieri. Buenos Aires: Galerna, 1999. 111–18.

———. "Voces de crisis: Tres dramaturgas mexicanas." *Teatro XXI* (Buenos Aires) 3.4 (1997): 27–30.

Burgess, Ronald D. *The New Dramatists of Mexico. 1967–1985.* Lexington: UP of Kentucky, 1991.

———. "Nuestra realidad múltiple en el drama múltiple de Sabina Berman." *Texto Crítico* 2.2 (1996): 21–28.

———. "Sabina Berman's Act of Creative Failure: *Bill.*" *Gestos. Teoría y Práctica del Teatro Hispánico* 2.3 (1987): 103–13.

———. "Sabina Berman's Undone Threads." *Latin American Women Dramatists. Theater, Texts, and Theories.* Ed. Catherine Larson and Margarita Vargas. Bloomington: Indiana UP, 1998. 145–58.

Costantino, Roselyn. "El discurso del poder en *El suplicio del placer* de Sabina Berman." *De la colonia a la postmodernidad: teoría teatral y crítica sobre teatro latinoamericano.* Ed. Peter Roster y Mario Rojas. Buenos Aires: Galerna, 1992. 245–52.

———. "Sabina Berman." *Latin American Writers on Gay and Lesbian Themes. A Bio-Critical Sourcebook.* Ed. David William Foster. Westport CT: Greenwood Press, 1994. 59–63.

Cypess, Sandra M. "Dramaturgia femenina y transposición histórica." *Alba de América* 7.12–13 (1989): 283–304.

———. "Ethnic Identity in the Plays of Sabina Berman." *Tradition and Innovation: Reflections on*

Latin American Jewish Writing. Ed. Robert DiAntonio and Nora Glickman. Albany: SUNY UP, 1993. 165–77.

Day, Stuart. "Berman's Pancho Villa versus Neoliberal Desire." *Latin American Theatre Review* 33.1 (1999): 5–23.

Gil, Lydia M. "Sabina Berman: Writing the Border." *Postcolonial Perspectives* (1994): 39–55.

Gladhart, Amalia. *The Leper in Blue. Coercive Performance and the Contemporary Latin American Theater*. Chapel Hill: U of North Carolina P, 2000.

———. "Playing Gender." *Latin American Literary Review* 24.47 (1996): 59–89.

Magnarelli, Sharon. "Masculine Acts/Anxious Encounters: Sabina Berman's *Entre Villa y una mujer desnuda*." *Intertexts* 1.1 (1997): 40–50.

———. "Tea for Two: Performing History and Desire in Sabina Berman's *Entre Villa y una mujer desnuda*." *Latin American Theatre Review* 30.1 (1996): 55–74.

Medina, Manuel F. "La batalla de los sexos: Estrategias de desplazamiento en *Entre Pancho Villa y una mujer desnuda de Sabina Berman*." *Revista Fuentes Humanísticas* 4.8 (1994): 107–11.

Meléndez, Priscilla. "Co(s)mic Conquest in Sabina Berman's *Aguila o sol*." *Perspectives on Contemporary Spanish American Theatre*. Ed. Frank Dauster. Lewisburg, PA: Bucknell UP, 1996. 19–36.

Moreno, Iani del Rosario. "La cultura 'Pulp' en dos obras: *Krisis* de Sabina Berman y *Pulp Fiction* de Quentin Tarantino." *Gestos. Teoría y Práctica del Teatro Hispánico* 13.26 (1998): 67–82.

Nigro, Kirsten F. "Inventions and Transgressions: A Fractured Narrative on Feminist Theatre in Mexico." *Negotiating Performance: Gender, Sexuality and Theatricality in Latin/o America*. Ed. Diana Taylor and Juan Villegas. Durham, NC: Duke UP, 1994. 137–58.

———. "Sabina Berman and Her Theatre." *Theatre Forum* 14 (1999): 88–90.

———. "Theatre, Women, and Mexican Society: A Few Exemplary Cases." *Perspectives on Contemporary Spanish American Theatre*. Ed. Frank Dauster. Lewisburg, PA: Bucknell UP, 1996. 53–66.

Rojas, Mario A. "*Krisis* (sic) de Sabina Berman y el escenario político mexicano." *Tradición, modernidad y posmodernidad*. Ed. Osvaldo Pellettieri. Buenos Aires: Galerna, 1999. 119–34.

Taylor, Diana. "*La pistola* de Sabina Berman: ¿violencia doméstica o envidia del pene?" *Antología crítica del teatro breve hispanoamericano. 1948–1993*. Ed. María Mercedes Jaramillo and Mario Yepes. Antioquia, Columbia: Editorial Universidad de Antioquia, 1997. 60–65.

Vargas, Margarita. "*Entre Villa y una mujer desnuda* de Sabina Berman." *Revista de Literatura Mexicana Contemporánea* 2.4 (1996): 76–81.

Versényi, Adam. "Sabina Berman und die Frage nach Identität." *Materialen zum mexikanischen Theater*. Ed. Kirsten Nigro. Berlin: Edition día, 1994. 76–84.

Woodyard, George. "La historia dramática de Luis de Carvajal: Perspectivas argentinas y mexicanas." *El teatro y su crítica*. Ed. Osvaldo Pellettieri. Buenos Aires: Galerna, 1998. 105–12.

Zachman, Jennifer A. "El placer fugaz y el amor agustiado: metateatro, género y poder en *El suplicio del placer* de Sabina Berman y *Noches de amor efímero* de Paloma Pedrero." *Gestos. Teoría y Práctica del Teatro Hispánico* 16.31 (2001): 37–50.

SABINA BERMAN is Mexico's most commercially successful and critically acclaimed female playwright. She has won the Mexican National Theatre Prize an unprecedented four times and written film scripts, poetry, prose, and journalism in addition to her work for the stage. Her collection of interviews with Mexican women in positions of power, *Mujeres y poder*, won the 2000 National Journalism Award.

ADAM VERSÉNYI is an associate professor of dramaturgy at the University of North Carolina–Chapel Hill and the dramaturg for PlayMakers Repertory Company. His translations of plays by Agustin Cuzzani, Griselda Gambaro, and Sabina Berman have appeared in *Modern International Drama, Performing Arts Journal,* and *Women and Performance.* Among his many writings on Latin American theatre is a book, *Theatre in Latin America: Religion, Politics, and Culture from Cortes to the 1980s.*

THEATER IN THE AMERICAS

The goal of the series is to publish a wide range of scholarship on theater and performance, defining theater in its broadest terms and including subjects that encompass all of the Americas.

The series focuses on the performance and production of theater and theater artists and practitioners but welcomes studies of dramatic literature as well. Meant to be inclusive, the series invites studies of traditional, experimental, and ethnic forms of theater; celebrations, festivals, and rituals that perform culture; and acts of civil disobedience that are performative in nature. We publish studies of theater and performance activities of all cultural groups within the Americas, including biographies of individuals, histories of theater companies, studies of cultural traditions, and collections of plays.